Issue | 129

RADICAL HISTORY *Review*

Unpacking Tourism

Editors' Introduction

Daniel Bender, Steven Fabian, Jason Ruiz,
and Daniel J. Walkowitz

People everywhere are on the move, albeit typically under very different circumstances. For staggering numbers of migrants and refugees, who have become the target of ire from resurgent far-right parties everywhere from Germany to the United States, travel is a necessity resulting from forced migration, fleeing war or dictators, or the desperate search for opportunity and economic survival. But as states and the Far Right increasingly challenge, restrict, and police this human mobility, millions of others travel as a leisure-time activity. Indeed, 2015 was the sixth year in a row of sustained growth in international tourism. With numbers rising 4.4 percent in 2015 alone, 1.184 billion people took to planes, trains, cruise ships, yachts, bicycles, and automobiles to experience resorts, hotels, airports, attractions, theme parks, restaurants, museums, monuments, conservation parks, battlefields, religious destinations, and heritage sites. Fifty million more people engaged in overnight travel trips in 2015 than the year before. Broken down by region, the numbers are even more astonishing. In a moment of vocalized concerns about threats from traveling strangers to traveling disease, tourist numbers rose everywhere but in Africa (which was still likely visited by 53 million people). The Middle East, the perceived center of the refugee crisis, was the destination for 54 million, an increase of 3 percent from the year before. Another 609 million mobile people arrived in Europe and 277 million in Asia and the Pacific. Visitors romped on beaches, snapped pictures of local peoples, thronged heritage sites, paid museum admissions, tasted "local"

Radical History Review
Issue 129 (October 2017)   DOI 10.1215/01636545-3920643
© 2017 by MARHO: The Radical Historians' Organization, Inc.

foods and drinks, found lovers, carried germs, and complained about or enjoyed local hospitality.[1]

So we are indeed a mobile species, but often, when we move, we tour. Beginning with the first temperance trains chartered by Thomas Cook in 1841, a vast global tourism infrastructure has emerged. Ruins become attractions; pilgrimages and cruises can be booked at the same agencies; guides in many languages variously entertain and instruct, explaining where to eat, what to drink, or how to behave; hotels dominate skylines and offer international standards of luxury; beaches become resorts. The rise of a tourist infrastructure is just as visible in universities and colleges. Some teach tourism to train its professionals—a "world of opportunity," advertises one such program. More critically, scholars across the humanities and social sciences have sought to understand the power relations created by this mass movement of (comparatively affluent) peoples; the knowledge created in the tourism encounter; and ways local peoples and their community have resisted the demands of a tourist economy.[2] Tourism histories are a reflection of tourism's fundamental impact on environment, politics, and economy. As Eric Zuelow has recently reminded us, one of every eleven jobs worldwide is tied in some way to the tourism economy. The history of tourism, he writes, "is to examine the modern age."[3]

Tourism shapes popular fantasies of adventure, structures urban and natural space, creates knowledge around difference, and demands an array of occupations servicing the insatiable needs of those who travel for leisure. A more critical approach also recognizes that tourism also increasingly represents a way of structuring encounters across constructed lines of nation, race, gender, class, region, and more. A radical approach to unpacking tourism highlights how tourism, as a form of paradigmatic modern encounter, bleeds into diplomacy, militarism, and empire building. After all, it was Cook's ships that ferried the British army up the Nile to relieve General Charles Gordon at Khartoum in 1884.

Of course, tourism since then has been less about exploration and more about economic exchange, and the industries associated with tourism now make up significant segments of many national economies (including the United States, which according to the World Tourism Organization of the United Nations is the world's second most visited country, after France).[4] As Hal Rothman has argued, tourism economies frequently represent a "devil's bargain" between tourists and those that he and others have called the "toured upon."[5] Rothman's phrasing has informed many subsequent studies of tourism because it so perfectly captures the uneven power relations between those who engage in tourism as tourists and those engaged in the service of the tourism industry. It is also a pithy reminder to those of us who act as tourists—as do we, the editors—to consider the ethics of our actions.

This issue of *Radical History Review* explores radical approaches to the study of tourism. From examinations of soldiers heading off to war with guns and tourist guides to tourism and heritage in holy sites, these essays understand tourism as both leisure activity and colonial project. Conceptualizing tourism as human mobility, these essays together ask pointed questions about the ways people and communities resist the exploitative aspects of the touristic encounter and the interrelationship of both diplomacy and empire-building with tourist industries. Tourism represents a critical way of producing knowledge about the "other," poverty, nature, and culture, and it is the task of radical historians to interrogate the underlying systems of power that shape that knowledge production.

This special issue is interested in both the history of tourism and history *in* tourism. What kinds of narratives about modernity, folklore, empire, and development are produced through tourist encounters? How does tourism, as a global industry with its own capitalist and labor history, relate to other forms of ethnographic leisure, such as museums and heritage? How do local actors decide which historical narratives are privileged in the marketing of a place? What stories do they (choose to) remember and forget, or ignore? How do tourists' demands for "authenticity," accessible infrastructure (including railroads, hotels, police, etc.), and adventure shape local and regional political economies? What modes of agency do the "locals" express—or lack—as they approach the touristic encounter?

The essays in this issue examine tourism from above and below, simultaneously as a strategy of development and diplomacy and as highly charged encounters. As tourism has increased both as an industry and as a form of mobility, it has emerged as a fundamental political priority everywhere from local towns to nations, even those rent by war and poverty. Notably, even as this issue goes to press, the battered, beleaguered, and brutal Syrian government made the headlines by posting YouTube videos promoting the beaches and historical ruins of the nation in the midst of a civil war—a nation literally in ruins.[6] Did Bashar Assad's government actually expect tourists to arrive? Or was it a claim to international legitimacy, arguing that a nation that can promote tourism must also have infrastructure (despite years of intense fighting)? Or was the campaign a desperate move to lure tourist cash when the rest of the economy has failed?

The tragic case of tourist development in the midst of a civil war raises questions about the desire of local and national governments to attract tourists which can have profound consequences. In this context, is Syria's campaign terribly different from that of other impoverished countries that still build yet one more resort or five-star hotel? What expectations does a tourist campaign impose on its residents, citizens transformed into hosts? Dean MacCannell has noted the effects of what he terms "staged authenticity"—demanding that local populations re-create or perform, often racialized, roles to meet tourists' expectations of an authentic or genuine experience.[7] If staging authenticity underlies so much of a global heritage industry, it also transforms living traditions and practices, such as those of indigenous or migrant populations, into everyday attractions.[8]

The example of a tourist campaign in the midst of a military campaign highlights the intersection of tourism with empire building, diplomacy, and militarism. A brief voyage to Hawaii reveals that mass tourism is linked to militarism. Since the 1950s, sprawling resorts have catered to tourists eager for a South Seas paradise. Yet the state is also the militarized hub of the United States' vast archipelago of military bases, stretching from Pearl Harbor to Guam to Okinawa. As Teresia Teaiwa has argued, tourism and the military work together to obscure long histories of colonial conquest, resource extraction, and violent labor relations. "*Militourism*," she defines, "is a phenomenon by which military or paramilitary force ensures the smooth running of a tourist industry, and that same tourist industry masks the military force behind it."[9] Thus, as Vernadette Vicuña Gonzalez has argued elsewhere, a typical Hawaiian holiday combines a visit to Pearl Harbor with plenty of time on the beach.[10] In this way, the tourist visit dangerously replicates military rest and recreation. Meanwhile, in the staged authenticity of the hotel "luau" or the "hula" performance, indigenous peoples become (re)cast less as colonized peoples than as willing hosts. The notion of militourism is broadly useful in many contexts including and beyond the tropical Pacific. From Cook's original alliance with the British army to the more recent transformation of former American military bases in the Philippines into hotels and military museums, tourist and military industries are entwined in the colonial project.

Contributors to this issue demonstrate how, in the past century and a half of the institutionalization of tourism as an imperative of national development, tourism has reshaped diplomacy and international relations. Richard Nixon, for example, first went to China playing the role of tourist (as much as wartime president). He walked the Great Wall, that paradigmatic Chinese tourist site, and tasted local foods. Then, like so many tourists who flocked to China in the years following, he shared his holiday snapshots with those back at home. So, too, are tourists reminded that they represent their countries abroad. This was at the heart of the arch anticommunist Conrad Hilton's zeal for placing his international hotels at the very front lines of the Cold War in places such as Athens and Istanbul. Even his fantasy of building a Hilton within sight of the Kremlin was driven by his zeal to counter communism with tourism. Tourists, he believed, were diplomats with dollars. From workers' paradise to tropical paradise, his Havana Hilton also became the destination for Fidel Castro and Cuban revolutionaries as they entered the capital. Soon the hotel, a towering example of tourist infrastructure and symbol of American soft power, housed revolutionaries, not vacationers.

The arrival of tourists—mobile people with money whose visit is encouraged by host states—can have localized effects, far beyond the money they bring. Despite contemporary pleas for sustainable tourist development, they alter environments with demands for new hotels, mountain paths, or beach access. One ongoing example is Venice, Italy. In a city that once boasted a population of over 160,000 in the 1930s, almost two-thirds of its residents have since been driven out by rising rents and property taxes, the conversion of multiple homes into Airbnb accommodations, and the general obstructions to everyday life caused by hordes of distracted tourists. The daily number of visitors now exceeds the entire local population. The Italian state and the citizens of Venice are practically at war with one another over the presence of cruise ships that threaten the city's fragile ecosystem. Venetians have donned wetsuits and placed themselves directly in the path of cruise ships and have placed hundreds of shopping carts in central tourist areas to draw attention to their plight. In July 2016, the United Nations declared that if this pattern continues, it will place Venice on the UN Educational, Scientific, and Cultural Organization's (UNESCO) list of endangered historic sites—a status typically reserved for places threatened by war.[11]

The issues discussed above intersect in multiple and diverse ways in all the articles featured in "Unpacking Tourism," making it a challenge to find the most appropriate way to organize them into thematic sections. Each of the sections does emphasize, however, a particular theme even as they speak in important ways to others. Our first section, "Subaltern Sightseeing," includes two featured articles that address tourism and marginalized groups. Julio Capó Jr. argues how transnational tensions between Miami and the Caribbean islands during the Prohibition era allowed a niche tourist economy to emerge in the Florida port that catered to queer cultures and networks, providing alternative or supplemental experiences to what the Caribbean offered. While Capó's subalterns are the sightseers, Katrina Phillips's are the sight-seen: Native American cultural performers situated as the focus of tensions between federal policy and state tourism initiatives in Wisconsin in the early twentieth century. As the federal government sought to suppress Indian cultures in their efforts to assimilate them into American society, both Wisconsin state officials and Native Americans themselves promoted indigenous cultural traditions, including those of the Winnebago, as a strategy to enrich both state and tribe.

The next section, "Diplomacy on Display," features three articles examining twentieth-century American alliance-building initiatives that used tourism. Mark Rice focuses on the Good Neighbor foreign policy of the United States in relation to Peru. Rice argues how "tourism development in Latin America served the aims of US foreign policy" by providing a less aggressive interventionist approach to winning over allies, while Peruvian state and indigenous elites took advantage of US financing to promote national symbols and local cultures to win over US visitors. The other two articles, by Scott Laderman and Rüstem Ertuğ Altınay, are both set during the Cold War era. Laderman's subjects reflect a more interventionist approach toward US foreign policy than Rice's: hundreds of thousands of US soldiers. Stationed in military bases in various countries around the world, the US Department of Defense gave its soldiers guidebooks to help them adjust to life abroad and promote American values. Laderman demonstrates how "the pocket guides stressed the various ways that these US military tourists would serve as grassroots diplomats or 'ambassadors of goodwill' in Washington's ongoing struggle against the putative communist menace." Altınay's article flips the focus on America's Cold War relationships by examining them from the perspective of Turkish foreign policy and its efforts to promote goodwill toward the United States. The Turkey Tourism Association organized a cruise to "introduce the 'people of the free world' to the 'friendly nation of Turkey.'" The Turks believed that all peoples represent their countries, and so they arranged multiple opportunities for everyday Americans to interact with the people of Turkey onboard the ship. Turkey, therefore, was brought to Americans to explore for themselves, blurring lines between host and guest, demonstrating how performances that project social identities "both reproduce and challenge the broader systems and manifestations of power."

The final section of featured articles is titled "Tourist Traps." This subtitle alludes to the kinds of predicaments in which the subjects of the research find themselves, in some ways as a result of Rothman's so-called devil's bargain. For example, Ryvka Barnard analyzes Bethlehem's Manger Square as a site of contested space between Palestinians and the Israeli state. The former are trapped by the latter's efforts to control the area as well as "surveil and censor the occupied population." While Palestinians are still able to use the site to stage resistance, the ways they rebel are, in a way, "trapped," or curtailed, by the nature of the place as a holy site of global importance. Max Holleran's subject, Spain, lost its devil's bargain by promoting its beaches to tourists from the wealthier members of the European Union as a means to create employment for its citizens, but ultimately wound up trapping itself in a peripheral relationship to Northern European countries. The recession of 2008 exacerbated this negative development even further since a significant part of the Spanish economy had come to rely on seasonal tourism.

Our Reflections segment, "Touring American Pasts and Presents," features two essays. Authors Rebecca J. Kinney and Vernadette Vicuña Gonzalez walk the reader through two different tourist experiences, Detroit and Pearl Harbor / Puʻuloa, reflecting on the tensions extant in reconciling diverse meanings and symbolisms represented in the same place. Whether evoking a nostalgic past while "reproduce[ing] the invisibility of institutional racism" in Detroit or foregrounding Native Hawaiian history in a space of "unabashed patriotism" in Puʻuloa / Pearl Harbor, the tours expose visitors simultaneously to divergent pasts and presents. Our issue closes with a book review examining four recent monographs connected by their focus on tourism in the US Southern states. Similar to the conflicting narratives found in the Reflections essays, Kim Cary Warren remarks how Southern US tourism presents "both a luxurious region promising leisure and nostalgia and a seemingly foreign territory unable to escape its inherent connection with slavery, secession, and racial violence." Taken together, the authors highlight how challenging it has been for the South to reform its image to visitors.

From the point of view of the traveler, tourism evokes something potentially positive: the promise of adventure, leisure, exploration, discovery, entertainment, relaxation, pleasure, and enjoyment. However, as this issue shows, when unpacked, tourism can represent a volatile convergence of multiple and divergent interests and concerns. Tourist sites are continually contested between consumers and citizens, states and communities, elites and subalterns, soldiers and civilians, and even between different nations. The cover image, a photograph taken by Brian McMorrow featuring a section of the West Bank wall in Bethlehem, embodies so many of these tensions. Bethlehem is an internationally significant tourist destination invested with a particular positive meaning to those who plan trips there; however, upon arrival, visitors discover a stark reality of concrete walls, barbed wire, armed soldiers, and security checkpoints. Stateless local residents contend with a highly militarized occupying power, while both seek to control the tourist pilgrimage site of Manger Square, which represents significant revenue. While a graffitied message, "I love tourists," could be interpreted as an attempt to reassure bewildered tourists, it could also be sarcastic given how their presence actually makes political resistance challenging for Bethlehem's Palestinians. Centered in the midst of this message is an image of a taxi cab perched roof-side down on the tip of a pyramid. Perhaps it represents a local understanding of Rothman's "devil's bargain": a local economy based on a tourism economy, but teetering uncertainly on the brink of disaster. Instead of offering an answer, we offer a challenge and an invitation to the reader to join us and our contributors in unpacking the meanings of tourism.

—Daniel Bender, Steven Fabian, Jason Ruiz, and Daniel J. Walkowitz

Daniel Bender is Canada Research Chair in Global Culture and professor of history at the University of Toronto. He is the author or editor of five books, most recently, of *Making the Empire Work: Labor and United States Imperialism* (coedited; 2015) and *The Animal Game: Searching for Wildness at the American Zoo* (2016). He is working on a study of taste, empire, and tourism in Asia, the Arctic, Africa, and the Pacific.

Steven Fabian is associate professor in the Department of History at the State University of New York at Fredonia. He is currently editing his book manuscript "Owners of the Town: Bagamoyo and Urban Identity on the Swahili Coast, 1840s–1960s." His articles have appeared in the *International Journal of African Historical Studies*, the *Canadian Journal of African Studies*, and the *Journal of Eastern African Studies*.

Jason Ruiz is associate professor of American studies at the University of Notre Dame, where he is affiliated faculty with the Program in Gender Studies and the Institute for Latino Studies. His research focuses on American perceptions of Mexico and Latin America with emphases on race, cultural and economic imperialism, tourism, gender, and sexuality. He is the author of *Americans in the Treasure House: Travel to Porfirian Mexico and the Cultural Politics of Empire* (2014). His articles have appeared in *Radical History Review*, *American Studies*, the *Journal of Transnational American Studies*, the *Oral History Review*, and *Aztlán*.

Daniel J. Walkowitz is emeritus professor of history and of social and cultural analysis at New York University. He is completing a book whose working title is "Jewish Heritage Tourism as Remembered and Forgotten: Looking for the Lost World of Jewish Socialism."

Notes

1. United Nations World Tourism Organization, "International Tourist Arrivals."
2. Ateljevic, Morgan, and Pritchard, *Critical Turn in Tourism Studies*; Kirshenblatt-Gimblett, *Destination Culture*; Seneca College, "School of Hospitality and Tourism."
3. Zuelow, *History of Modern Tourism*, x.
4. United Nations World Tourism Organization, "International Tourist Arrivals."
5. Rothman, *Devil's Bargains*.
6. Taylor, "Syria's Message to Tourists."
7. MacCannell, "Staged Authenticity," 589–603.
8. Raibmon, *Authentic Indians*; Imada, *Aloha America*.
9. Teaiwa, "Reading Paul Gauguin's *Noa Noa*," 251.
10. Gonzalez, *Securing Paradise*.
11. Haines, "Tempers Flare in Venice."

References

Ateljevic, Irena, Nigel Morgan, and Annette Pritchard, eds. 2012. *The Critical Turn in Tourism Studies: Creating an Academy of Hope*. London: Routledge.

Gonzalez, Vernadette Vicuña. 2013. *Securing Paradise: Tourism and Militarism in Hawai'i and the Philippines*. Durham, NC: Duke University Press.

Haines, Gavin. 2016. "Tempers Flare in Venice as Angry Protesters Block Cruise Ships." *Telegraph*, September 26. www.telegraph.co.uk/travel/news/tempers-flare-in-venice-as -angry-protesters-block-cruise-ships.

Imada, Adria L. 2012. *Aloha America: Hula Circuits through the U.S. Empire*. Durham, NC: Duke University Press.

Kirshenblatt-Gimblett, Barbara. 1998. *Destination Culture: Tourism, Museums, and Heritage*. Berkeley: University of California Press.

MacCannell, Dean. 1973. "Staged Authenticity: Arrangements of Social Space in Tourist Settings." *American Journal of Sociology* 79, no. 3: 589–603.

Raibmon, Paige. 2005. *Authentic Indians: Episodes of Encounter from the Late-Nineteenth-Century Northwest Coast*. Durham, NC: Duke University Press.

Rothman, Hal. 1998. *Devil's Bargains: Tourism in the Twentieth-Century American West*. Lawrence: University Press of Kansas.

Seneca College. 2017. "The School of Hospitality and Tourism." www.senecacollege.ca/school /tourism (accessed 1 May 2017).

Taylor, Adam. 2012. "Syria's Message to Tourists: Come Back, Enjoy Our Beaches." *Washington Post*, September 2. www.washingtonpost.com/news/worldviews/wp/2016/09/02/syrias -message-to-tourists-come-back-enjoy-our-beaches/?utm_term=.0f0cea96279e.

Teaiwa, Teresia. 1999. "Reading Paul Gauguin's *Noa Noa* with Epeli Hau'ofa's *Kisses in the Nederends*: Militourism, Feminism, and the 'Polynesian' Body." In *Inside Out: Literature, Cultural Politics, and Identity in the New Pacific*, edited by Vilsoni Hereniko and Rob Wilson, 249–63. Lanham, MD: Rowman and Littlefield.

United Nations World Tourism Organization. 2016. "International Tourist Arrivals Up 4% Reach a Record 1.2 Billion in 2015." Press release, January 18. http://media.unwto.org/press -release/2016-01-18/international-tourist-arrivals-4-reach-record-12-billion-2015.

Zuelow, Eric. 2016. *A History of Modern Tourism*. New York: Palgrave.

Sexual Connections

Queers and Competing Tourist Markets in Miami and the Caribbean, 1920–1940

Julio Capó Jr.

Patrons of Miami's La Paloma club expected a night of sexual thrills and entertainment. When national Prohibition ended in 1933, liquor flowed even more freely than before in dry-only-in-name Miami. Most fears of legal recourse for selling alcohol, particularly among small-time illicit traders who constituted the bulk of those harassed by authorities, dissipated. Bootlegging, however, did not. Prohibition taught Miami businesses that operating outside the law remained the most profitable enterprise. Such was the case with La Paloma. There, women wearing G-strings and brassieres danced and stripped for their audience's pleasure. Other "immoral performances" included female impersonators and queers who treated audiences to "indecent jokes and songs." La Paloma was, among other things, a queer establishment.[1]

So long as tourists and other patrons sought out titillating entertainment, Miami businessmen such as Al Youst, operator of La Paloma, were happy to oblige. On the evening of November 15, 1937, as music blared, backlights dimmed, dancers gyrated, and glasses clinked, dozens of women and men forced their way into the club. These figures, dressed in long, white, hooded robes, meant to strike fear in the hearts of the club's unsuspecting customers and staff. La Paloma had been raided.[2]

This raid was not conducted, at least not officially, by local law enforcement agents but rather by nearly two hundred members of the local Ku Klux Klan (KKK).

Radical History Review
Issue 129 (October 2017)   DOI 10.1215/01636545-3920655
From *Welcome to Fairyland: Miami's Queer Past from 1890 to 1940.*

The mob burned "a fiery cross" in front of the establishment, located in an unincorporated section of northwestern Miami. Reports claimed they stormed into the club, "smashed tables and chairs," and "ordered all patrons and employe[e]s . . . be searched for weapons." They then "compelled patrons to leave" and threatened to burn the place down if they did not comply. The terrorists believed that everyone connected to the establishment was guilty of immorality and threatened the city's moral fabric.[3]

With mounting pressure from such conservative forces, Miami-area law enforcement at least tacitly approved of the Klan's actions that night, but to little effect. Dade County sheriff David C. Coleman agreed that La Paloma was a "menace" to the city. "I am going to do everything in my power within the law to keep the club closed," he claimed. Youst had reportedly been arrested at least six times before, on charges varying from intercourse with a minor, the sale of liquor without a proper license, to assault and battery. Residents grew frustrated, however, because no charge ever seemed to stick.[4] Following the raid, Coleman ordered La Paloma to remain closed and temporarily "clamped the lid on nightspots . . . where intoxicating beverages" were sold.[5] Less than two weeks later, Coleman and his deputies conducted their own raid on the establishment. But La Paloma soon reopened. Coleman's far-reaching closing order was in effect for only two days before he reversed it. Miami's tourist economy depended on it.[6]

Miami underwent massive urban transformation in the 1920s and 1930s. In some ways, the city opened up and became far more egalitarian. Several urban crises during the mid-1920s had devastating effects on the local economy, which, a few years later, were compounded by the global Great Depression. Under these circumstances, Miami's white urban boosters and investors came to embrace new middle-class and even some working-class tourists. These visitors hitched rides on trains or came in automobiles and mobile trailers to partake in the leisure culture once only visible to them in literature, film, and on the stage. By the 1930s, the tourist season that had previously catered to wealthy northern snowbirds expanded to begin in October and end by mid-March. Economic necessity pushed urban boosters to at least market Miami as a year-round resort city for the bourgeoisie. They soon began aggressively marketing the area to tourists during summertime, assuring them that "Florida is really 'air-conditioned' by nature."[7]

Meanwhile, the rise of the aviation industry further promoted Miami as a tourist destination and hub for the Caribbean's many playgrounds. Incorporated as a city in just 1896, Miami thus is a relatively "new" urban space that has historically been shaped by the Caribbean.[8] Although Miami boosters had competed with Caribbean markets before, the advent of regular flights to Havana and other exoticized locales meant that the once-requisite stop in southern Florida increasingly became less crucial to tourists. US imperialism ensured that Cuba, in particular, became a site of racialized sex tourism connected to Miami's own markets. One

Cuban called Miami and Havana "rivals and even enemies" fighting for the upper hand in the tourist trade.[9]

These and several other transnational tensions nudged Miami further toward becoming "wide open," a status that allowed queers to carve out distinct spaces in the city. Competing visions pitted urban boosters who wanted a liberal policy against conservative residents invested in making Miami a "model city." Economic pressures ensured that a liberal policy won out, particularly during the city's high tourist season. As Miami increasingly became known as a wide-open city, queers utilized that notorious marketing scheme to sustain themselves. They became critical actors in keeping Miami profitable. Much like Miami's "exotic" connections to the Caribbean, queers made the city's tourist economy work, staffing the service industry and functioning as physical representations of the fantasy and transgression urban boosters marketed, keenly designed as an alternative or supplement to the racialized tourism available in the Caribbean.

Miami's entrenched relationship to the Caribbean provides a necessary transnational view of Prohibition-era politics and the uneasy urban battles that ensued upon the amendment's repeal—two key phenomena in the development of queer cultures and networks. George Chauncey, in his study on New York, has argued that the repeal of Prohibition in 1933 ultimately brought to light the gender and sexually transgressive culture that thrived in the shadows of illicit and underground economies. The repeal significantly curtailed New York's visible and vibrant gay culture, even if it did not fully eradicate it.[10] Something similar occurred in Chicago, where local law enforcement generally permitted the "pansy and lesbian craze" to go mostly undisturbed as a means to reap greater profits from visitors to the World's Fair there in 1933. As Chad Heap has argued, however, once Prohibition had been repealed in New York—and in Chicago, when repeal was coupled with the fair's closing the following year—this queer culture did not exactly disappear. Rather, it successfully relocated to the urban spaces' black entertainment districts.[11] While this temporarily extended the public visibility of New York's and Chicago's queer nightlife, Miami's liberal policy that catered to its king industry, tourism, gave its queer culture an even longer shelf life. Miami's own trajectory more closely resembled San Francisco's, where, as Nan Alamilla Boyd has uncovered, an *increase* in queer entertainment and culture proceeded repeal. This occurred, in large part, to help fill local and state coffers—not necessarily curb vice.[12] Miami's queer past, however, demonstrates the need to treat historical moments and processes such as Prohibition as transnational and global phenomena. Sexual and pleasure-seeking economies along with illicit trade connected to the Caribbean critically informed Miami's Prohibition and post-Prohibition cultural politics; urban power brokers responded to these transnational forces by rebranding the city as a more modern, more affordable, and safer version of the exoticized and more racialized playground places such as Havana offered.

This essay employs "queer" as a category of analysis that centers, more broadly, disruptions to normative gender and sexuality. Although several historians have unearthed localized usages and etymologies of the term *queer*, there is limited evidence to support the notion that it had a singular or dominant meaning in Miami prior to World War II.[13] Indeed, while some references are made in this essay to emerging identities, including lesbians and gays, this work uncovers several queer subjectivities that are not necessarily reducible to identities or do not hold any such currency with us today. They include those who fostered same-sex desires or sought out homosexual sex, transgender representations such as crossdressers and female and male impersonators, burlesque dancers and other sexualized stage performers, as well as escorts and prostitutes and other sex workers.[14]

A Transnational Tourist Paradise

Following a frenzied land boom in the 1920s, Miami's heavily inflated real estate market burst and put the city on the path to economic recovery a few years prior to the arrival of the Great Depression. Limited transportation, fraud, inflation, and general speculations that failed to yield a profit in the early 1920s bankrupted many investments.[15] In addition, a hurricane with winds over 125 miles per hour pummeled the city in September 1926. The estimated fiscal damage reached $76 million, excluding losses incurred to personal property.[16]

One of Miami's more significant enterprises for economic recovery, directly connected to its tourism, was the smuggling of prohibited alcohol. Although residents voted to make Miami "dry" in 1913—seven years before the Eighteenth Amendment to the United States Constitution—many observed "the ease with which liquor [could] be purchased" there.[17] Miami had long been promoted as a space where people could sow their oats. Prohibition did not curtail that image.

Most of the contraband that sustained this economy entered Florida via the Caribbean.[18] One 1923 article reported, "Rum running along the south Atlantic seaboard has assumed such tremendous proportions that the inhabitants of poverty stricken little islands have become rich almost over night and . . . become known as 'bootleggers paradise.'"[19] The Bahamian islands, with their hidden bays and inlets, were central to this business. One publication noted how "every outlaw, every thief, every criminal who can get the price and can give the password of bootleggery . . . has acquired a voting residence in Nassau."[20] In Bimini, vessels built in southern Florida "almost under the noses of government enforcement agents" transported cases of alcohol into Miami.[21]

While both the Bahamas and Cuba benefited from the liquor-smuggling business during Prohibition, US imperialist policies ensured that Cuba would be particularly primed to compete with Miami as a new tourist destination. New York hotelier John McEntee Bowman opened Hotel Sevilla–Biltmore in Havana in 1920 just as the United States implemented its antiliquor laws. He later purchased land in Miami during the boom and built the Biltmore Hotel in Coral Gables in 1926. While both hotels welcomed consumers seeking titillation and an escape from "dry" environments, Cuba provided the full security of no prohibition laws on its books (see fig. 1).[22]

Music composer Irving Berlin's 1920 song "I'll See You in C-U-B-A" captured the appeal of the sexual tourism made available to US Americans during Prohibition. The song observed: "Ever since the U.S.A. went dry / Ev'rybody's going there . . . / I'm on my way to Cuba / . . . where wine is flowing." As a nod to the "gay" culture of urban excess, it noted: "Cuba, where all is happy / Cuba, where all is gay." The sexual subtext was again suggested when the singer rhymed how Cuban women, or "dark-eyed Stellas," would "light their fellers' Panatelas," or their phallic cigars.[23]

As this emphasis on vice tourism from the United States may suggest, Cuban politics, economics, and social unrest played a central role in shaping Miami during this period. Cuban journalist, artist, scholar, and urban critic Armando Maribona revealed the island's intense competition with Miami for tourist dollars and pesos. Working for the island's national tourism office, Maribona noted how "many people see the matter as a sort of boxing match, 'Miami versus Cuba,' with no shortage, unfortunately, of Cubans placing their bets on Miami in hopes of seeing their own country's tourism fail in order to hurt a person or entity they dislike," likely a leftist-nationalist leader or organization.[24] In the age of rising *cubanidad* ("Cubanness," generally understood as constitutive of Cuban cultural and national identity), many Cuban venture capitalists invested in Miami's success to the detriment, Cuban nationalists maintained, of their land and people.[25]

Cuban nationalists as well as local and foreign investors frequently looked to Miami's markets and employed versions of Maribona's ideas to further advance the island's tourism industry prior to the 1959 communist revolution. Reinaldo López Lima, another government-sponsored tourism official in Cuba, built on Maribona's arguments in saying that tourism had the potential to become "Cuba's second harvest." He studied the success of Miami's tourism and concluded that it reaped roughly the same gains as Cuba's sugar industry *during the island's best years.* He believed that further developing Cuba's tourism would help break the monoculture.[26] Incidentally, the island's tourist season—which overlapped with Miami's because of their shared tropical climates—actually coincided with the *zafra,* or sugar cane harvest during the winter months, limiting tourism's potential impact at dismantling the monoculture or sustaining a viable year-round workforce in either industry. Maribona was a staunch nationalist who emphasized Cuba's natural beauty. He also sought to take advantage, albeit cautiously, of the island's intimate ties with the United States—particularly Miami.[27] It is important to note that Cuban designers' embrace of "modern" architecture and art predated Miami's own push for these styles. Indeed, perceptions of "modernity," or lack thereof, were heavily defined by concepts of race and empire.[28] As the title of his influential study, *Tourism and Citizenship,* suggests, Maribona understood this and argued that it was every Cuban's

Figure 1. An inebriated Uncle Sam gaily traveling to Cuba, where liquor flows freely. Note the juxtaposition to southern Florida, where a decree that reads "dry law" is depicted as severely limiting vice culture. Postcard, *Flying from the Desert*, c. 1930. Bacardi, publisher. Compañia Litográfica de la Habana, printer. 5.5 × 3.5 inches. Photo by David Almeida. XC2002.11.4.118, Vicki Gold Levi Collection, Wolfsonian–Florida International University, Miami Beach

civic duty to embrace tourism. He framed the island's push for tourism in nationalist terms, contending that it made Cuba modern by expanding its people's access
to education, health, cleanliness, social order, and urban planning.[29] He supported
opening Cuba as a means of bringing capital to the nation—not individuals—while
also resisting the idea that "Cuba should be ready to get used."[30]

Some Cuban boosters, however, believed it necessary to further develop the
island's sexual markets to remain competitive with Miami and other places marketed as exotic and tropical. One Cuban periodical called Cuba's "refined 'gigolo'" a
"necessary auxiliary of tourism." Both female and male escorts who would "dance,
converse, entertain, and drink with" unaccompanied foreigners were deemed
instrumental to building the island's tourism. Some women visiting the island might
seek a Cuban gigolo's companionship because their husbands were too "tired, over-
weight" or were "inept dancers." Maribona distinguished this "refined" service from
the perverse, but popular, trade that thrived in Havana. Indeed, sources suggested
that Cuban escorts offered a number of other nighttime services.[31]

Sexual tourism proved critical to Cuba's economic diversification. "In Cuba
we lack refined showgirls and 'escorts,'" argued Maribona. "Instead, there exists a
gross system that disgraces our country." On the island, tourists were offered the
"entertainment of '*cuadros plásticos*'"—defined in this source as the "lowest form
of immoral theater" and suggestive of a show that was sexual and exhibitionist in
nature—which were "open to the public with the authorization of the government,
and other bad or worse things that have given Barcelona and Marseilles such bad
reputations."[32] Maribona found blame in the United States and Cuba, as US promoters advertised the island as a metaphorical whore and Cuban capitalists obliged
such fantasies by exploiting their own people for personal gain.[33] He condemned US
periodicals and travel literature that "induce[d] tourists to visit Cuba only through
controlled excursions wherein, with the pernicious assistance of some Cuban tour
guides, travelers [got] to know the worst Havana ha[d] to offer, including porno-
graphic entertainment especially made for [that] double racket."[34]

These concerns were tied to changes in Cuban politics. Maribona emphasized the frustration of the Cuban Republic's first president, Tomás Estrada Palma:
"This is a republic without citizens." Maribona believed that the state had abandoned the needs of its most vulnerable people and that self-interest and greed often
prevailed among corrupt leaders and well-to-do Cubans. "Since the fall of Estrada
Palma," Maribona argued, "government officials and their cronies have had at their
fingertips the means by which to satisfy their personal ambitions. In this way the
republican period in Cuba has not impeded the extortion [that was] characteristic of
past political regimes." He even lamented, "Should communism ever be installed in
Cuba, the favors, corrupt patronage [*las botellas*], and the enrichment of a regime's
backers would continue," so long as "self-proclaimed decent people keep trying to
indulge in luxuries and physical pleasures, vices, and aristocratic trappings."[35] He

added, "If Cuba is not the 'Tourist Paradise' we advertise, it is also a far stretch from being the Eden Republic that the selfless heroes of our independence dreamed of."[36]

This reflected the political climate that led to Cuban dictator Gerardo Machado's ousting in 1933. Elected Cuba's president in 1925, Machado initially received widespread support despite his abuses of power, including extending his term as president. When the global economy tanked in 1929, so too did Cuba's sugar exports. Cubans had had enough. Diverse factions made up of student protesters, merchants, and labor defenders helped topple Machado's government and ushered in a short-lived revolution. The United States' abrogation of the Platt Amendment in 1934 and the progressive constitution of 1940 were among Cuba's nationalist gains. The former, however, actually solidified the US naval base in Guantánamo Bay. The latter reform was ultimately undercut by Sergeant Fulgencio Batista, who helped depose Machado. In fact, Batista usurped the Cuban government and ruled as a dictator-*caudillo*—at times as president himself and at times through puppet-presidents—until the 1959 revolution.[37]

This turmoil helped market Miami as a sinful paradise that could simultaneously guarantee its tourists' stability and safety. After all, the 1933 revolution and Machado's expulsion coincided with the repeal of Prohibition in the United States. Throughout Miami, rumors abounded that Cuba's troubles had drastically curtailed its tourism by the late 1920s.[38] Cuba's loss was Miami's gain. Novelist and elite Miami resident Elizabeth Goodnow Cooper flew to Havana in the midst of these changes and described the Cuban capital as "a city of departed glory." Demonstrating the imperial ethos espoused by many Miami investors who benefited from US involvement in Cuba, she speculated: "Perhaps it was American business that had pulled out, perhaps it was the repeal of prohibition that had, with the revolution, kept the tourists away, or the low price of sugar—anyway, neither the town nor the people looked happy."[39] Similarly, many Cubans blamed "Miami hoteliers," including those who built hotels in Cuba to the chagrin of nationalists seeking to purge foreign investments from the island. Cuban sources claimed that influential Miami boosters had exaggerated conditions on the island in the press to deter visitors from Havana and steer them to Miami, Havana's similarly tropical, but younger and more modern, sister city. While Miami boosters touted their city's tropical and Caribbean connection, they also emphasized the safety and nationalism US Americans might associate with visiting a city officially part of the United States.[40]

Even before the repeal of Prohibition, transnational tourist exploits—and the two cities' competition for dollars and pesos—particularly nudged Miami toward becoming a wide-open city that, while often mimicking the exoticism linked to Cuba, simultaneously emphasized southern Florida's safety in distinctly racialized terms. Indeed, selective and lax enforcement of laws became necessary for Miami to compete with Cuba as the most accommodating playground.[41] During a 1930 US congressional hearing over the effectiveness of the antiliquor law, the House of Representatives Committee on the Judiciary heard testimony from Bonnie Melbourne Busch of Miami, the vice chairwoman for Florida's chapter of the National Women's Democratic Law Enforcement League. When the committee asked her if "Florida . . . pays little or no attention to the prohibition statute," Busch replied: "No; because I think it is a tourists' country entirely now, and they are on the way to and from Cuba and other places." The congressmen pushed further: "Would you say aside from the very ideal climate and other native attractions, that the proximity of Florida to the Bahama Islands and the Republic of Cuba was also part of the attractions?" To that, Busch simply replied: "I do not know. The climate takes me there."[42] While Busch's testimony reveals the popular belief that cities such as Miami rarely enforced the law, it also connects its urban identity to the Caribbean and its racialized, exotic "attractions."

Visiting Miami and Havana, or both, could represent a form of "slumming," albeit to varying degrees linked to racialized ideas that were linked to safety, security, voyeurism, and pleasure. By the mid-1920s, Miami-based travel companies coordinated leisure trips from Miami to Havana. US travelers could board a cruise ship, a steamship, or, later, an airplane to Cuba. One company opened an office in the Cuban capital and hired local guides, drivers, and translators to conduct its business.[43] Romance and sex were key elements of this trade. One Miami-based tour company assured visitors: "To Latin people love and courtship are a romantic affair." Promoters stressed how Cuban women were a source of lust and deceit. The tour company warned: "Girls try to break men's hearts but not their own." Guidebooks inferred the availability of Cuban women to US American men. They assured men that chaperons were increasingly becoming "extinct," removing a significant hurdle for intimacy. One guidebook provided roughly two dozen Spanish phrases a traveler "might like to know." It included how to communicate "Give me a kiss" and "You are very charming."[44] US travel to Cuba, with the possibilities of sexual tourism, sparked new entrepreneurial ventures. Many Miami boosters understood Cuba as an important gateway that attracted tourists to their city, as a starting or end point for their tropical vacation. For their part in promoting sexual tourism, Cuban lawyers and doctors offered US visitors advice on local marriage laws and treating venereal disease, such as syphilis.[45] It is important to note that although these neocolonial efforts defined the Caribbean as a racialized site for sexual pleasure for US Americans, they similarly sought to safeguard the reproductive imperatives of white visitors and their progeny. Birth control and reproductive politics sought to regulate racialized populations, such as Cuban women, interpreted as genetically unfit and inferior.[46] That, too, helped distinguish Miami from Cuba, even though the former also sought to regulate its sexual tourism trade and the black, ethnic, and working-class women who operated and staffed it.[47]

Urban boosters understood that should Miami's vice culture cease, tourists "would go to Cuba" and indulge in its playground instead.[48] One journalist noted how "pleasures that do not come within the pale are so readily obtainable" in Miami in large part because Havana "is only three hours away by plane, and offers to do as you please." In this way, "Havana has become the *bête noir* [*sic*] of Miami." He believed that if "Miami retains the best features of the sin-cursed Cuban capital," another reference to the Caribbean's inherent racialized character, "the dollars that might fly across the Straits will stay where they will do the most good."[49] Similarly, during Prohibition playwright and journalist Basil Woon joked that he would "pop over to Florida and tell" tourists there "about Havana." "I will tell them that we have a perfect climate, and horse racing, and plenty of drinks, and open gambling, and a wonderful beach, and good roads." He then realized that Miami offered the very same. "It seems to me that about the only chance Havana stands [at competing with Miami's tourism] . . . is to organize a slush fund and elect another reform governor of Florida." He added, "And what a slim chance that would be."[50]

Queers and Shifting Urban Power

The corruption, graft, and vice associated with Cuba shared striking similarities with Miami's own urban politics. Many American mobsters "located in Havana" had direct connections to Miami and its underground economies.[51] This changing power structure did not go unnoticed by Miami elites, small-time merchants, middle-class residents, religious organizations, or terrorist groups such as the KKK. This tension was palpable in a southern Florida broadcast that observed: "Residents and businessmen of Miami Beach seem finally to have reached the point where they must choose between the wealthy conservative element, which has played so large a part in building up their community, and the flashy fly-by-night followers of Lady Luck, who are literally here today and gone tomorrow."[52] By the 1930s, a battle for urban power—one in which new community standards, morals, and identities would take shape—ensued unlike the city had ever seen.

Miami's conservative elites and members of the city's growing middle class in particular mobilized following the arrival of Northern and Midwestern syndicates, especially notorious gangster Alphonse "Al" Capone, or "Scarface." Although Capone earned his notoriety in Chicago, where the mob controlled much of the city's sexual demimonde, he, too, eventually took advantage of Florida's land boom.[53] He bought a luxurious home in 1928 on Miami Beach's Palm Island, where he escaped Chicago's law enforcement. Capone was not alone. Mafiosi Jake Guzik, Frank Erickson, Meyer Lansky, and Frank Costello also put down roots in southern Florida.[54] Conservative members of the city's ruling class, particularly anxious over their property investments, challenged this shift in Miami's urban power structure.[55]

Miami's vice culture that catered to the whims of tourists meant that residents had to choose: "Capone or civilization?" By 1929, a Florida reverend named Frank Nelson launched a publication titled *Sky Talk* "devoted to the moral and spiritual welfare of the State." It focused on the "evils" of bootlegging and gambling and lamented Miami's perceived decay. Unsavory characters "flocked to the state," Nelson claimed, "attracted by wide-open Miami, . . . where the law had been trodden underfoot with impunity." "Florida needs boosting," he concurred, but "[you] never can boost a thing unless you have something solid to stand on." He believed dependence on tourism created moral chaos and placed a welcome mat for "undesirables." Miami could not house "beer kings, hold-up men, prostitutes, and professional gamblers, and also have doctors, lawyers, merchants, and other varieties of law-abiding citizens."[56]

Miami's tourist-driven wide-open policy mobilized several moralist forces, including many middle-class residents and religious organizations. They looked to the Greater Miami Ministerial Association, which claimed to represent all Protestant churches in the area and had a membership of over thirty thousand, for guidance.[57] Local ministers implored their followers to dismantle the argument that a wide-open policy was necessary to grow Miami's economy. "Miami does not need the dollar so much as she needs the ideal. Of the two—financial or moral bankruptcy—may she never choose or experience the latter."[58]

Transgressive expressions of gender and sexuality were key targets of their moral crusade. Nelson placed women's "lack of clothes" alongside the pervasion of the speakeasy, gambling, "the arts of the underworld," red-light districts, and polygamy. A Miami pastor claimed that "disreputable characters" attracted to the city's vice culture were breaking into his church "to sleep and for worse purposes."[59] Similarly, "like flies at an open syrup spigot," "women of the street" waited for those with "their night's winnings" in their pockets.[60] One man wanted a return to the time when he could "walk on Miami Avenue," downtown's thoroughfare, "without being molested by" the "ladies of the evening."[61]

In 1931 conservative forces further mobilized when Florida legalized parimutuel gambling, which, rather than shine a light on the underground spaces in the city, helped increase and reinforce vice cultures in establishments that queers had long frequented. Illegal gambling had been commonplace for many years. The Miami Jockey Club, later renamed the Hialeah Race Course, opened in the midst of the area's boom. Lax law enforcement defined the race atmosphere, wherein spectators wagered on horses and dogs at the tracks. This enterprise attracted many tourists. In response to the Great Depression, Florida's legislature, opting to capitalize on the financial successes Miami found with this illegal venture, passed the "turf bill." It mandated that Florida's sixty-seven counties share the profits equally. The state received 2 percent of every legal wager and 15 percent of all admissions as a tax. In 1933 the counties split $308,531.56 from Hialeah's earnings alone. This number was quite small compared to the whopping $8 million that circulated the racetrack during that forty-five-day season.[62]

Queers proved instrumental to this tourist-driven and illicit culture. Wealthy New York mobster-bootlegger William "Big Bill" Vincent Dwyer opened a new racetrack in southern Miami. Although the Tropical Park Race Track opened in 1931, it did not have a proper season until 1933. Despite Dwyer's bootlegger reputation in the city, many supported his bid to expand horse-racing season. Many even saw him as a heroic figure helping the area bounce back from depression.[63] His supporters overlooked Dwyer's underground activities and lifestyle. This aggravated the county sheriff, who claimed that he received threatening phone calls from Dwyer urging law enforcement officials to permit him to operate his illicit businesses without police harassment.[64] Journalist Barbara Walters recalled Dwyer during her childhood in Miami, where, in a strange turn of events, she lived with the notorious gangster. Walters observed how Dwyer shared his bedroom with his "chauffeur/bodyguard" and that, in retrospect, "it seems somewhat logical" that he was "gay."[65]

Indeed, queers were among the so-called undesirables, unsavory characters, vagrants, and "colorful crowds" who staffed and fueled this tourist economy.[66] Miami's moral crusaders believed "the lice that follow the stables [at legal race-tracks] are unworthy of mixing with decent people." One man identified "coke fiends, crooks, pickpockets and parasites of every description."[67] During one of the raids at La Paloma, police arrested "four men employed . . . to wear feminine clothes and impersonate women in songs and dances." They all pleaded guilty and had to pay a fine of $25 or else serve "30 days on charges of vagrancy." The report suggests that Youst or club management regularly looked out for them. None of the men appeared in court and were instead represented by the club's attorney. Club personnel believed queer performers were instrumental to their businesses and often safeguarded them as investments for optimal profits. Similarly, a few days earlier, a judge fined several women who worked at another queer club, Kelly's Torch Club in Hialeah, with "indecent exposure" as well as several men "on charges of using obscene language."[68]

Their presence was further highlighted and became more central to Miami's playground image with the national repeal of Prohibition. Alternative newspaper *Friday Night* revealed how queers could be found in clubs, cabarets, speakeasies, and revues. In one cartoon (see fig. 2), a limp-wristed club bouncer throws out a patron, who asks him: "Why do you expel me so gently?" Stressing his effeminacy, the queer jokes that they are not allowed to put a "kick in 3.2 beer," referencing the alcohol-content permitted to be sold through the 1933 Cullen-Harrison Act, which started the repeal of Prohibition.[69] Similarly, author Leslie Charteris described the clientele and ambience at a Miami speakeasy in his 1940 novel *The Saint in Miami*. The club emcee was a "slim-waisted creature" whose "blond hair was beautifully waved, and he had a smudge under one eye that looked like mascara." He spoke with "an ingratiating lisp." The place was a site of "obvious queernesses." A character noted how "some of the groups of highly made-up girls who sat at inferior tables with an air of hoping to be invited to better ones were a trifle sinewy in the arms and neck," observing that they were cross-dressing men made available to the highest-paying customer. He also described how "some of the delicate-featured young men who sat apart from them were too well-developed in the chest for the breadth of their shoulders." This Miami club and gambling joint, then, also found queer women who passed as men among its clientele. One character noted how this sight was all too typical of Miami after dark: "Those eccentricities were standard in the honky-tonks of Miami."[70]

Other evidence reveals how queers were visibly featured at the races and gambling joints. One visitor noted how the men's "powder room" at the Tropical Park racetrack had "enough male aids to beauty to make an effeminate man happy." He warned, "If you don't watch out, you can come out of there feeling like a lady, and smelling like one too." He made another subtle reference to the effeminacy he attributed to these tourist spaces when he juxtaposed the rugged trees of California to the "swishy" and

"But, bouncer, why do you expel me so gently?"
"Listen, bo, don't you know we ain't allowed to put no kick in 3.2 beer?"

Figure 2. Queers, such as this limp-wristed club bouncer, had a visible presence in Miami's tourist-dependent nightlife. *Friday Night*, October 20, 1933, file 17, box 29, ser. 278, State Archives of Florida, Tallahassee

"sissy-like" pines he found in Miami.[71] Irving Young, a black man from Miami committed to the state asylum and deemed a "sexual pervert," had also been flagged for his excessive use of alcohol and habitual gambling.[72]

This queer-vice nexus reached numerous audiences and would-be visitors and slummers through popular culture, often entangled with more violent forms of criminal activity. The mystery plot of Walter Gibson's 1940 *Crime over Miami* (written under pen-name Maxwell Grant) centered on the city's jewel theft and *bolita* rackets. The latter was a transnational risk game rooted in the Cuban lottery that had been played in Miami since at least the 1920s.[73] One of the story's villains

More Casualties On The Local Battlefront

Figure 3. Newspaper reports and fictional accounts regularly relayed the often violent and vice-ridden association of Miami's queer joints located in the city outskirts. This cartoon referenced a "riot" at Kelly's Torch Club in Hialeah, editorialized as representative of the "causalities on the local battlefront," a nod to Miami's tourist-driven wide-open policy. Cartoon by Martin Dibner. *Miami Daily News*, October 5, 1939

played the "circuit as a female impersonator."[74] As this work and *The Saint in Miami* suggest, fictional detective tales with Miami as backdrop relied on queer characters for plot twists that added to the city's lure. In a 1936 crime serial titled *Murder off Miami*, gender and sexual transgression were also a central part of the city's criminal and underworld reputation, one that was particularly tailored for tourist consumption. In that fictional work, a bishop defended himself from a "public scandal" he had the "ill-fortune" of being involved in "with the troops in 1917"—heavily suggestive of the public scandals involving fairies and other "perverts" in naval institutions.[75] Similarly, 1939's *Murder Masks Miami* was full of gay subtext: hazed sailors wore mermaid costumes at sea, the murderer is thought to be a male cross-dresser, the author details the rippling muscles of his protagonists, a reference is made to a pansy playwright, and a fit man notes how "an artist from Provincetown" once persuaded him to model in the nude.[76] These queer, subversive, illegal, and often violent associations transcended fiction and had real-life equivalences. In October 1939, for instance, a "riot" ensued at the queer joint Kelly's Torch Club (see fig. 3). Three club employees were convicted of beating three patrons in the club; a female dancer testified that the violence ensued when her colleagues defended her against the men's attempt "to strip her of her clothing."[77] A month earlier, a "brawl" erupted at La Paloma's "men's washroom."[78] Altogether, these well publicized and reported after-dark associations proved popular and invited visitors to view Miami as a site for queer, titillating experiences tempered by the voyeuristic lure of potential danger.

As New York, where so many of Florida's tourists hailed from, turned up the heat on its gay nightlife following repeal, Miami boosters further embraced the marketability of its gender and sexually transgressive culture. Contemporary reviews and advertisements often depicted Miami's nightlife using the discernible language of New York City's gay heyday. In reference to the city's nightclubs, one critic noted, "This Miami area reeks with atmosphere. It features 'Greenwich Village' type spots such as the Jazzy Ha-Ha club and the La Paloma," two queer joints.[79] At the former, one could find "painted men" who "danced and profaned sweet songs."[80] By no means was this subtle. It was well known that Greenwich Village "hosted the best-known gay enclave in both the city and the nation."[81] The reviewer similarly observed how Miami and Miami Beach also featured "'Broadway' style places" and "'52nd street' type rendezvous," listing several popular and ritzy queer joints.[82] In this way, the gay subculture many middle-class folks saw publicly subdued in New York—or saw become less visible in public spaces—was marketed as relocated to the nation's playground.[83]

In Miami, although queers provided entertainment or staffed the clubs, many were often priced out as patrons—especially after repeal. More queers thrived in the less "plush establishments" that provided locals and tourists alike with vice, gambling, and sex. In this way, a rawer version of Miami after dark could be found in the municipal outskirts. As one contemporary recalled, "Some club-owners slit their gullets with ridiculous prices, or check-padding." Others, however, "found temporary sanctuary from bankruptcy by canceling standard acts and substituting strip-teasers" and queer performers who offered crude jokes onstage and perhaps other services on the side. *These* acts could "be lured at waitresses' pay" and were therefore safe investments for club owners and operators who tapped into the market of pleasure seekers priced out of the elaborate, Broadway-esque entertainment found in central Miami and Miami Beach. Some of these establishments "made a play for the homosexual trade." The evidence suggests that these spaces were more policed than the "expensive night-club[s]" in downtown Miami and Miami Beach that offered female impersonations, even as police also largely turned a blind eye to the smaller joints during winter months.[84] While most of the swankier tourist places located in Miami's and Miami Beach's main thoroughfares that featured queer entertainers boarded up during the off-season—or during the summers or warmer months—it appears that places like La Paloma and Kelly's Torch Club remained open, possibly year-round. This suggests that in addition to catering to tourist-slummers, these spaces were also sustained by local residents or prolonged snowbirds, including queers.[85]

Many operators of Prohibition-era speakeasies—which so many queers worked in and frequented—reacted to repeal and the renewed pressures of competing with Caribbean tourist markets by relocating to the city outskirts or to unincorporated parts of the county.[86] Miami bootleggers who dodged legal fees under Prohibition did not welcome the loss of profits and moved their establishments away from proper municipalities.[87] Tourists soon discovered that "'jook joints' were the Florida equivalent of Northern roadhouse: dives located outside the city limits, hence beyond the reach of the metropolitan police."[88] Unincorporated Dade County offered more loosely defined zoning regulations and no municipally mandated taxes and license fees, as well as one less law enforcement jurisdiction for entrepreneurs to deal with.[89] Like San Francisco, Miami's queer nightspots constituted a significant part of the city's urban economy, even as it balanced its embrace and separation from the racialized sex tourism the Caribbean offered its visitors.[90]

La Paloma was one of the queer and gambling nightspots located in unincorporated Dade County. Described as "dimly lit," its atmosphere catered to those willing to push the boundaries of their own gender and sexual expressions. One man recalled how its "low-ceilinged main room presented shows filthy beyond words." There you could find "homosexuals in evening gowns, trousered lesbians, and prostitutes." While La Paloma served as an alternative to the nightspots in Miami and Miami Beach proper for heterosexual tourists, queers also constituted its clientele. This is similarly suggested by the fact that La Paloma remained open longer, if not year-round, unlike ritzier establishments that operated only during peak season. Indeed, queer performers and staffers often "solicited customers for normal or abnormal sex practices."[91]

Those services may have been less known or legible to many of the clubs' heterosexual clientele, who seemed awestruck by the gender and sexual transgression and general derision queers offered through their performances. As Heap has argued, heterosexual men took women to view these performances in large part because they served as "the perfect counterpoint to highlight their own masculinity."[92] Their masculinity was particularly sharpened through the contrast of onstage pansies and female impersonators who offered "obscene simperings and gesturings." These Miami performers were described as "twisted caricatures of humanity."[93]

They challenged gender norms by caricaturing the so-called naturalness of masculinity and femininity.[94] Many of these performers—some of whom were not in
drag—joined "scantily clad" women in telling "smutty" stories, jokes, and songs,
some of which hinted at or referenced homosexuality.[95] They played to the audience's sexual sensibilities and, according to one spectator, "gain[ed] most of their
revenue from money tossed derisively [by the audience] during the public entertainment," not unlike drag performances today. While queers certainly patronized these
spaces, these performances proved incredibly popular among heterosexual slummers who represented the bulk of "the crowds jammed" into these clubs. One man
argued that the only reason such nightspots were tolerated in Miami was because
"people seem[ed] willing to pay for the privilege of visiting them."[96]

As the raid on La Paloma shows, the KKK represented a powerful force in
the moral crusade against the area's wide-open policy and the "undesirables" who
sustained it. Since the KKK reemerged in Miami during the 1920s, Klan women
and men employed violence and scare tactics—mob action, lynchings, bombings, parades, and abductions—to enforce the urban ideology of white power.[97]
This "reactionary populism" grew in intensity with Prohibition and further gained
momentum in Miami once repeal and competition from Cuba helped formalize a
liberal policy. The Klan revitalized its image during this period by shoring up support with middle-class whites who shared a commitment to "correct evils" in their
communities—"particularly vices tending to the destruction of the home, family,
childhood, and womanhood."[98]

The Klan's raid on La Paloma also reveals how, despite moral crusades, queers
and the leisure establishments they worked in and frequented thrived in service to
Miami's tourism industry. Although local police largely condoned the Klan's actions,
several forces clearly denounced it. The *Miami Herald* wrote a scathing column
where it reiterated, "Law enforcement has not been turned over to the Ku Klux Klan
in Dade County."[99] Meanwhile, newspapers throughout the country reported the
affair, which had the potential to affect the wide-open reputation tourists expected.
The *New York Times* concluded that, as a result of the raid, "the accent" for tourist
pleasure seekers "will be more on bathing, fishing, golf and tennis than on strip-tease
dancers, private 'clubs' where anything goes and heavy-tariff gambling emporiums."
It cited the closing or taming of several "once-famous hot spots," which were now
"apparently indefinitely off the list of Miami entertainment centers." This included La
Paloma. While the view that "tourists need not expect the hectic after-dusk amuse-
ment of the old days" reached many would-be tourists, it was far from accurate.[100]
County law enforcement failed to successfully prosecute any serious charges against
Youst or his nightclub. The club soon reopened, and Youst stayed true to his word that
La Paloma would "reopen . . . with spicier entertainment than ever."[101]

Despite sporadic raids, Youst and other queer joint operators offered risqué entertainment for tourists and residents for several more years. In one of the

more outrageous multisite raids, county sheriff Coleman disguised himself as "the gay fellow" and "hick" to clamp down on "female impersonators and strip teasers" in Kelly's Torch Club. At the same time, one of his deputies dressed up as a "gay blade in dyed hair and an open-throated sports shirt" to catch queer performers in the act at La Paloma.[102] The spectacle of these theatrically orchestrated raids—resplendent with costumes and dramatic reveals—made the raids seem as if part of an act, an exhilarating performance for audiences who rarely got arrested in the process.[103] Following another raid in 1939, a waiter, possibly a queer employee, uttered: "Although the show is pretty flat at present, we expect to reopen next week as soon as the heat is off."[104] Other entertainers interpreted the raids as "business as usual."[105] They represented a veiled attempt to placate conservative residents, but by no means did police seek to eradicate such nighttime offerings. Law enforcement more often allowed them to operate without fear of any long-term legal retaliation.

Police upheld an even more lax attitude during the winter months when most tourists visited Miami. All reported raids on queer joints in 1939 were conducted during the tourist off-season. That is why a report referred to one raid as "belated."[106] This became national knowledge. "Normally," police raided these spaces, bookie and queer joints alike, "on an average of about once a month and after paying a fine, [club owners or managers] return to business at the old stand." By March, police conducted what one newspaper referred to as "Miami's seasonal 'face washing,'" or raiding the city's vice dens.[107] Club operators and police often played a coy game of cat and mouse wherein clubs under heat tamed the shows just long enough to detract attention. Inevitably, they reintroduced their most risqué acts for tourists. Law enforcement officials seem to have indulged conservative residents' complaints from time to time, but only temporarily and without any long-term results. They did not want vacationers to lament the loss of their playground and, in turn, the mainstay of Miami's economy: tourism.

While some Miami police officers may not have necessarily approved of crude entertainment and instead may have even sympathized with the vigilante groups and residents that retaliated during this era, they understood that a wide-open policy and liberal attitude were necessary to promote tourism. This industry was particularly defined by its abandonment of conservative values and morality. It operated on the transgression of gender and sexual norms, which permitted the city's queer residents a space to work, congregate, and thrive. While New York City sought to curtail much of its gay subculture after repeal, the reverse occurred in Miami. In part to compete with the racialized sex tourism made available in particular Caribbean sites through the tentacles of US imperialism, Miami's boosters, lawmakers, and police further embraced a liberal moral code during its ever-expanding tourist season. This occurred to the chagrin of the city's conservative and religious forces that sought to curb, but could not eradicate, Miami's visible queer nightlife. Queers had become a central feature in making Miami a playground at the Caribbean-US borderlands.

Miami's liberal policy remained in place—albeit with some post-tourist-season or arbitrary crackdowns and raids—until the late 1940s. Among several other changes, by the early 1950s renewed competition from Cuba's pre-1959 revolution tourism industry, Cold War gender and sexual anxieties, and a more concerted effort to diversify Miami's economy radically altered the lives and experiences of the city's queers.[108] "We don't want [sexual] perverts to set up housekeeping in this county," claimed Dade County sheriff Thomas J. Kelly in 1954, representative of the area's shift in attitude toward queer individuals and communities.[109] Tourism would continue to control much of Miami's urban identity, however. For instance, by 1945 Miami had earned its badge as "the least industrialized metropolitan district in the United States." Even then, much of its limited manufacturing remained connected to the success of its tourism.[110] Although Kelly's perspective became the norm, if not the official policy, among most of the city's power brokers, the area's continued reliance on tourism allowed queers to carve out distinct spaces in the city and its pleasure-seeking economy. After all, Miami's tourism thrived on its ability to subvert established norms, including those manifest through gender and sexuality.

Julio Capó Jr. is assistant professor in the Department of History and Commonwealth Honors College at the University of Massachusetts, Amherst. He researches inter-American histories, with a focus on queer, sexuality, gender, urban, Latinx, race, (im)migration, and empire studies. His book *Welcome to Fairyland* chronicles Miami's transnational queer past from 1890 to 1940. His work has appeared in the *Journal of Urban History, Journal of American Ethnic History, Diplomatic History,* as well as *Time*, the *Washington Post*, and the *Miami Herald*.

Notes

The author would like to thank the editors of this issue, especially Jason Ruiz, for their guidance. He is also grateful to the two anonymous reviewers, Marc Stein, Melanie Shell-Weiss, and participants of the Five College History Seminar for their sharp feedback on earlier drafts of this work.

1. *Miami Herald*, "Club Klan Raided"; "La Paloma Ban Asked by State."
2. *Miami Herald*, "Club Klan Raided."
3. Ibid.
4. Ibid.
5. *Miami Herald*, "County Night Spots Closed."
6. "La Paloma Club Reopens."
7. Eastman, Scott and Company Summer Campaign; "Florida to Make Strong Bid for Summer Tourists."
8. Rose, *Struggle for Black Freedom*; Connolly, *World More Concrete*; Shell-Weiss, *Coming to Miami*; García, *Havana USA*; Mohl, "Black Immigrants."
9. *El mundo*, May 30, 1936 (my translation); reprinted in Maribona, *Turismo y ciudadanía*, 311.
10. Chauncey, *Gay New York*, chap. 12.
11. Heap, *Slumming*, chap. 6.
12. Boyd, *Wide-Open Town*, 47–48.

13. For more on distinct localized uses of the term, see Chauncey, *Gay New York*; Woolner, "'Woman Slain.'"

14. Sedgwick, *Epistemology of the Closet*; Cohen, "Punks, Bulldaggers, and Welfare Queens"; Stein, *Rethinking the Gay and Lesbian Movement*, 8–9.

15. Vanderblue, "Florida Land Boom II."

16. Sessa, "Miami in 1926," 34.

17. Dorman, "Miami Bootlegger."

18. Sáenz Rovner, "Prohibición norteamericana."

19. *St. Petersburg (FL) Evening Independent*, "Florida Gulf Coast."

20. *Literary Digest*, "Bootlegger's Bad Ways," 34.

21. Carter, "Florida and Rumrunning," 49.

22. Schwartz, *Pleasure Island*, 40, 45.

23. Berlin, "I'll See You in C-U-B-A."

24. Maribona, *Turismo y ciudadanía*, 95 (my translation).

25. Pérez, *On Becoming Cuban.*

26. López Lima, *Turismo y urbanismo*, 11–15 (my translation). See also Corporacíon Nacional del Turismo, "Boletín."

27. López Lima, *Turismo y urbanismo*, 116–17.

28. Rodríguez, "The Architectural Avant-Garde," 255–263.

29. Maribona, *Turismo y ciudadanía*, 296–97 (my translation).

30. Ibid., 206 (my translation).

31. *Avance*, September 29, 1935 (my translation), reprinted in Maribona, *Turismo y ciudadanía*, 135–37.

32. Ibid. (my translation). In some circles in Cuba today, the word *"cuadro"* can also refer to group sex that may be exhibitionist or performed for entertainment purposes. While its usage in Cuba during the 1930s carried the element of sexual exhibitionism, it is uncertain if the phrase may have held this specific meaning then too. Thank you to Annet Sanchez for helping me make this distinction.

33. Pérez, *Cuba in the American Imagination*, 235–37.

34. Maribona, *Turismo y ciudadanía*, 320 (my translation).

35. Ibid. (my translation).

36. Ibid., 296 (my translation).

37. De la Fuente, *Nation for All*; Dur and Gilcrease, "US Diplomacy."

38. Carson, "Ifs and Ands of Race Track Gambling."

39. Committee of One Hundred, *Newsletter.*

40. *El mundo*, May 30, 1936 (my translation), reprinted in Maribona, *Turismo y ciudadanía*, 311.

41. Matherly, "Primary Functions of Florida Advertising"; "Millions Are Being Spent to Take Business Away."

42. U.S. House of Representatives, *Prohibition Amendment*, 730–31.

43. Globe Tours, Inc., *Havana Tours.*

44. Davis Tours, Inc., *Havana.*

45. Schwartz, *Pleasure Island*, 70.

46. Briggs, *Reproducing Empire*, chap. 3. See also Kline, *Building a Better Race.*

47. *Miami Metropolis*, "Segregated District and Home for Disorderly Women Urged."

48. B. Angus to Governor David Sholtz.

49. Kofoed, "Miami," 673.

50. Quoted in "Greater Miami, World Resort."

51. Sheriff Dan Hardie to Governor David Sholtz, January 30, 1933. See also Schwartz, *Pleasure Island.*
52. "Excerpt from WQAM News Program."
53. Bergreen, *Capone,* 78–81.
54. Leslie, "Great Depression in Miami Beach," 44.
55. *Miami Daily News,* "City Commission Adopts New Vagrancy Ordinance."
56. Quoted in *Sky Talk,* "Florida and the Gamblers."
57. Greater Miami Ministerial Association to Governor David Sholtz.
58. Greater Miami Ministerial Association, statement issued.
59. Ibid.
60. "Miami Is Wide Open Again."
61. P. L. Dodge to Governor David Sholtz.
62. *St. Petersburg (FL) Times,* "Large Sum Bet."
63. Bell, "O'er the Sports Desk."
64. Sheriff Dan Hardie to Governor David Sholtz, January 30, 1932. Hardie to Sholtz.
65. Walters, *Audition,* 34–35; *New York Times,* "Bill Dwyer Dies."
66. "Colorful Crowd Sees Program of Six Races."
67. Anonymous to L. R. Railey.
68. "La Paloma 'Artists' Handed $25 Fines."
69. *Friday Night.*
70. Charteris, *Saint in Miami,* 140, 136–37.
71. Cross, "Race Plant at Tropical Park."
72. "Irving Young."
73. Connolly, *World More Concrete,* 80–81.
74. Grant, "Crime over Miami," 83–84.
75. Wheatley, *Murder off Miami*; Chauncey, "Christian Brotherhood or Sexual Perversion?"
76. King, *Murder Masks Miami,* 33, 58–60, 106, 156.
77. "Trio Convicted in Club Brawl."
78. "Club Brawl Jails Three."
79. Killen, "Miami Night Clubs"; *Time,* "Good Season."
80. *Time,* "Good Season."
81. Chauncey, *Gay New York,* 227–28.
82. Killen, "Miami Night Clubs."
83. Chauncey, *Gay New York,* chap. 12.
84. Kofoed, *Moon over Miami,* 229–31.
85. "Torch Is Told to Clean Show."
86. *Miami Herald,* "Night Spot Closing Order."
87. *Friday Night,* "Illegal or Legal Liquor."
88. Grant, "Crime over Miami," 62.
89. Laws of Florida, chap. 17833; *Miami Herald,* "Zoning Regulations."
90. Boyd, *Wide-Open Town,* 52–56, 73–83.
91. Kofoed, *Moon over Miami,* 229.
92. Heap, *Slumming,* 240.
93. Kofoed, "Boys in Girls' Clothes."
94. Butler, *Gender Trouble,* 175–193.
95. *Palm Beach Post,* "Miami Club Must Change Its Songs."
96. Kofoed, "Boys in Girls' Clothes."
97. Dunn, *Black Miami,* 117–24.

98.   MacLean, *Behind the Mask of Chivalry*, xiii, 98–99.

99.   *Miami Herald*, "Klan Is Not Law."

100. *New York Times*, "Miami Night Life."

101. *Miami Herald*, "Night Spot Closing Order"; *Miami Herald*, "Early Club Opening Is Seen."

102. "Sheriff Raids Two Night Clubs."

103. Heap, *Slumming*, 52–53.

104. "La Paloma Ban Asked by State."

105. "Sheriff Raids Two Night Clubs."

106. Ibid.; *St. Petersburg (FL) Evening Independent*, "Two Miami Clubs Raided."

107. McDermott, "Male Strip-Tease Act Too Raw."

108. Schwartz, *Pleasure Island*; Fejes, "Murder, Perversion, and Moral Panic"; Johnson, *Lavender Scare*; Capó, "'It's Not Queer to Be Gay.'"

109. *Miami Daily News*, "Raiders Seize Nineteen."

110. Wolff, *Miami*, 85.

References

Angus, B. 1933. Letter to Governor David Sholtz, February 27. File 8, box 4, ser. 278, State Archives of Florida, Tallahassee.

Anonymous. 1928. Letter to L. R. Railey, November 20. Railey Family Papers, HistoryMiami, Miami.

Bell, Jack. 1933. "O'er the Sports Desk." *Miami Daily News*, December 30.

Bergreen, Laurence. 1994. *Capone: The Man and the Era*. New York: Simon and Schuster.

Berlin, Irving. 1920. "I'll See You in C-U-B-A." Music and lyrics, item 45, box 78, Levy Sheet Music Collection, Johns Hopkins University, Baltimore.

Boyd, Nan Alamilla. 2003. *Wide-Open Town: A History of Queer San Francisco to 1965*. Berkeley: University of California Press.

Briggs, Laura. 2002. *Reproducing Empire: Race, Sex, Science, and U.S. Imperialism in Puerto Rico*. Berkeley: University of California Press.

Butler, Judith. 1990. *Gender Trouble: Feminism and the Subversion of Identity*. New York: Routledge.

Capó, Julio, Jr. 2011. "'It's Not Queer to Be Gay': Miami and the Emergence of the Gay Rights Movement, 1945–1995." PhD diss., Florida International University.

Carson, James. 1929. "The Ifs and Ands of Race Track Gambling in Florida." April. Railey Family Papers, HistoryMiami, Miami.

Carter, James A., III. 1969. "Florida and Rumrunning during National Prohibition." *Florida Historical Quarterly* 48, no. 1: 47–56.

Charteris, Leslie. 1944. *The Saint in Miami*. Philadelphia: Triangle Books. First published 1940 by Crime Club.

Chauncey, George. 1985. "Christian Brotherhood or Sexual Perversion? Homosexual Identities and the Construction of Sexual Boundaries in the World War One Era." *Journal of Social History* 19, no. 2: 189–211.

———. 1994. *Gay New York: Gender, Urban Culture, and the Making of the Gay Male World, 1890–1940*. New York: Basic Books.

"Club Brawl Jails Three." n.d. Newspaper clipping, box 1, Robert R. Taylor Scrapbooks, HistoryMiami, Miami.

Cohen, Cathy J. 1997. "Punks, Bulldaggers, and Welfare Queens: The Radical Potential of Queer Politics?" *GLQ: A Journal of Lesbian and Gay Studies* 3, no. 4: 437–65.

"Colorful Crowd Sees Program of Six Races." n.d. Newspaper clipping, Railey Family Papers, HistoryMiami, Miami.

Committee of One Hundred. 1934. *Newsletter*, May 4. Box 20, Committee of One Hundred Records, HistoryMiami, Miami.

Connolly, N. D. B. 2014. *A World More Concrete: Real Estate and the Remaking of Jim Crow South Florida*. Chicago: University of Chicago Press.

Corporacíon Nacional del Turismo. 1935. "Boletín." December. Folder 1, box 27, ser. 278, State Archives of Florida, Tallahassee.

Cross, Austin F. 1936. "Race Plant at Tropical Park, Miami." *Ottawa (ONT) Evening Citizen*, April 13.

Davis Tours, Inc. c. 1930. *Havana*. Guidebook, XC2002.11.4.219, Vicki Gold Levi Collection, Wolfsonian–Florida International University, Miami Beach.

de la Fuente, Alejandro. 2001. *A Nation for All: Race, Inequality, and Politics in Twentieth-Century Cuba*. Chapel Hill: University of North Carolina Press.

Dodge, P. L. 1933. Letter to Governor David Sholtz, November 10. File 17, box 29, ser. 278, State Archives of Florida, Tallahassee.

Dorman, Bob. 1924. "Miami Bootlegger Is a Businessman." *Bluefield (WV) Daily Telegraph*, December 14.

Dunn, Marvin. 1997. *Black Miami in the Twentieth Century*. Gainesville: University Press of Florida.

Dur, Philip, and Christopher Gilcrease. 2002. "US Diplomacy and the Downfall of a Cuban Dictator: Machado in 1933." *Journal of Latin American Studies* 34, no. 2: 255–82.

Eastman, Scott and Company Summer Campaign. n.d. File 3, box 4, ser. 278, State Archives of Florida, Tallahassee.

"Excerpt from WQAM News Program." 1936. February 29. File 7, box 28, ser. 278, State Archives of Florida, Tallahassee.

Fejes, Fred. 2000. "Murder, Perversion, and Moral Panic: The 1954 Media Campaign against Miami's Homosexuals and the Discourse of Civic Betterment." *Journal of the History of Sexuality* 9, no. 3: 305–47.

"Florida to Make Strong Bid for Summer Tourists." n.d. Newspaper clipping, file 3, box 4, ser. 278, State Archives of Florida, Tallahassee.

Friday Night. 1933. October 20. File 17, box 29, ser. 278, State Archives of Florida, Tallahassee.

———. 1933. "Illegal or Legal Liquor." November 10. File 17, box 29, ser. 278, State Archives of Florida, Tallahassee.

García, María Cristina. 1996. *Havana USA: Cuban Exiles and Cuban Americans in South Florida, 1959–1994*. Berkeley: University of California Press.

Globe Tours, Inc. c. 1925. *Havana Tours*. Brochure, XC2002.11.4.13, Vicki Gold Levi Collection, Wolfsonian–Florida International University, Miami Beach.

Grant, Maxwell. 2014. "Crime over Miami." In *The Shadow, No. 83*, 58–111. San Antonio: Sanctum Books. Originally published 1940.

"Greater Miami, World Resort." n.d. Newspaper clipping, Railey Family Papers, HistoryMiami, Miami.

Greater Miami Ministerial Association. 1927. Statement issued. January. Railey Family Papers, HistoryMiami, Miami.

———. 1933. Letter to Governor David Sholtz, July 14. File 15, box 29, ser. 278, State Archives of Florida, Tallahassee.

Hardie, Dan (Sheriff). 1932. Letter to Governor David Sholtz, January 30. File 2, box 30, ser. 278, State Archives of Florida, Tallahassee.

Hardie, Dan (Sheriff). 1933. Letter to Governor David Sholtz, January 30. File 2, box 30, ser. 278, State Archives of Florida, Tallahassee.

Heap, Chad. 2009. *Slumming: Sexual and Racial Encounters in American Nightlife, 1885–1940*. Chicago: University of Chicago Press.

"Irving Young." n.d. C-17584, box 95, ser. 1063, State Archives of Florida, Tallahassee.

Johnson, David K. 2004. *The Lavender Scare: The Cold War Persecution of Gays and Lesbians in the Federal Government*. Chicago: University of Chicago Press.

Killen, James L. 1940. "Miami Night Clubs Drawing the Spenders." *Hammond (IN) Times*, January 19.

King, Rufus. 1939. *Murder Masks Miami*. New York: Popular Library.

Kline, Wendy. 2005. *Building a Better Race: Gender, Sexuality, and Eugenics from the Turn of the Century to the Baby Boom*. Berkeley: University of California Press.

Kofoed, Jack. 1929. "Miami." *North American Review* 228, no. 6: 670–73.

———. 1939. "Boys in Girls' Clothes Open Another Problem." *Miami Daily News*, March 22.

———. 1955. *Moon over Miami*. New York: Random House.

"La Paloma 'Artists' Handed $25 Fines." n.d. Newspaper clipping, box 1, Robert R. Taylor Scrapbooks, HistoryMiami, Miami.

"La Paloma Ban Asked by State." n.d. Newspaper clipping, box 1, Robert R. Taylor Scrapbooks, HistoryMiami, Miami.

"La Paloma Club Reopens." n.d. Newspaper clipping, box 1, Robert R. Taylor Scrapbooks, HistoryMiami, Miami.

Leslie, Vernon M. 1980. "The Great Depression in Miami Beach." Master's thesis, Florida Atlantic University.

Literary Digest. 1922. "The Bootlegger's Bad Ways and Big Profits." December 30, 31-34.

López Lima, Reinaldo. 1949. *Turismo y urbanismo*. Havana. G155.C9L6, Cuban Heritage Collection, University of Miami, Coral Gables, FL.

MacLean, Nancy. 1994. *Behind the Mask of Chivalry: The Making of the Second Ku Klux Klan*. New York: Oxford University Press.

Maribona, Armando. 1942. *Turismo y ciudadanía*. Havana: Editorial Alrededor de América. G155.C9M3, Cuban Heritage Collection, University of Miami, Coral Gables, FL.

Matherly, Walter J. n.d. "Primary Functions of Florida Advertising." File 4, box 4, ser. 278, State Archives of Florida, Tallahassee.

McDermott, John B. 1944. "Male Strip-Tease Act Too Raw." *St. Petersburg (FL) Times*, March 24.

Miami Daily News. 1930. "City Commission Adopts New Vagrancy Ordinance." May 23.

———. 1954. "Raiders Seize Nineteen in Pervert Roundup." August 14.

Miami Herald. 1937. "Club Klan Raided Closed Down after Sheriff's Warning." November 17.

———. 1937. "County Night Spots Closed by Sheriff." November 19.

———. 1937. "Early Club Opening Is Seen by Manager." November 18.

———. 1937. "Klan Is Not Law." November 17.

———. 1937. "Night Spot Closing Order Is Modified." November 20.

———. 1937. "Zoning Regulations in County Discussed." November 18.

"Miami Is Wide Open Again." n.d. Newspaper clipping, Railey Family Papers, HistoryMiami, Miami.

Miami Metropolis. 1918. "Segregated District and Home for Disorderly Women Urged." November 30.

"Millions Are Being Spent to Take Business Away from Florida." n.d. File 4, box 4, ser. 278, State Archives of Florida, Tallahassee.

Mohl, Raymond A. 1987. "Black Immigrants: Bahamians in Early Twentieth-Century Miami." *Florida Historical Quarterly* 65, no. 3: 271–97.

New York Times. 1937. "Miami Night Life Loses 'Hot Spots.'" November 22.

———. 1946. "Bill Dwyer Dies; 'Bootlegger King.'" December 11.

Palm Beach Post. 1937. "Miami Club Must Change Its Songs." July 21.

Pérez, Louis A., Jr. 1999. *On Becoming Cuban: Identity, Nationality, and Culture*. Chapel Hill: University of North Carolina Press.

———. 2008. *Cuba in the American Imagination: Metaphor and the Imperial Ethos*. Chapel Hill: University of North Carolina Press.

Rose, Chanelle N. 2015. *The Struggle for Black Freedom in Miami: Civil Rights and America's Tourist Paradise, 1896–1968*. Baton Rouge: Louisiana State University Press.

Sáenz Rovner, Eduardo. 2004. "La prohibición norteamericana y el contrabando entre Cuba y los Estados Unidos durante los años veinte y treinta." *Innovar: Revista de ciencias administrativas y sociales*, no. 23: 147–57.

Schwartz, Rosalie. 1997. *Pleasure Island: Tourism and Temptation in Cuba*. Lincoln: University of Nebraska Press.

Sedgwick, Eve Kosofsky. 1990. *Epistemology of the Closet*. Berkeley: University of California Press.

Sessa, Frank B. 1956. "Miami in 1926." *Tequesta*, no. 16: 15–36.

Shell-Weiss, Melanie. 2009. *Coming to Miami: A Social History*. Gainesville: University Press of Florida.

"Sheriff Raids Two Night Clubs." n.d. Newspaper clipping, box 1, Robert R. Taylor Scrapbooks, HistoryMiami, Miami.

Sky Talk. 1929. "Florida and the Gamblers." May 25. Railey Family Papers, HistoryMiami, Miami.

St. Petersburg (FL) Evening Independent. 1923. "Florida Gulf Coast Is Called Paradise for Bootleggers." July 10.

———. 1939. "Two Miami Clubs Raided by Cops." March 23.

St. Petersburg (FL) Times. 1933. "Large Sum Bet during Hialeah Racing Program." March 15.

Stein, Marc. 2012. *Rethinking the Gay and Lesbian Movement*. New York: Routledge.

Time. 1941. "Good Season." March 17.

"Torch Is Told to Clean Show or Close Club." n.d. Newspaper clipping, box 1, Robert R. Taylor Scrapbooks, HistoryMiami, Miami.

"Trio Convicted in Club Brawl." n.d. Newspaper clipping, box 1, Robert R. Taylor Scrapbooks, HistoryMiami, Miami.

U.S. House of Representatives. 1930. *Prohibition Amendment: Hearings before the House Committee on the Judiciary, Part 2*. 71st Cong., 2nd sess, April 2. Washington, DC: Government Printing Office.

Vanderblue, Homer B. 1927. "The Florida Land Boom II." *Journal of Land and Public Utility Economics* 3, no. 3: 252–69.

Walters, Barbara. 2009. *Audition: A Memoir*. New York: Vintage Books.

Wheatley, Dennis. 1936. *Murder off Miami*. London: Hutchinson.

Wolff, Reinhold P. 1945. *Miami: Economic Patters of a Resort Area*. Coral Gables, FL: University of Miami, Inc.

Woolner, Cookie. 2015. "'Woman Slain in Queer Love Brawl': African American Women, Same-Sex Desire, and Violence in the Urban North, 1920–1929." *Journal of African American History* 100, no. 3: 406–27.

Performance over Policy

Promoting Indianness in Twentieth-Century Wisconsin Tourism

Katrina Phillips

In 1921 the *Milwaukee Sentinel* excitedly informed its readers that the town of Wisconsin Rapids in central Wisconsin had been "peacefully invaded" by hundreds of Indians whose arrival gave the city "the appearance of a frontier town."[1] The Indians had come to town for a powwow that offered non-Native residents and tourists the chance to see reconstructed tepees on the outskirts of town where the Indians would "live as of yore" while partaking in Indian games and dances. Another newspaper, the *Milwaukee Journal*, expected that the powwow would draw nearly one thousand Indians, including warriors in "war paint and feathers" with Indian ponies pulling camp equipment, tents, and rations.[2] It would be, the *Superior Telegram* boasted, "one of the greatest Indian celebrations ever held," attracting enough Indian participants to be considered "the biggest [powwow] in this state, since the days of the scalping knife and tomahawk."[3]

The events in Wisconsin Rapids were not the only ones aimed at tourists in early twentieth-century Wisconsin. In fact, Wisconsin newspapers promoted numerous Indian powwows, dances, and historical pageants in 1921 alone, from Green Bay and Wisconsin Rapids to Keshena and the Wisconsin Dells, that sought to open the floodgates of tourists. This article demonstrates how Wisconsin's tourism industry in the late nineteenth and early twentieth centuries created an economy that was entirely at odds with federal Indian policy edicts at the turn of the century

Radical History Review
Issue 129 (October 2017)   DOI 10.1215/01636545-3920667
© 2017 by MARHO: The Radical Historians' Organization, Inc.

by highlighting the strategic incorporation of Indians and Indian imagery, the rise in the number of tourist endeavors in Wisconsin that featured, showcased, or referenced American Indians, and the similarly strategic participation of Indians in tourism endeavors.

John Troutman has shown how music shaped federal Indian policy and the federal government's citizenship agenda for American Indians, which focused on allotment and assimilation in the late nineteenth and early twentieth centuries. The Office of Indian Affairs (OIA), along with reformers and church and government officials, believed that the continued, nearly unabated performances of songs, dances, and ceremonials—part of what Troutman calls "expressive culture"—had become barriers to citizenship. For the OIA and its compatriots, restricting or banning these apparent barriers were ways to hasten indigenous citizenship. Troutman's intervention lies in his assertion that many American Indians resisted these calls for civilization programs and citizenship despite the decrees and legislation that came down from government agencies. It is also critical to note that the government's intentions were not always mirrored by the general public, many of whom traveled near and far to witness performances of expressive culture by American Indians across the country.[4]

This article, then, builds on Troutman's analysis to argue that, in turn-of-the-century Wisconsin, many of these productions, often—but not always—staged by non-Native boosters and businesspeople, were not wholly grounded in romanticism or nostalgia for the Indians of days of yore. Tourism endeavors in the mid- to late nineteenth century often promoted the state's natural resources, from peaceful lakes and streams to quaint resorts in the wilderness, while ignoring regional Indians. By the turn of the century, however, Indians became an integral part of numerous tourism ventures even as government officials worked to ban indigenous culture and assimilate Indians. These Indian performances staged in Wisconsin in the early twentieth century highlight the struggle at the intersection of federal policies and state tourism initiatives. Town businesses and boosters looked for ways to lure tourists to growing towns, while government agents saw Indian songs, dances, and other cultural productions as the clearest markers of indigenous savagery.

"Both the Indians and the Officials Welcome You":
Indian-Centered Tourism and Federal Policy

In 1921, the same year Wisconsin Rapids promoted what the *Marshfield News* called "the invasion of the Indian delegation," the *Portage Democrat* reported that more than 150 Indians would stage a powwow, a harvest dance, and an "old-time Scalp Dance" at Stand Rock in the Wisconsin Dells.[5] The powwow and dance grounds in the Dells, on the same spot "that was used by their ancestors more than a hundred years ago for war councils, religious ceremonies and tribal feasts and festivals," could accommodate fifteen hundred visitors. Admission, including round-trip fare on a steamer, would cost visitors $1.15. The *Portage Democrat* did not balk at the price of admission, noting that "the Indians, with all the financial acumen of their white brothers, are conducting the pow-wow along strictly commercialized lines and are looking after the dollars—which is all well and good, because in this age the Indian as well as the paleface must pay when he eats."[6] A few weeks later, the *Milwaukee Journal* admitted that, while the admission price to the Wisconsin Rapids powwow would not be known until the opening day, it would be more than the $0.25 and $0.50 charged in 1917 and 1920, respectively.[7] The *De Pere Democrat* boasted that the 1921 Oneida Indian Centennial was "the biggest celebration by Indians ever held in this country." The newspaper outlined a dizzying array of events, including lacrosse and baseball games, Indian pony races, Indian cooking demonstrations, and dances, along with Indian camps and villages where visitors could see participants "making baskets of all kinds, bead work, moccasins, bows and arrows and other articles peculiarly Indian as to origin."[8]

These statewide events, however, coincided with the issuance of Circular 1665 in the spring of 1921. Commissioner of Indian Affairs Charles Burke addressed the circular to superintendents at Indian agencies, noting that, while Indian dances seemed to be less frequent than before, there were still enough "evil" and "degrading tendencies" in these performances to warrant increased supervision and "punitive measures" to discourage indigenous participation.[9] Burke's proclamation was not a blanket condemnation of all dancing, but focused instead on the Sun Dance and related religious ceremonies. Moreover, he also insisted that superintendents work to regulate what he called "frequent or prolonged periods of celebration which bring the Indians together from remote points to the neglect of their crops, livestock, and home interests."[10]

The assimilation-minded commissioner might have been positively apoplectic if he had learned that Indians had traveled from Minnesota, the Dakotas, Montana, Nebraska, and Idaho, as well as within Wisconsin, for the Wisconsin Rapids powwow or that the Indians at Stand Rock would interpret old tribal rites "in savage costume."[11] Broadly speaking, assimilation policies intended to integrate American Indians into US society by removing the influences of indigenous language, culture, religion, and social, economic, and political structures. Assimilation proponents often targeted Indian songs and dances because these cultural elements highlighted the supposed savagery of Indianness.[12] Circular 1665 was just one of many pieces of federal Indian policy that sought to further assimilate American Indians into non-Native society in the late nineteenth and early twentieth centuries. While Clyde Ellis and John Troutman have demonstrated that Circular 1665 lacked statutory authority and failed to reduce or control Native dances, Burke's stance in 1921 and a similar, subsequent circular in 1923 reveal the widespread federal sentiments toward these performances.[13]

In 1883 Secretary of the Interior Henry Teller wrote that "the debauchery, diabolism, and savagery of the worst state of the Indian race" was most evident in "the continuance of the old heathenish dances," and he insisted that these performances must meet a swift and permanent death.[14] Several years later, Commissioner of Indian Affairs Robert Belt argued that Indian dances were "ruinous evils" and that Indians should "remain at home and engage in more civilizing avocations."[15] Circular 1665 echoed these prevailing sentiments among many government officials, underscoring the continued attempts—and perhaps emphasizing the failure of—these endeavors to stop Indians from dancing, singing, holding traditional ceremonies, and making traditional items. The opportunities to dance, give demonstrations on Indian handicrafts, and reconnect with friends and family at events such as the one staged in Wisconsin Rapids would not have furthered the assimilation and detribalization objectives of the OIA.[16] Indian reformers fought to control and monitor displays of Indianness including songs and dances, hoping to direct Indians' attention toward apparently proactive, progressive activities such as "officially mandated agricultural, mechanical, or domestic arts."[17] Hopeful tourism promoters, however, recognized the allure of these indigenous cultural markers, performances, and handicraft demonstrations that still characterized Indians as unassimilated. Federal Indian policy sought to bring Indians into the present, while tourist endeavors sought to keep Indians in the past.

"Under the Spotlights": Adding Indians to the Tourist Landscape

In October 1921, six months after Burke's circular, the *Antigo Daily Journal* emphasized the "wonderful beauty and fertility of the Lake Superior plains, together with the unsurpassed attractions to be offered the tourists of the Middle West and the East."[18] The *Superior Telegram* followed suit, claiming that an estimated three hundred thousand cars full of tourists headed west every summer, but only "rivulets from this mighty stream have heretofore flowed into Wisconsin and but a slight trickle has reached the furthermost parts of the state where the forests and the streams and the lakes are the most attractive."[19] The state's tourism industry had initially eliminated Indians from the landscape but soon turned toward Indians in order to show "snapshots of a disappearing primitive past."[20] While government officials promoted policies and practices intended to erase indigeneity, the public did not always share their views. Non-Natives leapt at opportunities to see live performances of traditional songs and dances performed by Indians before assimilation policies and Euro-American progress overtook the Indians. Federal policies such as Circular 1665 sought to indirectly undercut state attempts to build and grow a tourist economy that sought to capitalize on a nationwide fascination with Indians.

Hal Rothman has argued that tourist economies often create a "devil's bargain" between those who are tourists and those who are "toured upon." Wisconsin's deliberate use of Indians, Indian places, and Indian history in the development of its tourism industry produced a similar problem.[21] This path toward a profitable tourist economy was at odds with federal Indian policy and often required Indian participation to authenticate these tourism endeavors. Historians have questioned the motivations of Indian performers in seemingly exploitative arenas, questioning why indigenous people would *willingly* put themselves and their cultures on display, often dressing and acting in ways that non-Natives would consider authentic but that may not have aligned with indigenous perspectives. Scholars have also raised questions regarding the agency of and opportunities for indigenous performers, citing evidence of duplicitous and often unscrupulous tactics employed by producers and managers of touring productions and local tourist promoters.[22]

The widespread participation of American Indians in tourism endeavors that are also distinctly capitalistic enterprises has led Brian Hosmer to wryly examine the "rather commonsensical proposition that Indian people could understand the workings of the capitalist market system and at least attempt some adaptations."[23] At the same time, however, it would be unwise to unilaterally grant agency to indigenous participants in Wisconsin tourism endeavors writ large or assume that subversion of larger settler colonial projects, such as the widespread assimilation and citizenship programs, was the primary motivation behind Indian involvement in these enterprises. It is possible, though, to demonstrate that a vast array of tourism initiatives relied on the use of American Indians to draw tourists to a particular part of the state.

Even as white audiences symbolically and economically consumed Native bodies through touristic enterprises, indigenous performers were able, in varying degrees, to control their commodification in the wake of stringent federal regulations and restrictions surrounding Indian performances. Looking more closely at what James C. Scott calls "hidden transcripts," or the ways subordinated groups push back against public transcripts of domination, scholars such as Adria L. Imada discover counter-colonial movements in the spaces between acquiescence and outright resistance to colonialism.[24] Michael D. McNally argues that, even as Native actors performed "a romanticized Indianness for pay in lean times, they were not determined by that script or rendered wholly absent."[25] Despite contemporary scholars' concerns regarding the potential exploitation of indigeneity for the sake of economic profits, Indians in Wisconsin echoed the larger movement of indigenous participation in performative arenas by, in a sense, capitalizing on financial as well as social opportunities that allowed them to increase their personal profits by performing Indianness.[26] Indians throughout Wisconsin and across the nation hosted dances, powwows, pageants, and other celebrations that were open to the non-Native public. Visitors flocked to these events regardless of admission prices—and regardless of federal attempts to restrict or ban these performances.

Newspaper articles archived by the Wisconsin Historical Society, and on which this article draws, provide a bevy of information regarding the promotional attributes of these productions, as well as occasionally offering insight into the types of events and performances produced throughout the state. Those from the early twentieth century rarely emphasize what more recent scholarship has sought to understand: the agency and motivation of the indigenous peoples who participated in these tourist endeavors. Therefore, this essay centers on the promotional aspect of Indian-centered tourism and the development of the tourist industry around Wisconsin amid the tug-of-war between state interests and federal policies.

"Into the Wild and Silent Wilderness": The Rise of the Tourism Industry

Tourism was a flourishing industry in the eastern United States by the 1820s, emerging at a pivotal moment in US society when Americans were working to define their national identity in opposition to Europe.[27] In Wisconsin and elsewhere, the tourist industry initially sought to capitalize on Americans' fascination with the nation's landscape and its original inhabitants. Kilbourn City in south-central Wisconsin eventually renamed itself "Wisconsin Dells" to capitalize on the popularity of the Dells on the Wisconsin River. The Dells were known as the region's greatest natural wonder as early as the mid-1840s and quickly became one of the state's first tourist destinations.[28] By 1849, when Wisconsin naturalist Increase A. Lapham toured the region, the area already boasted an exciting history to draw tourists in, a hotel, and residents eager to entertain visitors. While Lapham's somewhat dry, geologically centered descriptions of the "many fantastic shapes in the cliffs" may not have been thrilling entries in a tourists' guidebook, the early fascination with the area soon turned into a booming business.[29]

These early tourist manuals and promotional materials rarely featured Indians. Instead, they emphasized the area's natural landscape and beauty. Lakes and rivers held bountiful fish to catch, and the woods hid game animals for hunting. Those not inclined toward hunting and fishing could tour breathtaking sites whose innate splendor had clearly been preserved. According to these materials, Wisconsin Indians had disappeared from the historical narrative and the landscape, implicitly assuring tourists that their pilgrimages to "wild-seeming scenic spots" were, in fact, to places that were now considered "well-tamed."[30] While this early erasure and denial of Wisconsin's indigenous populations was usually presented as a natural process, it underscores the dramatic shift to the later incorporation of, if not reliance on, Indians, Indian places, and Indian histories in the growth and expansion of the state's tourism industry.

Tourists started inching into what is now the Midwest by the middle of the nineteenth century. By the late 1860s, lakes in southern Wisconsin were fashionable vacation spots, attracting tourists from Milwaukee, Chicago, Memphis, and New Orleans.[31] By the 1870s, railroad companies and local entrepreneurs led concerted efforts to attract tourists to Wisconsin. An 1875 tourists' guide to the Wisconsin Dells embraced the "prose, romance and poetry of this wonderful region," teasing the general public with stories of "the natural wonders and beauties of the scenery surrounding Kilbourn City, and more especially the notable Dells of the Wisconsin [River] and the strange, wild glens and canyons which enter the Dells from either side."[32] Established business owners and entrepreneurs, encouraged by the early success at the Dells, quickly began building cabins, cottages, and resorts and contracting with railroad and steamship companies. Soon after, wealthy urban tourists began traveling to Wisconsin to avail themselves of the numerous opportunities for outdoor recreation and relaxation. Newspaper writers swooned over "the clean air, breathtaking sunsets, and wondrous meetings of soaring red bluffs and deep blue water" that held "even more allure for visitors."[33] An 1875 guide to summer resorts in Wisconsin, Minnesota, and Michigan, published as a supplement to a railroad routes and rates book, listed more than a dozen Wisconsin destinations. The guide, for instance, extolled sailing, rowing, and fishing near Milwaukee, which also had "the full benefit of the cool and refreshing lake breeze." The Water Cure at the Bidwell House in Palmyra, Wisconsin, promised to offer "speedy and permanent relief" for diseases that had "baffled the skill of man, and have been pronounced incurable."[34]

For most of the nineteenth century, tourism in Wisconsin was a parallel industry operating alongside fishing, logging, and quarrying, among other industries, especially in the northern part of the state.[35] As the nineteenth century barreled toward the twentieth and extractive resource industries declined, the state needed to find a new direction toward economic prosperity. An infrastructure for tourism already existed throughout most of the state, thanks to the proliferation of railroad lines that crisscrossed the state and the burgeoning automobile industry.[36] Abandoning these pathways was not an option after all the time and money spent building railway lines, locks and docks for steamships, and roads. Rather than exporting resources out of the state, tourism intended to import people—primarily people from larger cities, such as Chicago, Milwaukee, Minneapolis, and St. Paul, and even from cities as far south as St. Louis, who hoped to escape the "noise, congestion, and pace of urban life."[37] In an effort to appeal to more potential visitors, the state promoted palliative cures for city living, such as the Wisconsin Dells and the restorative resorts that capitalized on painting their land, water, and air as pristine, while outdoor recreation endeavors offered tourists the chance to fish, swim, dive, surf, trap shoot, play golf and tennis, and take motorboat trips and automobile excursions.[38]

"The Story Must Be True": Incorporating Indians into Wisconsin Tourism

The Indians of Wisconsin soon proved to be as economically viable as the state's lakes, rivers, and forests, all of which were marketed toward a traveling US public that had become disillusioned with the burgeoning urban environment and had the time and money to travel.[39] As large cities became more crowded, the country life came to be more appealing to urban whites. City folks hopped in their cars, boarded a steamship, or bought a train ticket to a destination that promised fresh air and a respite from the daily toils of city life. Increasing numbers of city folks throughout the industrialized United States fled their "bureaucratized lives in steamy hot cities for the northern edges of civilization, where they hoped to brush up against something refreshing and authentic."[40] This idea of the "refreshing and authentic" became, in many instances, tied either directly or indirectly to the ideals of Indianness that cast indigenous peoples and cultures as the pinnacle of authenticity in the midst of what seemed to be an increasingly inauthentic and modern world.[41]

In 1880 Chicago attorney John Lyle King boasted that the northern wildernesses offered a "grateful reprieve and a speedy reparation" from the "exhaustion that comes of the inordinate and exacting frets and activities of business, the languor and inertia of summer fervors, the *ennui* and satiety that follow the dissipations of social life."[42] Historian Chantal Norrgard has shown that non-Native tourists in Wisconsin, envisioning a vacation in a true wilderness, insisted that the Indians they employed cater to their expectations of "a primitive people who were close to nature," a people who built and paddled birch-bark canoes, danced in traditional regalia, made moccasins for visitors, told stories around the campfire, and used "traditional" tracking methods to guide hunters and fishermen.[43] Outdoor adventures freed Chicago lawyers and capitalists such as King and his companions from the restraints and stress of the city and civilization, proffering instead the imagined freedom and simplicity of a rural idyll. The men relied on two Menominee Indian guides, whom King asserted were the most critical tools at the tourists' disposal. They were natural foresters and skilled canoeists, men with acute senses whom he deemed "the navigator of the birch-bark, the carrier of the luggage, the tent-builder, the log-heap fireman, the cook, the baker, the scallion, in fact the indispensable general utility man and brother."[44]

The Menominee guides King and his fellow outdoorsmen employed were not the only ones who worked for tourists and travelers, and they would not be the only ones whose everyday lives became entangled in the up-and-coming tourist industry in Wisconsin. An 1897 bicycling guide encouraged cyclists to visit the "Chippewa Indian reservation" in Odanah, in the northern part of the state, calling it "an enjoyable trip for wheelmen who desire to see the red man at home."[45] The tourists who trekked to northern Wisconsin in the late 1800s and early 1900s wanted to see a primitive wilderness, and they also wanted to see the seemingly primitive Indians who lived in that wilderness. Tourists eagerly traveled to Indian villages and reservations, excitedly commenting on what they deemed "the barbarous and uncivilized conditions of the reservations."[46]

Railroads, hotels, and resorts also made arrangements for and promoted Indian performances to offer their guests the wilderness experiences that urban tourists craved. In 1896 Indian agent William Mercer and William F. "Buffalo Bill" Cody brought Bad River Ojibwe leaders together with Cody's employed Dakota performers to sign a "peace treaty" on the grounds of Ashland's grand Hotel Chequa-megon, built on the shores of Lake Superior in the 1870s by Wisconsin Central Railroad interests. Mercer and Cody believed that a dramatic signing of a peace treaty would thrill and delight non-Natives in the surrounding region.[47] Nearly nine hundred Bad River and Lac du Flambeau Ojibwe came to Ashland for the event and, according to Eric Olmanson, the sheer number of Ojibwe at the Hotel Chequa-megon also became something of a tourist attraction. Hundreds of Ashland residents went down to Front Street to see "the dusky men and women whose presence had converted the Chequamegon into a veritable Indian reserve."[48]

American Indians worked in the Wisconsin tourism industry as fishing and hunting guides and, likely to the chagrin of government officials such as Commissioner Burke, participated in public performances staged by both Natives and non-Natives. Indians throughout the state worked in the tourism industry as performers, vendors, domestic workers, or hunting and fishing guides.[49] Others became hosts, willingly or otherwise, to passing motorists. In October 1922, four travelers drove to Keshena Falls. The trip, according to an Oshkosh newspaper, was of particular interest to Arthur Kannenberg, whom the newspaper called "an active student of Indian folklore" and "an official of the Wisconsin Archeological society [*sic*] and also secretary of the Winnebago County Historical and Archeological society." Their visit coincided with a medicine dance. Upon their arrival, a Menominee Indian named Charlie Dutchmann escorted them to the ceremony site. Kannenberg called Dutchmann a personal friend and praised him for his hospitality. While Kannenberg's delight is palpable, the newspaper makes no mention of any Indians other than Dutchmann and a couple who entertained the travelers before they made their way to the dance. The newspaper emphasizes not only the unusual privilege but also the party's fascination with the ceremony they happened upon. It paints the party's experience as a chance encounter to see twentieth-century Indians revert "back to the customs of their ancestors," noting the rare opportunity to see such a ceremony.[50]

"Rich in Historical Lore": Using Indians and Indian History in Tourist Endeavors

Tourist performances ranged from small, local productions to ones of epic proportions that required weeks, if not months, of practice and preparation.[51] Others simply sought to capitalize on the idea of the Indian without actual Indians. A 1920s brochure from the Chamber of Commerce in Marinette, a town near the Wisconsin-Michigan border on the shores of Lake Michigan, proudly claimed a Native woman as its namesake, encouraging visitors to see the home of "the Indian queen" and "many other interesting and historical spots."[52] While the brochure sadly noted that "the good Queen has passed to the happy hunting grounds of her people," it cheerily promised that the waters that had been the "abiding place of the red man" remained ready for tourist enjoyment, even if the Indians were no longer present. The bungalows at the town's auto tourist camp boasted modern amenities, such as shower baths, lavatories, water fountains, and a writing desk. The camp itself was within twenty miles of Indian gardens and other relics worth visiting, as well as public lake resorts, camping sites, and fishing grounds. For towns such as Marinette, its mere association with Indians of the past was enough to hook potential tourists. The chamber of commerce adroitly used the idea of the Indian past to give cash value and allure to its campground and fishing waters. It subtly assured would-be visitors that exciting tourist opportunities of a kind of vicarious Indianness awaited them in a tamed wilderness, the same streams and fields Indians had once fished and hunted.

In July 1921, the *Milwaukee Journal* trumpeted an upcoming historical pageant and Indian centennial in Green Bay. Promoters and boosters, the article noted, hoped that the trifecta of a homecoming, a historical pageant, and an Indian centennial, including four thousand pageant participants and five thousand Indians, would draw twenty thousand visitors over six days.[53] The Indian centennial commemorated the movement of Oneida Indians from New York to Wisconsin led by Reverend Jedidiah H. Morse, the father of telegraph inventor Samuel Morse.[54] The *Milwaukee Sentinel* boasted that Indians who set up camp at the fairgrounds between Green Bay and De Pere would demonstrate the "primitive methods employed in making bows and arrow, stone axes, baskets, rugs, Indian bread, corn meal, dolls, bead work, and other products of a hundred years ago," even though most of the Indians "engaged in farming and business have forgotten how these things were made." The newspaper was hopeful, however, that the Oneida reservation would be searched "in an effort to find a few of the patriarchs of the tribe "who have not forgotten old Indian customs and whose fingers still possess the cunning to fashion utensils and weapons from crude materials."[55]

Other centennial events included a water carnival, a "Pageant of Progress" parade, and Indian events.[56] Hosted by the Oneida, a huge Indian village arose at the fairgrounds to serve as a gathering place for dances and powwows. Some visiting Indians participated in the pageant, but many seemed to focus on the Oneida Indian Centennial celebration. The *De Pere Democrat* called it "one of the biggest events in the history of the red man," and the schedule of events included lacrosse and baseball games, pony races, dancing, and performances by Robert Bruce, dubbed "the nationally famous Indian cornetist," and Red Cloud, "the great sousaphone player of Sousa's Band," considered "one of the greatest among the many bass horn players which this country has produced," according to John Philip Sousa himself.[57] Even as federal Indian policy continually tried to undermine Indian culture through assimilation, town boosters continued planning, promoting, and hosting events that celebrated Indians and Indian history, and the tourists kept coming.

The Power of Performance over Policy

In 1924 Superintendent W. E. Dunn of the Grand Rapids Agency in Wisconsin Rapids sent a letter to the Commissioner of Indian Affairs. The Indians had held not one, but two powwows the year before, and Dunn noted that they had made "considerable money" on the gate receipts charged to the non-Native audience. Performers had also been hired out by more than half a dozen cities. The Indians earned good money when they left the reservation for these performances, often making more than they could from farming or raising livestock. Dunn, therefore, was unsure how to prevent the Indians from dancing in the absence of other economic opportunities.[58]

As noted throughout this essay, reticence such as Dunn's toward indigenous performances was not always a popular stance. Wisconsin newspapers eagerly publicized upcoming performances throughout the 1920s, often publishing detailed schedules and assuring visitors of the quality of the performances and the accommodations. In 1921 the *Baraboo Daily News* announced that the "Winnebago Indians of the Northwest" had decided to move their annual powwow from Valley Junction to Kilbourn, perhaps to accommodate potentially larger crowds. The year before, the event drew more than three thousand visitors from around the region.[59] In 1922 the *Clintonville Tribune* confidently announced that roads near Wittenberg were in good condition, guaranteeing easy travel for visitors hoping to catch the daily powwows. The powwows, held in addition to a local tribe's annual get-together meeting, were scheduled for every afternoon and every evening at a price of $0.50 for adults and $0.25 for children.[60] In 1924 the annual Indian powwow in Reserve, Wisconsin, drew thousands of tourists determined to catch a glimpse of Indians who "danced with a fevered abandon throughout the four days and nights, oblivious to the staring crowds, the intense heat, bodily fatigue."[61] The *Superior Telegram* wistfully noted that the city-dwelling visitors would leave with only "vivid memories of a few flaring colors, the smoke of the powwow fires along the lake edge and the mumbled chant of the toothless chief who has had handed down to him the sacred legendry of his forefathers of the wilderness." Despite these connotations of the vanishing Indian, the newspaper also outlined the construction of "a new powwow wigwam" that would be much more convenient for the tourists who crowded the reservation, some of whom had traveled a great distance to see the dances.[62]

Despite Burke's best efforts, Circular 1665 did not have its desired effect.[63] The commissioner found himself forced to issue a supplement in 1923 that added half a dozen recommendations for Indian agents, including one that encouraged a propaganda campaign to educate the US public about the ills of Indian dancing and to provide what he called a "healthy substitute."[64] Another recommendation called for a determined effort by government officials, in cooperation with missionaries, to persuade fair management and towns adjacent to reservations to stop commercializing the Indians by soliciting them for show purposes. However, Burke and his fellow government officials did not succeed in wholly banning performances of Indian songs, dances, and ceremonies. In Wisconsin, Indian-centered tourist events continued into the 1930s. In 1931 Indians at Odanah performed a historical pageant depicting their history, and three months later they hosted a celebration of the Treaty of 1854, which established four reservations in Wisconsin: Bad River, Red Cliff, Lac Courte Oreilles, and Lac du Flambeau; gave the US access to the Mesabi Iron Range along Lake Superior; and held that the Ojibwe retained usufructuary rights in the ceded areas.[65] In 1930 more than three hundred Winnebago Indians performed in a pageant for tourists, and in 1931 some Winnebago danced at the Lake Hallie Fourth of July celebration.[66]

While the multitude of Indian-centered tourism endeavors hosted in Wisconsin in the early twentieth century may not have purposely sought to defy federal Indian policies of the era, they signal the important role that Indians and their distinct cultural components played in the development of the state's tourism industry. Town boosters and local newspaper writers wholly believed that Indian performances would draw tourists from within Wisconsin as well as from surrounding states. In 1922 the *Wisconsin State Journal* published several articles about a ten-day Indian festival held at Stand Rock in the Wisconsin Dells, claiming that thousands of tourists had come to witness the fifth annual festival that featured a multitude of dances. The newspaper described performances by old warriors who had "donned their gay buckskin costumes and beat their weird drums under the spotlight from the white man's steamer."[67] In 1930, several years after Burke had again attempted to quash Indian dances, the *La Crosse Tribune-Leader* bemoaned the loss of the Red Cross powwow near Watermill. The powwow had once raised more than $200 for the Tomah chapter of the Red Cross, but "the all-night beating of the tom-tom is no longer heard. . . . Thus time works changes, even to the people of the red race, who have learned to commercialize the ceremonials and handwork peculiar to themselves." The powwow had not dissolved because the Indians had disappeared or turned their backs on their songs, dances, and traditions. Instead, the Indians had simply started traveling to Kilbourn, which likely offered the opportunity to attract more visitors, for "the famous Indian pageant."[68] Like countless promoters of performances and productions throughout the nation, the Indians of the Red Cross powwow continued to capitalize on the non-Native visitors' fascination with indigenous culture. Their move to Kilbourn was likely intentional, and that decision emphasizes the power of performance over policy in the state's tourism industry.

Katrina Phillips (Red Cliff Band of Lake Superior Ojibwe) is assistant professor of history at Macalester College. Her current research focuses on the role of American Indian historical pageantry in the development of regional tourist economies in North Carolina, Oregon, and Ohio in the twentieth and twenty-first centuries.

Notes

1. *Milwaukee Sentinel*, "Redskins Arrive for Big Pow Wow."
2. *Milwaukee Journal*, "Indians of Seven States Don Tribal Dress"; *Superior Telegram*, "Winnebago Indians to Hold Mammoth Pow-Wow."
3. *Superior Telegram*, "Winnebago Indians to Hold Mammoth Pow-Wow."
4. See Troutman, *Indian Blues*.
5. *Marshfield News*, "Wis. Rapids Welcomes First of Powwow Indians"; *Portage Democrat*, "Big Pow-Wow at Stand Rock." The phrase quoted in the essay's subhead is from Shawano Chamber of Commerce, *Wisconsin's Playground*.
6. *Portage Democrat*, "Big Pow-Wow at Stand Rock."
7. *Milwaukee Journal*, "Indians of Seven States Don Tribal Dress."
8. *De Pere Democrat*, "Indians All Ready to Give Their Big Show."
9. Charles A. Burke, "Circular no. 1665: Indian Dancing," April 26, 1921 (Department of the Interior, Office of Indian Affairs. Indian Rights Association papers, 1864-1973, Reel 40).
10. Ibid.
11. *Milwaukee Journal*, "Indians of Seven States Don Tribal Dress"; *Portage Democrat*, "Big Pow-Wow at Stand Rock."
12. See Theisz, "Putting Things in Order," 92; Axtmann, *Indians and Wannabes*, 12. For more information on the creation of the circular—and the indigenous response to it—see Wegner, *We Have a Religion*.
13. Ellis, "Five Dollars a Week," 197; Troutman, *Indian Blues*, 74.
14. Quoted in Ellis, "Sound of the Drum," 12–13.
15. Quoted in Ellis, "Five Dollars a Week," 185.
16. Troutman, *Indian Blues*, 152.
17. Ellis, "Five Dollars a Week," 188.
18. *Antigo Daily Journal*, "Annual Pageant on Apostle Islands." The phrase in the essay's subhead is quoted from *Wisconsin State Journal*, "Tourists Flock to Indian Festival."
19. *Superior Telegram*, "Thousands to See Pageant."
20. Raibmon, *Authentic Indians*, 146.
21. See Rothman, *Devil's Bargains*.
22. See, among others, Moses, *Wild West Shows*; Moses, "Performative Traditions in Indian History"; Raibmon, *Authentic Indians*; Arndt, "Ho-Chunk 'Indian Powwows'"; Troutman, *Indian Blues*; McNenly, *Native Performers*; Imada, *Aloha America*; Desmond, *Staging Tourism*; McNally, "Indian Passion Play"; Ellis, "Five Dollars a Week"; Ellis, "Sound of the Drum."
23. Hosmer, *American Indians in the Marketplace*, xi.
24. Imada, *Aloha America*, 18; see Scott, *Domination and the Arts of Resistance*.
25. McNally, "Indian Passion Play," 107.
26. Cothran, "Working the Indian Field Days," 197; Raibmon, *Authentic Indians*; Norrgard, *Seasons of Change*.
27. See, e.g., Gassan, *Birth of American Tourism*; Sears, *Sacred Places*; Nash, *Wilderness and the American Mind*; Aron, *Working at Play*. The phrase quoted in the essay's subhead is from Lanman, *Summer in the Wilderness*, 45.
28. Hoelscher, *Picturing Indians*, 18–23.
29. *Baraboo Daily News*, "Trip through the Dells"; *Baraboo Daily News*, "Early Journey through Sauk County."
30. Gassan, *Birth of American Tourism*, 2–4.
31. McCann, *This Superior Place*, 116; Feldman, *Storied Wilderness*, 92–93; Aron, *Working*

at Play, 52. The Wisconsin Central Railroad reached Ashland in 1877, but the Chicago, St. Paul, Minneapolis and Omaha Railway would not reach Bayfield—slightly farther north on Lake Superior's south shore—until 1883. McCann, *This Superior Place*, 117.

32. Wisner, *Dells of the Wisconsin*, 3.

33. Feldman, *Storied Wilderness*, 95; Norrgard, *Seasons of Change*, 110; McCann, *This Superior Place*, 115.

34. Charlton, *Guide to Summer Resorts in Wisconsin*, 22.

35. Cronon, "Irrevocable Lessons of Vanishing Fields," 10.

36. McCann, *This Superior Place*, 117–18; Feldman, *Storied Wilderness*, 111.

37. Norrgard, *Seasons of Change*, 109. See also Feldman, *Storied Wilderness*, 112; Shapiro, "Up North on Vacation."

38. "Apostle Islands Indian Pageant."

39. The phrase in the subhead is quoted from Wisner, *Dells of the Wisconsin*, 61.

40. McNally, "Indian Passion Play," 108.

41. See Troutman, *Indian Blues*, 154; Deloria, *Indians in Unexpected Places*.

42. King, *Trouting on the Brulé River, or Summer-Wayfaring in the Northern Wilderness*, iii.

43. Norrgard, *Seasons of Change*, 121.

44. King, *Trouting on the Brulé River*, iii–v.

45. Ryan, *Wisconsin Tour and Hand Book*, 31.

46. Feldman, *Storied Wilderness*, 97.

47. Norrgard, *Seasons of Change*, 114.

48. Olmanson, *Future City on the Inland Sea*, 170–71.

49. Norrgard, *Seasons of Change*, 8.

50. "Winnebago County Motorists See a Real Indian Powwow." The article does not indicate what portions of the ceremony the visitors were privy to, nor does it entertain the idea that the visitors were not allowed to witness some elements that may have been considered more sacred than others.

51. The phrase quoted in the subhead is from the *Milwaukee Journal*, "Twenty Thousand to View Historical Pageant."

52. Marinette Chamber of Commerce, *Come to the Land of Queen Marinette*.

53. *Milwaukee Journal*, "Twenty Thousand to View Historical Pageant."

54. *Milwaukee Sentinel*, "State Celebrates Advance of Red Man."

55. Ibid.

56. *Milwaukee Journal*, "20,000 to View Historical Pageant and Indian Centennial at Green Bay."

57. *De Pere Democrat*, "Indians All Ready to Give Their Big Show."

58. Troutman, *Indian Blues*, 101.

59. *Baraboo Daily News*, "Badger Indians Big Pow-Wow."

60. *Clintonville Tribune*, "Winnebago Indians Will Celebrate."

61. *Superior Telegram*, "Weird Dances of Indian Braves."

62. Ibid.

63. Troutman, *Indian Blues*, 74.

64. Burke, "A Message to All Indians," cited in Troutman, 74. Troutman notes that this typewritten copy of the circular, with additional recommendations at the end, was likely intended solely for superintendents, missionaries, and "other interested organizations or parties" instead of for distribution among the Indians (see: Troutman, fn 25, p. 275).

65. Feldman, 46.

66. *Marinette Eagle-Star*, "Sixty Indians to Give Historical Pageant"; *Ashland Daily Press*,

"Odanah Indians to Celebrate Treaty of 1854"; *Ashland Daily Press*, "Indians Plan 1854 Treaty Celebration"; *Eau Claire Daily Leader*, "Indian Tribal Dances at Fourth Celebration"; *La Crosse Tribune-Leader*, "Three Hundred Winnebago Indians off to Kilbourn." Troutman has argued that Indians often requested permission from agents and superintendents to hold dances on dates that held particular meaning for US Americans, such as the Fourth of July, as Indians recognized the significance of these holidays and understood that government officials tended to be more lenient due to indigenous displays of what they saw as patriotism.

67. *Wisconsin State Journal*, "Tourists Flock to Indian Festival"; *Wisconsin State Journal*, "Indian Tribal Dances Weave Old Spell."

68. *La Crosse Tribune-Leader*, "Three Hundred Winnebago Indians off to Kilbourn."

References

Antigo Daily Journal. 1921. "Annual Pageant on Apostle Islands to Attract Thousands." October 10. Wisconsin Historical Society, Madison.

"Apostle Islands Indian Pageant." n.d. Bayfield Heritage Association, Bayfield, WI.

Arndt, Grant. 2005. "Ho-Chunk 'Indian Powwows' of the Early Twentieth Century." In *Powwow*, edited by Clyde Ellis, Luke Erik Lassiter, and Gary H. Dunham. Lincoln: University of Nebraska Press.

Aron, Cindy S. 2001. *Working at Play: A History of Vacations in the United States*. New York: Oxford University Press.

Ashland Daily Press. 1931. "Indians Plan 1854 Treaty Celebration." September 26. Wisconsin Historical Society, Madison.

———. 1931. "Odanah Indians to Celebrate Treaty of 1854." September 24.

Axtmann, Ann M. 2013. *Indians and Wannabes: Native American Powwow Dancing in the Northeast and Beyond*. Gainesville: University of Florida Press.

Baraboo Daily News. 1912. "An Early Journey through Sauk County." January 4. Wisconsin Historical Society, Madison.

———. 1912. "A Trip through the Dells in 1849." January 4. Wisconsin Historical Society, Madison.

———. 1921. "Badger Indians Big Pow-Wow for Kilbourn." June 27. Wisconsin Historical Society, Madison.

Burke, Charles H. 1921. "Circular no. 1665: Indian Dancing." April 26. Department of the Interior, Office of Indian Affairs. Indian Rights Association papers, 1864–1973, Reel 40. Held by Minnesota Historical Society and Wisconsin Historical Association.

———. 1923. "Supplement to Circular no. 1665: Indian Dancing." February 14. Department of the Interior, Office of Indian Affairs. Indian Rights Association papers, 1864–1973, Reel 40. Held by Minnesota Historical Society and Wisconsin Historical Association.

Charlton, James. 1875. *Guide to summer resorts in Wisconsin, Minnesota, Michigan, etc., etc.* (S.I.: J. Charlton). Wisconsin Historical Society.

Clintonville Tribune. 1922. "Winnebago Indians Will Celebrate." May 19. Wisconsin Historical Society, Madison.

Cothran, Boyd. 2010. "Working the Indian Field Days: The Economy of Authenticity and the Question of Agency in Yosemite Valley." *American Indian Quarterly* 34, no. 2: 194–223.

Cronon, William. 2011. "Irrevocable Lessons of Vanishing Fields." In *A Storied Wilderness: Rewilding the Apostle Islands,* by James W. Feldman, ix-xiii. Seattle: University of Washington Press.

Deloria, Philip J. 2004. *Indians in Unexpected Places*. Lawrence: University Press of Kansas.

De Pere Democrat. 1921. "Indians All Ready to Give Their Big Show." July 28. Wisconsin Historical Society, Madison.

Desmond, Jane. 1999. *Staging Tourism: Bodies on Display from Waikiki to Sea World*. Chicago: University of Chicago Press.

Eau Claire Daily Leader. 1931. "Indian Tribal Dances at Fourth Celebration." June 26. Wisconsin Historical Society, Madison.

Ellis, Clyde. 2004. "Five Dollars a Week to Be 'Regular Indians.'" In *Native Pathways: American Indian Culture and Economic Development in the Twentieth Century*, edited by Brian Hosmer and Colleen O'Neill, 184–208. Boulder: University Press of Colorado.

———. 2005. "The Sound of the Drum Will Revive Them and Make Them Happy." In Ellis et al., *Powwow*, 3–25.

Feldman, James W. 2011. *A Storied Wilderness: Rewilding the Apostle Islands*. Seattle: University of Washington Press.

Gassan, Richard H. 2008. *The Birth of American Tourism: New York, the Hudson Valley, and American Culture, 1790–1830*. Amherst: University of Massachusetts Press.

Hoelscher, Steven D. 2008. *Picturing Indians: Photographic Encounters and Tourist Fantasies in H. H. Bennett's Wisconsin Dells*. Madison: University of Wisconsin Press.

Hosmer, Brian. 1999. *American Indians in the Marketplace: Persistence and Innovation among the Menominees and Metlakatlans, 1870–1920*. Lawrence: University Press of Kansas.

Imada, Adria L. 2012. *Aloha America: Hula Circuits through the U.S. Empire*. Durham, NC: Duke University Press.

King, Jon Lyle. 1880. *Trouting on the Brulé River, or Summer-Wayfaring in the Northern Wilderness*. New York: Orange Judd Company.

La Crosse Tribune-Leader. 1930. "Three Hundred Winnebago Indians off to Kilbourn to Participate in Pageant Planned for Tourists." June 15. Wisconsin Historical Society, Madison.

Lanman, Charles. 1847. *A Summer in the Wilderness; Embracing a Canoe Voyage up the Mississippi and Around Lake Superior*. New York: D. Appleton & Company; Philadelphia: Geo. S. Appleton. (Reprint: 2015.)

Marinette Chamber of Commerce. c. 1923. *Come to the Land of Queen Marinette*. Marinette, WI: Chamber of Commerce. Wisconsin Historical Society, Madison.

Marinette Eagle-Star. 1931. "Sixty Indians to Give Historical Pageant." June 24.

Marshfield News. 1921. "Wis. Rapids Welcomes First of Powwow Indians." August 11. Wisconsin Historical Society, Madison.

McCann, Dennis. 2013. *This Superior Place: Stories of Bayfield and the Apostle Islands*. Madison: Wisconsin Historical Society Press.

McNally, Michael D. 2006. "The Indian Passion Play: Contesting the Real Hiawatha in *Song of Hiawatha* Pageants, 1901–1965." *American Quarterly* 58, no. 1: 105–35.

McNenly, Linda Scarangella. 2012. *Native Performers in Wild West Shows: From Buffalo Bill to Euro Disney*. Norman: University of Oklahoma Press.

Milwaukee Journal. 1921. "Indians of Seven States Don Tribal Dress for Two Badger Pow-Wows." August 7. Wisconsin Historical Society, Madison.

———. 1921. "Twenty Thousand to View Historical Pageant and Indian Centennial at Green Bay." July 31.

Milwaukee Sentinel. 1921. "Redskins Arrive for Big Pow Wow." August 11. Wisconsin Historical Society, Madison.

———. 1921. "State Celebrates Advance of Red Man to Wisconsin." July 31.

Moses, L. G. 1996. *Wild West Shows and the Images of American Indians, 1883–1933*.

Albuquerque: University of New Mexico Press.

———. 2004. "Performative Traditions in Indian History." In *A Companion to American Indian History*, edited by Philip J. Deloria and Neal Salisbury, 193–208. Malden, MA: Blackwell.

Nash, Roderick Frazier. 2001 [1967]. *Wilderness and the American Mind* (4th edition). New Haven: Yale University Press.

Norrgard, Chantal. 2014. *Seasons of Change: Labor, Treaty Rights, and Ojibwe Nationhood*. Chapel Hill: University of North Carolina Press.

Olmanson, Eric. 2007. *The Future City on the Inland Sea: A History of Imaginative Geographies of Lake Superior*. Athens: Ohio University Press.

Portage Democrat. 1921. "Big Pow-Wow at Stand Rock." July 18. Wisconsin Historical Society, Madison.

Raibmon, Paige. 2005. *Authentic Indians: Episodes of Encounter from the Late-Nineteenth-Century Northwest Coast*. Durham, NC: Duke University Press.

Roscoe, Will. 1999. *The Zuni Man-Woman*. Albuquerque: University of New Mexico Press.

Rothman, Hal. 1998. *Devil's Bargains: Tourism in the Twentieth-Century American West*. Lawrence: University Press of Kansas.

Ryan, Samuel J. 1897. *Wisconsin Tour and Hand Book*. Appleton, WI: Wisconsin Division, League of American Wheelmen.

Scott, James C. 1990. *Domination and the Arts of Resistance: Hidden Transcripts*. New Haven: Yale University Press.

Sears, John F. 1998. *Sacred Places: American Tourist Attractions in the Nineteenth Century*. Amherst: University of Massachusetts Press.

Shapiro, Aaron. 1994. "Up North on Vacation: Tourism and Resorts in Wisconsin's North Woods, 1900–1945." *Wisconsin Magazine of History* 77, no. 3: 2–13.

Shawano Chamber of Commerce. c. 1925. *Wisconsin's Playground: Shawano Lake and Menominee Indian Reservation*. Shawano, WI: Chamber of Commerce. Wisconsin Historical Society, Madison.

Superior Telegram. 1921. "Winnebago Indians to Hold Mammoth Pow-Wow in August." June 8. Wisconsin Historical Society, Madison.

———. 1923. "Thousands to See Pageant." September 27. Wisconsin Historical Society, Madison.

———. 1924. "Weird Dances of Indian Braves Bring Tourists to Reservation." July 9. Wisconsin Historical Society, Madison.

Theisz, R. D. 2005. "Putting Things in Order." In Ellis et al., *Powwow*, 85–109.

Troutman, John. 2012. *Indian Blues: American Indians and the Politics of Music, 1879–1934*. Norman: University of Oklahoma Press.

Wegner, Tisa. 2009. *We Have a Religion: The 1920s Pueblo Indian Dance Controversy and American Religious Freedom*. Chapel Hill: University of North Carolina Press.

"Winnebago County Motorists See a Real Indian Powwow." 1922. Newspaper clipping, October 3. Wisconsin Historical Society, Madison.

Wisconsin State Journal. 1922. "Indian Tribal Dances Weave Old Spell at Wisconsin River." August 6. Wisconsin Historical Society, Madison.

———. 1922. "Tourists Flock to Indian Festival at Dells Cliffs; Chiefs Welcome Harvest." July 29. Wisconsin Historical Society, Madison.

Wisner, Frank O. *The Dells of the Wisconsin: An Illustrated Handbook, embracing the Prose, Romance and Poetry of This Wonderful Region*. Kilbourn City, WI: Frank O. Wisner. Wisconsin Historical Society, Madison.

Good Neighbors and Lost Cities

Tourism, the Good Neighbor Policy,
and the Transformation of Machu Picchu

Mark Rice

On a Sunday in October 1948, Hiram Bingham returned to Machu Picchu for the first time in over three decades. Accompanied by a group of dignitaries, Bingham, who had gained fame for his claim of discovering the "lost city of the Incas," cut the ribbon to a new highway to Machu Picchu built with the hopes of receiving new waves of tourists and visitors. Speeches and press coverage of the visit celebrated the completion of the new road. The event also lauded Bingham, who, in the accounts of both visitors and Peruvian officials, was the heroic explorer who discovered Machu Picchu in 1911, thus bringing national and global attention to an important symbol of Peruvian identity.[1] Lost in the fanfare was the fact that such an event would have been impossible to imagine thirty years earlier, when Bingham left Peru under a cloud of mistrust and many national leaders viewed Machu Picchu as an unimportant relic located in an economic and cultural backwater.

The remarkable transformation of Machu Picchu and Bingham was no accident, but was intertwined with the efforts to promote the Inca archaeological site into a tourist destination during the Good Neighbor era between Peru and the United States. Peru was not the only Latin American country to employ tourism and touristic narratives in the creation of national symbols.[2] However, the emergence of Machu Picchu as both a tourist destination and a national symbol was the product of a transnational effort that linked US goals to foment hemispheric solidarity with

Radical History Review
Issue 129 (October 2017) DOI 10.1215/01636545-3920679
From Making Machu Picchu: A History of Tourism, Region,
and Nation in Cusco, Peru by Mark Rice. Copyright © 2018 by the University
of North Carolina Press. Used by permission of the publisher. www.uncpress.unc.edu

activities of the Peruvian state, as well as local aims to promote the Cuzco region, the former heart of the Inca empire where Machu Picchu is located. The rise of Machu Picchu during the Good Neighbor era points to the importance of understanding how tourism development in Latin America served the aims of US foreign policy while creating a transnational space for national and local actors to assert their own cultural and political goals.

This essay explores how the 1930s and the 1940s offered a unique moment when diplomatic, economic, and cultural actors outside of Peru, especially those associated with the Good Neighbor policy, helped reinvent Machu Picchu as a national symbol and Bingham as a benevolent Pan-American figure who discovered the site. The Good Neighbor policy, a diplomatic commitment by President Franklin D. Roosevelt to nonintervention and hemispheric cooperation between Latin America and the United States, has long attracted the interest of historians. The Good Neighbor policy has also received renewed attention for its cultural policies and their influence in the United States and Latin America.[3] However, relatively little is known concerning the great influence the Good Neighbor policy had in the development of tourism in Latin America.[4] The rise of Machu Picchu points to the important effects of the Good Neighbor policy in providing new institutional support for cultural and tourist activities in Latin America. Equally important, this essay illustrates how local and national actors employed the language and climate of the Good Neighbor policy to pursue their cultural and political goals.

The diplomatic and cultural tools of the Good Neighbor policies offered residents of the Cuzco region (known as *cusqueños*) the support to promote Cuzco and Machu Picchu as travel destinations, cultural contact zones, and, more importantly, national symbols. The influence of tourism in the elevation of Cuzco and Machu Picchu as national symbols affirms scholarship by Mary Louise Pratt and Claudio Lomnitz that highlights the importance of transnational contact zones in the formation of national identity in Latin America.[5] In Latin America, where state-sponsored nationalism projects often have faced economic and political challenges, transnational contact zones can prove influential in the creation of national symbols. The case of Machu Picchu calls attention to the need to recognize the role tourism has played in the creation of transnational exchanges and national symbols.

Far from one-sided, these transnational contact zones were formed from mutual, if unequal, negotiations. The remaking of Machu Picchu in the 1930s and 1940s followed a similar process. *Cusqueños* employed the institutions and cultural climate of the Good Neighbor era to highlight Machu Picchu and their region as an important tourist destination. These transnational contact zones not only promoted travel to Machu Picchu but also allowed *cusqueños* to assert their region's *indigenismo* cultural movement celebrating indigenous history and folklore as the true representation of Peru on a national and hemispheric stage.

Yet Machu Picchu's reliance on transnational forces posed risks, especially if hemispheric political conditions shifted. Tourism promoters discovered this unfortunate fact as Peruvian-US relations rapidly shifted from an era of Good Neighbors to Cold Warriors by the end of the 1940s. A more important risk, however, was the legacy of the problematic narrative constructed to promote tourism at Machu Picchu. If tourism had the power to create new national narratives, it also held the power to distort existing ones. Dean MacCannell has notably described tourism as "staged authenticity," which strives to meet the tourist's expectations of what is genuine more than actually portraying reality.[6] In the case of Machu Picchu, the staged authenticity created by tourism serves the interests not only of travelers but also of much larger political aims and purposes.

In Peru, Cuzco's regional elites, allies in the Peruvian national state, and US diplomats created narratives that bolstered their political goals, commodified Machu Picchu for tourist consumption, and silenced alternative or conflicting views. These actors employed tourism to promote an imagined, utopian Inca past that appealed to local and national elites as well as travelers and US consumers. While this did make Machu Picchu into an iconic national symbol of Peru, that narrative largely ignored the contemporary political demands of Cuzco's exploited indigenous population. Meanwhile, Bingham was reinvented as a sympathetic Pan-American figure, while his dubious claims of discovery and unapologetic support for imperialism were altered to provide a positive narrative of US-Peruvian cooperation and hemispheric political solidarity. During the 1930s and 1940s, tourism thus aided Machu Picchu's emergence as a global symbol of Peru, but also as a site that was unmoored from the social and political realities of the nation it represented.

Rediscovering the Lost City

Bingham's 1911 Yale Peruvian Expedition brought global attention to Machu Picchu. However, scholars have shown that Machu Picchu was never actually "lost," nor was Bingham the first foreigner to visit the site.[7] Less known is the fact that Machu Picchu returned to relative obscurity after the burst of global interest in the site following Bingham's initial announcement. Several factors explain why Machu Picchu became a "re-forgotten" city outside of Cuzco, but many are related to the questionable conduct of Bingham. Between 1911 and 1915, Bingham organized three expeditions to Machu Picchu. He was adept at publicizing his expeditions, making use of advances in photography and publishing to introduce Machu Picchu to North American readers in the pages of *Harper's Magazine* and *National Geographic Magazine*. Yet Bingham erroneously concluded that Machu Picchu was both Tampu-tocco, the birthplace of the Inca, as well as Vilcabamba, the final Incan capital that fell to the Spanish in 1572.[8] Most archaeologists now believe that Machu Picchu was constructed in the mid-1400s to serve as a royal estate.[9] In addition to factual errors, Bingham's accounts often downplayed the role of *cusqueños* in his expeditions, despite the fact that local knowledge and labor were critical to his success.

Instead, Bingham used his experiences to advocate for the growth of US economic and political power in Latin America.[10]

Of more concern to *cusqueños*, Bingham consistently—and illegally—exported artifacts from Peru. During his final expedition to Machu Picchu in 1915, he was charged with theft. Although Bingham escaped prosecution, he abruptly left Peru following the dispute.[11] In 1922 Bingham published a book that documented his expeditions to Peru titled *Inca Land*.[12] The book contained relatively little information on Machu Picchu. Although Bingham promised publishers he would write more extensively about Machu Picchu in the future, the prospects of a political career changed his focus.[13] After serving in World War I, Bingham returned to Connecticut to pursue a political career, eventually becoming a United States senator in 1925. During his political campaigns, Bingham exploited his fame from the expeditions but held little nostalgia for Peru. In an article in the *Boston Daily Globe* in 1924, Bingham asserted: "[Peruvians] have no consuming curiosity about the past. Accordingly they were suspicious of our undertaking and their efforts, I assure you, were far from helpful."[14] *Cusqueños* were hardly saddened to see Bingham depart either. In 1926 the Universidad Nacional de San Antonio Abad del Cusco (UNSAAC) rescinded the honorary degree it granted to Bingham.[15] That same year, *cusqueño* archaeologist José Gabriel Cosio stated to *El Comercio de Lima*: "I absolutely don't lament the departure of Bingham."[16] Although never forgotten, Machu Picchu remained largely isolated from global interest and travel. When the British travel writer Anthony Dell visited the site in 1925, he commented that Machu Picchu was "overgrown with vegetation and is the haunt of poisonous snakes and spiders."[17]

Although global and local interest in Machu Picchu appeared to wane, Cuzco's regional political and intellectual leaders continued to harbor interest in using their region's past as a cultural and economic resource. In the 1920s, Cuzco had emerged as an active center of the *indigenismo* cultural movement that sought to rehabilitate the image of the Indian and the Andes. Cuzco was not the only center of *indigenismo* thought. In fact, the cultural and political movement had roots dating to the late nineteenth century and, during the 1920s, was employed by multiple political figures and movements in Peru that included the socialist thinker José Carlos Mariátegui, the populist American Popular Revolutionary Alliance-Peruvian Aprista Party (APRA), and even President Augusto Leguía and his authoritarian government. In addition to cultural endeavors, the diverse efforts of *indigenistas* sought to place the role of the Indian at the center of social reform and modernization in Peru. However, despite its valorization of Andean culture, *indigenismo* remained a largely urban and elite-oriented movement.[18] As scholars have noted, in the wake of agrarian uprisings against Cuzco's landed elite that rocked the region in the 1920s, *indigenista* intellectuals downplayed the social demands of Indians while emphasizing cultural indigeneity instead. This movement, sometimes termed neo-*indigenismo*, emphasized a utopian Incan past and folklore over the social and economic demands of contemporary indigenous communities. By the start of the 1930s, many *indigenistas* embraced the possibility of creating a "New Indian" through education, urbanization, and modernization.[19] Despite its urban and elite origins, Zoila S. Mendoza has noted that *indigenismo* in Cuzco also enjoyed popular support, especially in urban folkloric groups that hoped to use the cultural movement to assert their belonging in modern Peru.[20]

For Cuzco's *indigenistas* and their supporters, the narrative of tourism could emphasize their vision of an idealized Inca past as well as promote their region and its culture as compatible in a modern Peruvian nation-state. Tourism literature and promotion has long supported and crafted a selected historical narrative.[21] The first local call to employ tourism in the promotion of Cuzco and its cultural identity appeared in August 1921 when the rector of UNSAAC, Albert A. Giesecke, published an essay in his institution's *Revista Universitaria* titled "El Cuzco: Meca del turismo de la América del Sur" ("Cuzco: Mecca of Tourism in South America").[22] Giesecke, originally from Philadelphia, was appointed rector of UNSAAC in 1910 with a mandate to modernize the university, and he encouraged students, many who would go on to be prominent *indigenistas*, to focus their intellectual efforts on Cuzco society and history. Giesecke's experience made him a key transnational figure who enjoyed cultural contacts in the United States, Lima, and Cuzco. These links helped Giesecke aid Bingham's initial expeditions to Machu Picchu by placing the explorer in contact with locals with knowledge of the site.[23] In his call for Cuzco to realize its tourism potential, Giesecke highlighted two themes that would be echoed in later efforts to develop travel in the region: first, that Cuzco's ability to attract global travelers would lend proof of its modernity to Lima-based elites who still dismissed the region as a cultural and economic backwater and, second, that tourism promotion could help support the larger claims of local *indigenistas* that Cuzco's heritage and cultural folklore represented the "true" Peru as opposed to Lima.[24] In the next two decades, many *indigenista* intellectuals authored guidebooks that, like Giesecke's call, emphasized Cuzco's modernization and its Inca past while overlooking the often-desperate social conditions of its rural indigenous population.[25]

However, *cusqueños* had to confront geographic and political obstacles to tourism development. Peru's distance from the United States discouraged the emergence of a state-driven national tourism policy that had begun to develop in Mexico and Cuba.[26] Even within Peru, travel between Lima and Cuzco proved difficult. The first railroad line arrived in Cuzco in 1908, but well into the 1930s the journey to Lima required at least two full days of travel by train to the coast followed by another two days via ship to arrive at the national capital. When the first airplane touched down in Cuzco in 1925, the nearly monthlong civic celebration illustrated how important locals viewed the need to connect their region to the national and global community.[27] Even more important, Cuzco's geographical isolation was

Figure 1. *Ciudad y campo y caminos*, **1927. Hemeroteca de la Biblioteca Nacional del Perú**

employed by Lima intellectuals to argue that Peru's future lay in its industrializing coastal cities that would slowly absorb and eliminate Andean populations into a national mestizo identity.[28] The cover of the February 1927 travel and auto magazine *Ciudad y campo y caminos* best depicted how many Lima residents viewed travel in Peru's Andean interior (fig. 1). The illustration showed a well-to-do family having to navigate their auto between Indian peasants, llamas, and mountainous geography. Everything representing Andean culture appeared to stand in the way of modern traveling and, in the eyes of many, a modernizing nation.[29]

Yet by the mid-1930s, changes in national and hemispheric politics began to open up opportunities for *cusqueños* to expand their regional tourism efforts on a larger scale. The turbulent years at the start of the Great Depression in Peru were not kind to supporters of competing strains of *indigenismo*. Mariátegui died in 1930, the Leguía government fell from power that same year, and the former president died in 1932. Following a failed uprising in 1932, the APRA party was suppressed and banned by the national government.[30] However, in Cuzco, by the early 1930s the indigenous agrarian uprisings were eclipsed by the work of *indigenistas* that emphasized culture and folklore over grassroots political demands. Hoping to reassert their control in the tumultuous 1930s, Lima's national elites reached out to their regional counterparts. Many Cuzco-based *indigenistas* gained positions in national cultural institutions in Lima, while Giesecke moved to the capital to work at various educational posts and with the US embassy.[31] The neo-*indigenismo* message of Cuzco's folklore and tourism promotion appealed to Peru's leaders looking for a populist, but not radical, national narrative. While other regional and populist projects had come under strain, in the 1930s Cuzco folklore institutes, artists, and thinkers began to project their *indigenista* cultural project on a national scale as the true representation of Peru.[32] When the national government passed law no. 7688 declaring Cuzco the "Archaeological Capital of South America" on January 23, 1933, it affirmed for *cusqueños* the importance of their city and region to national concepts of Peruvianness.[33]

Equally important cultural links between Cuzco and the outside world also grew throughout the 1930s. In 1929 the United States Senate censured then senator Bingham for ethics violations. Although he remained in the Senate, his political future was damaged. Bingham rededicated his activities to archaeology and published *Machu Picchu, a Citadel of the Incas* in 1930.[34] By that time, Machu Picchu had faded from North American public awareness so much that the *New York Times* review of the book began by reminding readers, "Fifteen years ago, Machu Picchu, the white and beautiful citadel on a narrow ridge high above the rushing Urubamba River in Southern Peru, *was* well known by name and by picture to all Americans."[35] Bingham's publication did not prevent his electoral defeat in 1932, but it began a process that renewed public interest in the explorer and Machu Picchu.[36] It is hard to estimate to what degree Bingham's publication stoked popular interest in Machu Picchu, but there is no doubt that, starting in the 1930s, a renewed US interest in the exploration of South America began to blossom. Part of North American intrigue with the Andes stemmed from the overall popularization of the fields of archaeology and anthropology.[37] It also reflected increased interest in indigeneity in North American scholarly and cultural circles in the 1930s and 1940s, with a particular focus on the US Southwest and Mexico.[38] Growing tourism in the United States, particularly in the West, emphasized romantic images of indigenous and Hispanic culture and led to the creation of new national parks and initiated preservation campaigns in Santa Fe, New Mexico.[39] The *New York Times* noted in 1931: "South America is becoming a favorite haunt for explorers and adventurers. . . . Men are cutting their way through the menacing forest of the Gran Chaco; they are delving into the ancient ruins of the Inca."[40]

To channel increasing global awareness of Cuzco and Machu Picchu into larger tourist and cultural development, *cusqueños* found an ally in the Good Neighbor policy of the United States toward Latin America. In August 1940, Roosevelt created the Office for Coordination of Commercial and Cultural Relations between the American Republics to direct US cultural diplomacy efforts in the region to act as a central part of the Good Neighbor policy. Nelson A. Rockefeller headed the new office, renamed the Coordinator of Inter-American Affairs (CIAA) in July 1941.[41] Even before the creation of the CIAA, US diplomats and their Peruvian allies looked to create institutions to promote Pan-American cooperation. Although fascism was not as influential as in countries such as Argentina or Brazil, it did have some prominent followers in Peruvian national politics and media. In addition, Peru enjoyed extensive economic links to Japan and Germany. As a result, the United

States and its Peruvian allies were keen to shore up Pan-American sentiment. Good Neighbor relations with Peru were also aided by the strong pro-US political stance after the 1939 election of President Manuel Prado.[42]

Cooperation between the CIAA and the Peruvian government quickly helped to increase cultural awareness of Peru abroad in the 1940s. More importantly, and partly thanks to the influence of *cusqueños* in prominent cultural institutions in Lima, the Peru presented by Good Neighbor–era institutions emphasized Machu Picchu and other signs of Cuzco's regional *indigenista* folklore as representations of Peru. The CIAA produced hundreds of Latin America teaching aids and exhibits for US schools that focused on the Andean culture of Peru.[43] CIAA efforts to increase US awareness of Peru extended to radio and film. These also emphasized Peru's Andean culture over coastal cities.[44] CIAA-sponsored film shorts on Peru from 1942 included features on Lake Titicaca and "Cuzko" and an MGM-produced piece titled *Inca Treasure*.[45] Another CIAA-produced film, *Heart of the Inca Empire*, directed by Howard Knapp, was released in 1943 and featured numerous color shots of Cuzco and Machu Picchu.[46] With the assistance of the CIAA, in 1942 Walt Disney Productions completed the feature-length animated film *Saludos Amigos*, which included a segment on Peru that featured Donald Duck in Andean settings as he visited Lake Titicaca as an inquisitive—and comically dumbfounded—tourist.[47]

Pan-American Tourism

The visit of Donald Duck as a tourist reflected another trend of the Good Neighbor policy that appealed to backers of Cuzco tourism. Even before the creation of state institutions such as the CIAA, Peruvians sought to exploit the growing cultural awareness of their country to increase tourism. Several locally and nationally funded infrastructure projects were already under way to bring tourists to Machu Picchu. In 1928 the Santa Ana Railway reached Machu Picchu, dramatically improving access to the site, and a new airport for Cuzco was inaugurated in 1934.[48] That same year, the government funded the construction of a small lodge adjacent to Machu Picchu to permit small parties to stay overnight.[49] One of the more influential voices that called for increased state investment in tourism was the Touring y Automóvíl Club del Perú (Touring and Automobile Club of Peru; TACP). The TACP president, Eduardo Dibós Dammert, had extensive ties to the United States due to his control over the Goodyear Tire Company in Peru. Under his leadership, the TACP inaugurated its own magazine, *Turismo*, in July 1936. *Turismo* reflected the rising prominence of Cuzco and Machu Picchu as symbols of touristic Peru by placing the ruin on its front cover in its first year of publication (fig. 2).[50]

The edition featured an article (published in English) promoting Cuzco, stating, "To visit Peru and not include in your itinerary, what is at once the center and circumference of Incaic and Spanish Colonial history, is an unpardonable sin, a foolish lapse."[51] This sentiment, still prevalent in present-day travel literature, reflects how tourism had helped solidify Cuzco and Machu Picchu as singularly important representations of Peru.

Responding to ongoing calls for a coordinated tourism policy, Peru's Ministry of Foreign Relations commissioned Giesecke to travel to the United States in 1936 to study possible strategies for tourism development. Although independent of the United States, the Giesecke mission clearly demonstrated the diplomatic tone of the Good Neighbor–era emphasis on using commercial and cultural ties to create closer US-Peruvian relations. The ministry's instructions to Giesecke explicitly stated its goal, that "he form connections with North American tourism offices."[52]

Figure 2. Cover of *Turismo*, July 1936

Giesecke, in a report, concluded that Peru needed to craft a tourism policy to appeal to the United States and emphasized the importance of Cuzco as a future tourism destination.[53] Responding to these recommendations, the government finalized in November 1938 legislation quickly dubbed the "Hotel Law," which selected thirteen sites for new state-owned hotels and acquired the small Machu Picchu lodge as part of the new system.[54]

National efforts to increase state investment in tourism were encouraged by the United States, which also viewed tourism as an additional tool to support its economic and political goals in Latin America. Often identified with the Cold War era, the use of tourism to extend soft US economic and political influence can be traced to the Good Neighbor policy.[55] Beginning in 1939, the Pan American Union held regular inter-American travel conferences to promote hemispheric tourism, most of which were attended by representatives in the TACP.[56] The Pan American Union continually endorsed travel to Cuzco as one of the more attractive and viable tourism possibilities in the hemisphere and even featured the city's Plaza de Armas on its bulletin's cover in July 1941 (fig. 3).[57]

The United States government also used the State Department and the CIAA to explore the possibilities of transforming cultural cooperation into economic results through tourism.[58] One 1943 CIAA report on transportation infra-

Figure 3. Cover of the July 1941 *Bulletin of the Pan American Union* featuring Cuzco

structure in Peru predicted that "the tourist will play a large part in the financial future of the Republic [of Peru]."[59] As early as July 1943, the CIAA had contacted the Peruvian embassy's commercial councillor to inquire about possibilities for US investment in tourism in Peru.[60] Efforts to promote US tourism in Peru increased as World War II reached its conclusion. By 1945 director Rockefeller personally instructed the CIAA (renamed the Office of Inter-American Affairs, or OIAA) to focus on increasing tourism in all of Latin America.[61] By May 1945, the OIAA issued an internal planning report, titled "Suggested Program for the Development of Inter-American Tourist Travel." In the report, the OIAA encouraged continued hemispheric cooperation in tourism development, noting that "any project under-taken by the Office of Inter-American Affairs to promote travel of our citizens to other American Republics will, therefore, result in better economic and cultural relationships for us all."[62] For proponents of tourism development in Peru, the time to act had arrived.

US diplomats were not alone in anticipating a postwar tourism boom. As early as November 1943, the editors of *Turismo* predicted an optimistic future for their industry and lobbied the national government to "prepare with all foresight and orga-nization its plans for tourism for the postwar era."[63] The goal of postwar tourism preparation was best summarized in the January 1944 edition of *Turismo*, which stated, "We will prepare for the invasion." The editorial welcomed the postwar "inva-sion" of tourists. "It will arrive principally from the North, blond, happy, and wealthy," predicted the opening line of the essay. "Uncle Sam, acting as commander in chief, will give the order to attack. They will arrive with the most powerful and well-known arms: money, money, money." *Turismo* anticipated that "once again the Inca Empire will fall" and that "the flags of the tourists will fly above Macchupicchu [*sic*] next to ours. What a beautiful defeat!"[64] *Turismo* assured Peruvians that they could look for-ward to a new postwar era when talk of invasion would connote not violence but the peaceful invasion of cultural interaction and investment with the United States, as promised by the propaganda of the Good Neighbor era. Tourism, which represented both cultural and economic exchange, became a perfect means of achieving this opti-mistic vision. For *Turismo* and the interests it represented, the planned second con-quest of Peru would be welcome and, more importantly, profitable.

New state investment in tourism and its promise for Cuzco received a boost in 1944 as the new state-built Hotel Cuzco prepared for its opening. The hotel was the largest and grandest of the planned state lodgings.[65] The relationship between Cuzco folklore and tourism reached a new climax on June 24, 1944, when Cuzco held its first celebration of Inti Raymi—a folkloric presentation recreating the Incan winter solstice ceremony—in coordination with the inauguration of the new hotel.[66] Although the celebration of Inti Raymi had remained in the consciousness of *cusque-ños* since colonial times, the promise of tourism played a key role in the decision to begin an annual celebration. Even President Prado personally arrived in the city for the celebrations.[67] The dramatic Inti Raymi ceremony performed at the Sacsayhua-man archaeological complex overlooking Cuzco's urban center evoked depictions of a utopian Incan past translated for the consumption of modern observers. As noted by scholars, the ceremony was driven (and continues to be defined) not by historical accuracy but by local and national efforts to assert the importance of Cuzco folklore through tourism.[68] Lima's *La Crónica*, reporting on the first Inti Raymi, reinforced this sentiment by declaring, "In no other city besides Cuzco can one find a more reliable expression of what we can understand to be Peruvianness."[69] *Cusqueños*, of course, reveled in the national spotlight, and the assembled crowd became so enthu-siastic that a large group of residents lifted Prado on their shoulders and carried him back to the newly inaugurated hotel.[70]

The careful coordination between state policy and cultural tourism that debuted at the opening of the Hotel Cuzco accelerated with the election of José Bustamante y Rivero as president in 1945. Bustamante y Rivero's successful electoral platform called for populist reforms and a particular focus on state-led economic development. Equally important, Bustamante y Rivero's government permitted the participation of once-suppressed populist movements, especially APRA, which had also promoted *indigenista* symbolism.[71] Much to the delight of *cusqueños*, the new government promised increased state participation in tourism as a way to bring both increased economic development and cultural attention to the region.[72] The pro-posals of Bustamante y Rivero mixed both the Good Neighbor policy's encourage-ment to use international travel as part of hemispheric solidarity and a new effort to expand domestic tourism as part of a larger populist project. Bustamante y Rivero was not alone in these efforts. For example, the Ramón Grau government in Cuba also pledged to use tourism as a source of social development in the postwar era.[73]

On June 5, 1946, the Congress of Peru created the Corporación Nacional del Turismo (National Tourism Corporation; CNT)—the nation's first state-supported institution tasked with developing a tourism industry.[74] The first general director of the CNT, Benjamín Roca Muelle, set an aggressive agenda to use state resources to promote tourism in Peru. Prior to his appointment, Roca Muelle had worked as general manager of the TACP between 1939 and 1941 as well as the editor of *Turismo*. In both positions, Roca Muelle emerged as an enthusiastic advocate for greater government involvement in tourism investment, planning, and promotion with a focus on Cuzco.[75] From the organization's start, CNT leadership asserted that "the conservation and restoration of historical and archaeological monuments in the city of Cuzco, although outside the specific mission of the corporation, has deserved preferential attention."[76]

The "Discoverer of Machu Picchu" Returns

In 1948 another hemispheric initiative provided the CNT with an opportunity to promote travel to Machu Picchu. Cuzco was selected as the site of the second Inter-

American Indigenista Congress, which would gather political and cultural leaders from around the hemisphere to debate indigenous concerns. Promoters of the conference promised that the event would reaffirm Cuzco as the archaeological, folkloric, and touristic capital of South America.[77] The national government and the CNT successfully proposed funding a new access road to Machu Picchu in preparation for the congress.[78] Roca Muelle and Giesecke viewed the opening of the highway as an optimal moment to exploit the growing global interest in Machu Picchu. To do so, they turned to Bingham and, in the process, rehabilitated the reputation of the explorer.

By March 1948, the CNT and Giesecke had persuaded the government to name the new access road to Machu Picchu in honor of Bingham and to invite the explorer for the inauguration of the highway.[79] When presented with the opportunity to return to open the Machu Picchu highway, Bingham eagerly accepted.[80] With Giesecke's help, the CNT office in New York translated Bingham's speeches into Spanish prior to his departure.[81] To capitalize on the media attention surrounding Bingham's visit, *Turismo* published a special English-language article for North American readers describing Cuzco as "the millenary capital of the Inca Empire" and a "Peruvian city of major attraction to tourists."[82] Bingham's visit promised to be a major coup for both the CNT and tourism at Machu Picchu.

In addition to the transportation logistics, promoters of the Bingham visit faced another challenge; they had to rewrite the narrative of the "discovery" of Machu Picchu to reflect the Pan-American goodwill on which the visit sought to capitalize. However, in 1948, both *cusqueños* and Bingham had a mutual interest in overlooking their acrimonious past. When Bingham arrived in Lima accompanied by his wife, Suzanne, on October 6, 1948, Giesecke reported that he "was received with real affection by the people."[83] Even Cuzco's archaeological scholars who had advocated for Bingham's prosecution for theft in 1915 referred to him as a "romantic North American archaeologist, enchanted by the past" in their 1948 bulletin.[84] In Cuzco, Bingham gave a lecture on the history of Machu Picchu at UNSAAC on October 14, 1948. Bingham reasserted his original theories regarding Machu Picchu, arguing that the city was both Tampu-tocco, the legendary origin of the Inca, and Vilcabamba. Although both facts were seriously disputed by archaeologists, no one offered public criticism of Bingham's theories.[85]

The highway inauguration took place on October 17, 1948.[86] Suzanne Bingham lifted a veil to reveal a plaque celebrating Bingham as the "discoverer of Machu Picchu" and broke a bottle of champagne against the rocks near the marker. Hiram Bingham gave a short speech in Spanish thanking all those in attendance. *El Comercio del Cusco* reported glowingly on the speech, noting that "Bingham remembered his first ascension through these mountains, in the middle of a dense jungle, carried by the faith of a man of science."[87] After the ceremonies, the entire party, including the US ambassador, lunched in the tourist lodge. *El Comercio de Lima* observed, "The stone city of Machupicchu has suffered the first impact of civilization, but we

Figure 4. Bingham returning to Machu Picchu as a hero in 1948 to open the new tourist highway, as reported in *El Comercio de Lima*, October 20, 1948. Biblioteca Nacional del Perú.

speak of an impact that will not do damage, because [the ruin] finds itself destined to fulfill its archaeological importance and its admirable beauty" (fig. 4).[88] Much to the pleasure of the CNT, the event also gained press coverage in US markets, thus fulfilling the central objective of inviting Bingham.[89] Leaving Cuzco denounced as a thief in 1915, Bingham had returned in 1948 as a benevolent, Pan-American discoverer of Machu Picchu. This transformation was the product less of Bingham's own actions than of a transnational network of multiple actors who all saw benefits in employing tourism to elevate Machu Picchu as a national symbol of Peru.

Bingham's return in 1948 not only opened access to Machu Picchu but also rehabilitated his professional career and image. The visit certainly aided Bingham's efforts to publish a final book on his exploits at Machu Picchu. Printed in 1948, *Lost City of the Incas: The Story of Machu Picchu and Its Builders* would be Bingham's final publication.[90] Unlike Bingham's earlier publications that cast an imperial gaze on the Andes and its resources, his final book emphasized the Pan-American narratives crafted for his return to Cuzco. Although the book drew mixed critical responses, the archaeologist Victor W. von Hagen's review credited Bingham with drawing much-needed public interest to archaeology and the Inca and kindly concluded that "the fabulous city of Machu Picchu, as revealed here, will forever stand as Dr. Hiram Bingham's archaeological monument."[91]

Conclusion

Machu Picchu's emergence as "Bingham's archaeological monument" by the late 1940s occurred less due to the activities of the explorer than thanks to the shared interests of regional leaders, tourism promoters, and US diplomats. Although each group had different motivations, all saw their goals fulfilled in the promotion of Machu Picchu and Bingham as symbols of an idealized past and the promise of an amicable Pan-American future. More importantly, these efforts elevated Machu Picchu and Cuzco's regional folklore as national representations of Peru. The transnational networks of regional and hemispheric actors that aligned to promote tourism at Machu Picchu had redefined Peru's national identity to emphasize a highly regionalized history and culture of Cuzco. Unlike many European countries that feared postwar tourist visits would threaten their national identity, in the case of Peru, many viewed tourism as a key tool in reinforcing a new sense of nationalism.[92] As Pratt and Lomnitz have argued, understanding the dynamics of transnational contact zones remains critical to our understanding of the development of national identity in Latin America.[93] The case of Machu Picchu's transformation into a national symbol of Peru calls us to examine the powerful role tourism has played in the creation of these transnational networks and exchanges.

Of course, the transformation of Machu Picchu into both a tourist destination and a national symbol created conflict as well as consensus. The staged authenticity of tourism crafted to publicize Machu Picchu overlooked the grassroots political and cultural demands of Cuzco's indigenous communities that neo-*indigenistas* had either altered or obscured. The same interests also silenced local connections to Machu Picchu while heralding Bingham and disseminating his erroneous claims about the site and his expeditions. However, these efforts did not completely silence alternative narratives that used Machu Picchu as a potent symbol. Machu Picchu has always served as a symbol of alternate visions of the Andes and indigenous identities.[94] Pablo Neruda visited Machu Picchu in 1943 at the height of the site's Good Neighbor reinvention. Returning to Chile, Neruda reflected on his experience in the poem "Heights of Machu Picchu" to draw inspiration from the monument in a call for class unity of Latin America's oppressed.[95] Ernesto "Che" Guevara also drew a similar inspiration, visiting Machu Picchu on his now-famous motorcycle tour of Latin America in 1952. For Guevara, Machu Picchu was "an arm outstretched to the future, a stony voice with continental reach that shouts 'citizens of Indo-America, reconquer the past!'"[96] Although tourism promoters succeeded in exploiting Machu Picchu to support their political and economic goals, they were unable to strictly control the narrative of its symbolism to other observers.

However, *cusqueños* and tourism backers had more immediate concerns to consider during Bingham's visit. As the highway was being completed, the reformist Bustamante y Rivero government, shaken by political revolts and economic downturns, had begun to falter. The Indigenista Conference was delayed until 1949, and

Giesecke and Roca Muelle barely managed to avoid the cancellation of Bingham's visit. Shortly after Bingham's departure, Bustamante y Rivero's government fell to a military coup led by General Manuel Odría. The new Odría regime was backed by Peru's economic elite, who aimed to return Peru to an orthodox liberal economy and withdraw from the state-led development initiatives endorsed by Bustamante y Rivero.[97] The Odría regime wasted little time dissolving the CNT and the tourism development plans promoted by the Bustamante y Rivero government.

Quickly, the reliance of Cuzco tourism backers on the cooperation of the now-disappearing Good Neighbor policy became a liability. After the fall of Bustamante y Rivero, the national state had little initiative to fund the proposed inclusive development strategies that had largely bypassed it in favor of transnational institutions and links. Also, the United States began to transition from the Good Neighbor era to an aggressive Cold War focus that imperiled these efforts. Institutions such as the OIAA were quickly dissolved, and, even more important, the overall language and spirit of the Good Neighbor era faded. Now the United States viewed the nationalist and populist projects of Bustamante y Rivero's government with suspicion. Dwight D. Eisenhower's administration, endorsing a mantra of "trade not aid," also withdrew support for state-driven tourism development in favor of private investment.[98] Although tourism gradually increased at Machu Picchu through the 1950s, it would have to wait until the 1960s when the nationalist military government of Juan Velasco Alvarado once again invested state resources into tourism development. Illustrating the powerful influence of the touristic narrative developed decades earlier, the leftist and highly nationalist Velasco regime largely maintained the Pan-American narrative that celebrated Bingham.[99]

In recent years, even as the Peruvian state has litigated to return Machu Picchu artifacts collected by Bingham and stored at Yale University, the touristic narrative celebrating Bingham has been largely repeated in guidebooks and official activities.[100] Highlighting the influence of the tourism narrative to define sites and even national identities, the Peruvian national government in 2011 celebrated the centennial of Bingham's "discovery" of Machu Picchu. Speaking at the ceremony, President Alan García lauded Machu Picchu as the "synthesis of all things Peruvian."[101] Machu Picchu had indeed emerged as the synthesis of many aspects of Peruvian national identity by the twenty-first century. Less acknowledged, however, is the historical transnational synthesis between regional politics and the culture, hemispheric diplomacy, and tourism that created the modern—and problematic—image of Machu Picchu.

Mark Rice is assistant professor of history at Baruch College, City University of New York. His forthcoming book examines the history of tourism in Machu Picchu and Cusco, Peru. He studies modern Latin America with a focus on Peru and the Andean region as well as the history of travel and tourism.

Notes

I want to thank the anonymous reviewers for their insightful comments and suggestions. Part of this essay was presented as a paper at the New York City Latin American History Workshop. I am grateful for the comments made at the gathering. I am also grateful to Paul Gootenberg, Brooke Larson, Deborah Poole, and Eric Zolov for their advice. Unless otherwise noted, all translations are mine.

1. *El Comercio del Cusco*, "Ceremonias en la histórica Machu-Picchu"; Heaney, *Cradle of Gold*, 212–13.
2. For a snapshot of the burgeoning scholarly studies on tourism in Latin America, see Babb, *Tourism Encounter*, 1–13; Berger and Wood, "Introduction"; Bowman, *Peddling Paradise*, 1–12; Wilson, "Impacts of Tourism in Latin America."
3. Sadlier, *Americans All*.
4. Berger, "Goodwill Ambassadors."
5. Pratt, *Imperial Eyes*, 6; Lomnitz, *Deep Mexico, Silent Mexico*, 125–44.
6. MacCannell, *Tourist*, 91–107.
7. See Mould de Pease, *Machu Picchu*; Heaney, *Cradle of Gold*, 83–96.
8. Heaney, *Cradle of Gold*. For Bingham's own accounts, see Bingham, "Discovery of Machu Picchu"; Bingham, "Story of Machu Picchu"; Bingham, "In the Wonderland of Peru"; Bingham, "Further Explorations."
9. Salazar, "Machu Picchu," 25–46.
10. Salvatore, "Local versus Imperial Knowledge," 67–80.
11. Bingham, *Portrait of an Explorer*, 304–13; Heaney, *Cradle of Gold*, 75–77.
12. Bingham, *Inca Land*.
13. Hiram Bingham to F. H. Allen; Bingham to Ferris Greenslet; Bingham to Gilbert Grosvenor. Bingham wrote to Grosvenor, the editor of the *National Geographic Magazine*, that he initially planned to write an additional volume to *Inca Land* that would document Machu Picchu and his 1912 and 1915 expeditions.
14. Quoted in *Boston Daily Globe*, "Climbed Andes."
15. Hiram Bingham to Albert A. Giesecke, 1926.
16. *El Comercio de Lima*, "Machupicchu."
17. Dell, *Llama Land*, 200.
18. Coronado, *Andes Imagined*; Kristal, *Andes Viewed from the City*; Tamayo Herrera, "Prólogo," 9–19.
19. For more on *indigenismo* and neo-*indigenismo*, see de la Cadena, *Indigenous Mestizos*, 44–176; Lauer, *Andes imaginarios*, 107–10.
20. Mendoza, *Creating Our Own*.
21. Koshar, "'What Ought to Be Seen,'" 339–40.
22. Giesecke, "Cuzco."
23. Bingham, *Portrait of an Explorer*, 124–57; Oral History Research Office, "Reminiscences of Albert A. Giesecke," 31–32; Heaney, *Cradle of Gold*, 79–82; Tamayo Herrera, *Historia regional del Cuzco republicano*, 123–26.
24. Giesecke, "Cuzco."
25. See Cosio, *Cuzco histórico y monumental*; García, Valcárcel, and Giesecke, *Guía histórico-artística del Cuzco*; Valcárcel, *Cuzco*.
26. Berger, *Development of Mexico's Tourism Industry*; Schwartz, *Pleasure Island*.
27. Hiatt, "Flying 'Cholo.'"
28. De la Cadena, *Indigenous Mestizos*, 63–64; Drinot, *Allure of Labor*.
29. *Ciudad y campo y caminos*.

30. Klarén, *Peru*, 262–76.

31. De la Cadena, *Indigenous Mestizos*, 131–32; Tamayo Herrera, *Historia regional del Cuzco republicano*, 149–50; Tantaleán, *Peruvian Archaeology*, 67–68.

32. De la Cadena, *Indigenous Mestizos*, 131–76; Mendoza, *Creating Our Own*, 93–123.

33. Mendoza, *Creating Our Own*, 73–74.

34. Heaney, *Cradle of Gold*, 201–11; Bingham, *Machu Picchu, a Citadel of the Incas*.

35. Means, "Ancient City of the Incas."

36. Bingham, *Portrait of an Explorer*, 337.

37. Di Leonardo, *Exotics at Home*, 145–98.

38. Rosemblatt, "Other Americas."

39. Rothman, *Devil's Bargains*, 50–112; Shaffer, *See America First*, 40–129.

40. Naylor, "South America Calls to the Explorer."

41. Rowland, *History of the Office of the Coordinator of Inter-American Affairs*.

42. Klarén, *Peru*, 279–82.

43. McSpadden, *People Who Live in Thin Air*; CIAA, "Project Authorization."

44. Walter E. Krause to Robert C. Wells, memorandum, "Subject: Local Programs."

45. Motion Picture Society for the Americas, "Weekly Report Ending May 14, 1942"; Motion Picture Society for the Americas, "Weekly Report Ending August 26, 1942."

46. *Heart of the Inca Empire*.

47. *Saludos Amigos*.

48. *El Comercio de Lima*, "Fiestas del cuarto Centenario del Cuzco."

49. *El Comercio de Lima*, "En un tren especial."

50. Dammert, "Palabras del presidente."

51. Snyder, "Cusco."

52. Ministerio de Relaciones Exteriores, Resolución Suprema.

53. Giesecke, Informe, 4, 26–27.

54. Ministerio de Fomento y Obras Públicas, *Nuevos hoteles del Perú*, 4.

55. Endy, *Cold War Holidays*.

56. Pan American Union, *Final Act*; Lack, "Suggested Program," 3.

57. *Bulletin of the Pan American Union* 75, no. 7, cover.

58. US Department of State, "Regarding Decree of March 1937 Designating a Special Commission to Prepare the Draft of a Tourist Law"; US Embassy Lima to Washington, DC, memorandum, "Subject: Encouragement of Tourist Traffic by the Government of Peru."

59. F. D. Rugg to J. Stanton Robbins, report, "Transmittal of Report of Transportation Survey," 22.

60. Dorothy Lack to Juan Chávez D.

61. Nelson A. Rockefeller to Wallace K. Harrison.

62. Lack, "Suggested Program," 11.

63. *Turismo*, editorial, Nov. 1943.

64. Ayax, "Preparemonos para la invasión."

65. Ministerio de Fomento y Obras Públicas. *Nuevos hoteles del Perú para el turismo*.

66. De la Cadena, *Indigenous Mestizos*, 157–162; Mendoza, *Creating Our Own*, 150–55.

67. *La Crónica*, "Día del Cusco."

68. Dean, *Inka Bodies*, 200–218; de la Cadena, *Indigenous Mestizos*, 157–72.

69. Ventocilla, "Sentido del Cusco en la peruanidad."

70. *El Sol* (Cuzco), "Días de fervoroso peruanismo ha vivido el Cuzco."

71. Klarén, *Peru*, 289.

72. *Turismo*, "Notas y comentarios."

73. Skwiot, *Purposes of Paradise*, 146–47.
74. Fondo Ministerio de Hacienda, "Memoria de la Corporación Nacional de Turismo," 9.
75. *Turismo*, "Benjamín Roca Muelle."
76. Fondo Ministerio de Hacienda, "Memoria de la Corporación Nacional de Turismo," 17.
77. *La Prensa*, "Segundo Congreso Indigenista Interamericano," 2.
78. Fondo de Asuntos Indígenas, "Resolución Suprema, 15 de mayo de 1948."
79. *El Comercio de Lima*, "Ruinas de Machu-Pichu abiertas al turismo mundial."
80. Albert A. Giesecke to John Clifford Folger, May 17, 1948.
81. Hiram Bingham to Albert A. Giesecke, 1948.
82. *Turismo*, "Cuzco, Imperial Incaland."
83. Albert A. Giesecke to John Clifford Folger, November 22, 1948.
84. Cosio del Pomar, "Machupijchu," 138.
85. *El Comercio del Cusco*, "Machupicchu es la antigua Vilcabamba."
86. Giesecke, "Data by Albert A. Giesecke," 4.
87. *El Comercio del Cusco*, "Ceremonias en la histórica Machu-Picchu."
88. *El Comercio de Lima*, "Carretera 'Bingham' une el Cuzco y Machupicchu."
89. *Newsweek*, "Highway to Antiquity," 45.
90. Bingham, *Lost City of the Incas*.
91. Von Hagen, "Machu Picchu."
92. Endy, *Cold War Holidays*, 72–80.
93. Pratt, *Imperial Eyes*, 6; Lomnitz, *Deep Mexico, Silent Mexico*, 125–44.
94. Poole, "Landscape and the Imperial Subject."
95. Feinstein, *Pablo Neruda*, 173–76.
96. Quoted in Heaney, *Cradle of Gold*, 219–20.
97. Klarén, *Peru*, 289–99.
98. Skwiot, *Purposes of Paradise*, 169–76.
99. Rice, "Selling Sacred Cities," 138–84.
100. Taylor, "Yale and Peru Sign Accord"; Heaney, *Cradle of Gold*, 222–30.
101. *La República*, "Alan García."

References

Ayax. 1944. "Preparemonos para la invasion." *Turismo*, January. Hemeroteca de la Biblioteca Nacional del Perú, Lima.

Babb, Florence E. 2011. *The Tourism Encounter: Fashioning Latin American Nations and Histories*. Stanford, CA: Stanford University Press.

Berger, Dina. 2006. *The Development of Mexico's Tourism Industry: Pyramids by Day, Martinis by Night*. New York: Palgrave Macmillan.

———. 2010. "Goodwill Ambassadors on Holiday: Tourism, Diplomacy, and Mexico-U.S. Relations." In *Holiday in Mexico: Critical Reflections on Tourism and Tourist Encounters*, edited by Dina Berger and Andrew Grant Wood, 107–29. Durham, NC: Duke University Press.

Berger, Dina, and Andrew Grant Wood. 2010. "Introduction: Tourism Studies and the Tourism Dilemma." In Berger and Wood, *Holiday in Mexico*, 1–20.

Bingham, Alfred M. 1989. *Portrait of an Explorer: Hiram Bingham, Discover of Machu Picchu*. Ames: Iowa State University Press.

Bingham, Hiram. 1912. Letter to F. H. Allen, June 12. Box 1, folder 292, 9886, Yale Peruvian Expedition Papers.

———. 1913. "The Discovery of Machu Picchu." *Harper's Magazine*, April, 709–19.

———. 1913. "In the Wonderland of Peru." *National Geographic Magazine*, April, 387–573.

———. 1915. "The Story of Machu Picchu: The National Geographic Society–Yale University Explorations in Peru." *National Geographic Magazine*, February, 172–86, 203–17.

———. 1916. "Further Explorations in the Land of the Incas." *National Geographic Magazine*, May, 431–73.

———. 1922. *Inca Land: Explorations in the Highlands of Peru*. Boston: Houghton Mifflin.

———. 1922. Letter to Ferris Greenslet, June 15. Box 17, folder 292, 9889, Yale Peruvian Expedition Papers.

———. 1922. Letter to Gilbert Grosvenor, October 2. Box 17, folder 296, 9903, Yale Peruvian Expedition Papers.

———. 1926. Letter to Albert A. Giesecke, May 6. AG-0140, Colección Giesecke, Archivo Histórico Riva-Aguero, Lima.

———. 1930. *Machu Picchu, a Citadel of the Incas; Report of the Explorations and Excavations Made in 1911, 1912, and 1915 under the Auspices of Yale University and the National Geographic Society*. New Haven, CT: Yale University Press.

———. 1948. Letter to Albert A. Giesecke, September 29. AG-0140, Colección Giesecke, Archivo Histórico Riva-Aguero, Lima.

———. 1948. *Lost City of the Incas: The Story of Machu Picchu and Its Builders*. New York: Duell, Stone, and Price.

Boston Daily Globe. 1924. "Climbed Andes on the Way to the Governor's Chair." December 7.

Bowman, Kirk S. 2013. *Peddling Paradise: The Politics of Tourism in Latin America*. Boulder, CO: Lynne Rienner.

Bulletin of the Pan American Union. 1941. Vol 75, no. 7: cover.

———. 1942. "Project Authorization: Exhibits of Materials on Other American Republics." Record group 229, entry 1, Office of Inter-American Affairs, box 14, AIA-4186, 0–Educational Programs, United States National Archives, College Park, MD.

Ciudad y campo y caminos. 1927. February, no. 26.

Coronado, Jorge. 2009. *The Andes Imagined: Indigenismo, Society, and Modernity*. Pittsburgh: University of Pittsburgh Press.

Cosio, José Gabriel. 1924. *El Cuzco histórico y monumental*. Cuzco: n.p.

Cosio del Pomar, Felipe. 1948. "Machupijchu." *Revista del Instituto y Museo Arqueológico*, no. 12, n.p. Biblioteca del Museo Inka, Cuzco.

Dammert, Eduardo Dibós. 1936. "Palabras del presidente." *Turismo*, no. 105: n.p. Hemeroteca de la Biblioteca Nacional del Perú, Lima.

Dean, Carolyn. 1999. *Inka Bodies and the Body of Christ: Corpus Christi in Colonial Cuzco, Peru*. Durham, NC: Duke University Press.

de la Cadena, Marisol. 2000. *Indigenous Mestizos: The Politics of Race and Culture in Cuzco, Peru, 1919–1991*. Durham, NC: Duke University Press.

Dell, Anthony. 1926. *Llama Land: East and West of the Andes in Peru*. London: Geoffrey Bless.

di Leonardo, Micaela. 1998. *Exotics at Home: Anthropologies, Others, American Modernity*. Chicago: University of Chicago Press.

Drinot, Paulo. 2011. *The Allure of Labor: Workers, Race, and the Making of the Peruvian State*. Durham, NC: Duke University Press.

El Comercio del Cusco. 1948. "Las ceremonias en la histórica Machu-Picchu." October 18. Hemeroteca de la Biblioteca Municipal del Cusco.

———. 1948. "Machupicchu es la antigua Vilcabamba y en esa importante ciudad estuvo Manco II." October 16. Hemeroteca de la Biblioteca Municipal del Cusco.

El Comercio de Lima. 1926. "Machupicchu." September 10. Hemeroteca de la Biblioteca Nacional del Perú, Lima.

———. 1934. "En un tren especial cedido por el gobierno se efectuó ayer la excursión hacia Machupicchu." August 2. Hemeroteca de la Biblioteca Nacional del Perú, Lima.

———. 1934. "Las fiestas del cuarto Centenario del Cuzco." March 23. Hemeroteca de la Biblioteca Nacional del Perú, Lima.

———. 1948. "La carretera 'Bingham' une el Cuzco y Machupicchu." October 20. Hemeroteca de la Biblioteca Nacional del Perú, Lima.

———. 1948. "Las ruinas de Machu-Pichu abiertas al turismo mundial." March 4. Hemeroteca de la Biblioteca Nacional del Perú, Lima.

El Sol (Cuzco). 1944. "Días de fervoroso peruanismo ha vivido el Cuzco en torno a Manuel Prado celebrando el Día de la Ciudad." June 26. Hemeroteca de la Biblioteca Municipal del Cusco.

Endy, Christopher. 2004. *Cold War Holidays: American Tourism in France*. Chapel Hill: University of North Carolina Press.

Feinstein, Adam. 2004. *Pablo Neruda: A Passion for Life*. New York: Bloomsbury.

Fondo de Asuntos Indígenas. 1948. "Resolución Suprema, 15 de mayo de 1948." Legajo, 3.13.2.9, fol. 123, Achivo General de la Nación del Perú, Lima.

Fondo Ministerio de Hacienda. 1946. "Memoria de la Corporación Nacional de Turismo, correspondiente al año 1946." H-6, lejado 2444, Achivo General de la Nación del Perú, Lima.

García, José Uriel, Luis E. Valcárcel, and Albert A. Giesecke. 1925. *Guía histórico-artística del Cuzco*. Lima: Editorial Garcilaso.

Giesecke, Albert A. 1921. "El Cuzco: Meca del turismo de la América del Sur." *Revista universitaria* 10, no. 35: 3–17.

———. 1936. Informe, July 24. AG-D-071, Colección Giesecke, Archivo Histórico Riva-Aguero, Lima.

———. 1948. Letter to John Clifford Folger, May 17. AG-0521, Colección Giesecke, Archivo Histórico Riva-Aguero, Lima.

———. 1948. Letter to John Clifford Folger, November 22. AG-0521, Colección Giesecke, Archivo Histórico Riva-Aguero, Lima.

———. 1961. "Data by Albert A. Giesecke." February 13. AG-D-209, Colección Giesecke, Archivo Histórico Riva-Aguero, Lima.

Heaney, Christopher. 2010. *Cradle of Gold: The Story of Hiram Bingham, a Real-Life Indiana Jones and the Search for Machu Picchu*. New York: Palgrave Macmillan.

Heart of the Inca Empire. 1943. Produced by Howard Knapp, Wendell Clark Bennett, and U.S. Office of Inter-American Affairs. Directed by Howard Knapp. [Washington, DC]: Office of the Coordinator of Inter-American Affairs. 25 min.

Hiatt, Willie. 2007. "Flying 'Cholo': Incas, Airplanes, and the Construction of Andean Modernity in 1920s Cuzco, Peru." *Americas* 63, no. 3: 327–58.

Klarén, Peter. 2000. *Peru: Society and Nationhood in the Andes*. New York: Oxford University Press.

Koshar, Rudy. 1998. "'What Ought to Be Seen': Tourists' Guidebooks and National Identities in Modern Germany and Europe." *Journal of Contemporary History* 33, no. 3: 323–40.

Krause, Walter E. (assistant director, Radio Division). 1943. Memorandum to Robert C. Wells (chairman, Coordination Committee for Argentina), "Subject: Local Programs," March 15. Record group 229, Office of Inter-American Affairs, box 255, B-RA 1515, 3–Radio Programs-Dramatic, United States National Archives, College Park, MD.

Kristal, Efraín. 1987. *The Andes Viewed from the City: Literary and Political Discourse on the Indian in Peru, 1848–1930*. New York: Peter Lang.

Lack, Dorothy. 1943. Letter to Juan Chávez D., commercial councillor, July 26. Record group 229, entry 1, box 202, 2–Peru, Economic Development, Tourists, United States National Archives, College Park, MD.

———. 1945. "Suggested Program for the Development of Inter-American Tourist Travel." Washington, DC: Office of Inter-American Affairs. Record group 229, entry 40, box 657, United States National Archives, College Park, MD.

La Crónica. 1944. "El Día del Cusco." June 24. Hemeroteca de la Biblioteca Nacional del Perú, Lima.

La Prensa. 1948. "El Segundo Congreso Indigenista Interamericano debe ser celebrado en el Cuzco el 24 de julio." January 2. Hemeroteca de la Biblioteca Nacional del Perú, Lima.

La República. 2011. "Alan García: 'Machu Picchu es la síntesis de la peruanidad.'" July 7. www.larepublica.pe/07-07-2011/alan-garcia-machu-picchu-es-la-sintesis-de-la-peruanidad.

Lauer, Mirko. 1997. *Andes imaginarios: Discursos del indigenismo 2*. Cuzco: Centro de Estudios Regionales Andinos Bartolomé de las Casas.

Lomnitz, Claudio. 2001. *Deep Mexico, Silent Mexico: An Anthropology of Nationalism*. Minneapolis: University of Minnesota Press.

MacCannell, Dean. 1976. *The Tourist: A New Theory of the Leisure Class*. New York: Schocken Books.

McSpadden, Anne. 1941. *People Who Live in Thin Air: A Study of Life in the Andes Mountains of South America*. October 1. Record group 229, Office of Inter-American Affairs, box 399, OEM-CR 1, 3–Education Teaching Aides, United States National Archives, College Park, MD.

Means, Philip Ainsworth. 1930. "An Ancient City of the Incas: Dr. Bingham Sums Up the Results of the Machu Picchu Expedition." *New York Times*, May 4.

Mendoza, Zoila S. 2008. *Creating Our Own: Folklore, Performance, and Identity in Cuzco, Peru*. Durham, NC: Duke University Press.

Ministerio de Fomento y Obras Públicas. 1941. *Nuevos hoteles del Perú para el turismo*, September. Record group 229, entry 40, box 657, United States National Archives, College Park, MD.

Ministerio de Relaciones Exteriores. 1936. Resolución Suprema, March 14. AG-D-071, Colección Giesecke, Archivo Histórico Riva-Aguero, Lima.

Motion Picture Society for the Americas. 1942. "Weekly Report Ending August 26, 1942." Record group 229, entry 1, Office of Inter-American Affairs, box 218, United States National Archives, College Park, MD.

———. 1942. "Weekly Report Ending May 14, 1942." Record group 229, entry 1, Office of Inter-American Affairs, box 218, United States National Archives, College Park, MD.

Mould de Pease, Mariana. 2003. *Machu Picchu y el código de ética de la Sociedad de Arqueología Americana: Una invitación al diálogo intercultural*. Lima: Consejo Nacional de Ciencia y Tecnología; Pontificia Universidad Católica del Perú, Fondo Editorial; Instituto Nacional de Cultura; Universidad Nacional de San Antonio Abad del Cusco.

Naylor, Douglas. 1931. "South America Calls to the Explorer." *New York Times*, November 1.

Newsweek. 1948. "Highway to Antiquity: Carretera Hiram Bingham to Open Machu Picchu to the World." November, 45.

Oral History Research Office, Columbia University. 1963. "The Reminiscences of Albert A. Giesecke." New York: Columbia University.

Pan American Union. 1941. *Final Act: Second Inter-American Travel Conference, Mexico, DF,*

September 15–24. Washington, DC: Pan American Union Travel Division. Record group 229, entry 40, box 656, United States National Archives, College Park, MD.

Poole, Deborah. 1998. "Landscape and the Imperial Subject: U.S. Images of the Andes, 1859–1930." In *Close Encounters of Empire: Writing the Cultural History of U.S.–Latin American Relations*, edited by Gilbert M. Joseph, Catherine C. Legrand, and Ricardo D. Salvatore, 107–38. Durham, NC: Duke University Press.

Pratt, Mary Louise. 1992. *Imperial Eyes: Travel Writing and Transculturation*. New York: Routledge.

Rice, Mark. 2014. "Selling Sacred Cities: Tourism, Region, and Nation in Cusco, Peru." PhD diss., Stony Brook University.

Rockefeller, Nelson A. 1945. Letter to Wallace K. Harrison, director, Office of Inter-American Affairs, April 20. Record group 229, box 656, United States National Archives, College Park, MD.

Rosemblatt, Karin Alejandra. 2009. "Other Americas: Transnationalism, Scholarship, and the Culture of Poverty in Mexico and the United States." *Hispanic American Historical Review* 89, no. 4: 603–41.

Rothman, Hal. 1998. *Devil's Bargains: Tourism in the Twentieth-Century American West*. Lawrence: University Press of Kansas.

Rowland, Donald W. 1947. *History of the Office of the Coordinator of Inter-American Affairs*. Washington, DC: Government Printing Office.

Rugg, F. D. 1944. Report to J. Stanton Robbins, "Transmittal of Report of Transportation Survey of Peru." October 23. Record group 229, entry 1, Office of Inter-American Affairs, box 202, United States National Archives, College Park, MD.

Sadlier, Darlene J. 2012. *Americans All: Good Neighbor Cultural Diplomacy in World War II*. Austin: University of Texas Press.

Salazar, Lucy C. 2004. "Machu Picchu: Mysterious Royal Estate in the Cloud Forest." In *Machu Picchu: Unveiling the Mystery of the Incas*, edited by Richard L. Burger and Lucy C. Salazar, 21–47. New Haven, CT: Yale University Press.

Saludos Amigos. 1942. Produced by Walt Disney. Directed by Norman Ferguson, Wilfred Jackson, Jack Kinney, Hamilton Luske, and William Roberts. Burbank, CA: Walt Disney Productions. 42 minutes.

Salvatore, Ricardo D. 2003. "Local versus Imperial Knowledge: Reflections on Hiram Bingham and the Yale Peruvian Expedition." *Nepantla: Views from South* 4, no. 1: 67–80.

Schwartz, Rosalie. 1997. *Pleasure Island: Tourism and Temptation in Cuba*. Lincoln: University of Nebraska Press.

Shaffer, Marguerite S. 2001. *See America First: Tourism and National Identity, 1880–1940*. Washington, DC: Smithsonian Institution Press.

Skwiot, Christine. 2010. *The Purposes of Paradise: U.S. Tourism and Empire in Cuba and Hawai'i*. Philadelphia: University of Pennsylvania Press.

Snyder, Phyllis. 1936. "Cusco." *Turismo*, no. 105: n.p. Hemeroteca de la Biblioteca Nacional del Perú, Lima.

Tamayo Herrera, José. 1981. "Prólogo." In *El pensamiento indigenista*, edited by José Tamayo Herrera, 9–19. Lima: Mosca Azul Editores.

———. 2010. *Historia regional del Cuzco republicano: Un libro de síntesis, 1808–1980*. 3rd ed. Lima: n.p.

Tantaleán, Henry. 2014. *Peruvian Archaeology: A Critical History*. Translated by Charles Stanish. Walnut Creek, CA: Left Coast.

Taylor, Kate. 2011. "Yale and Peru Sign Accord on Machu Picchu Artifacts." *ArtsBeat* (blog),

New York Times, February 11. http://artsbeat.blogs.nytimes.com/2011/02/11/yale-and-peru
-sign-accord-on-machu-picchu-artifacts.

Turismo. 1943. Editorial. November, n.p. Hemeroteca de la Biblioteca Nacional del Perú, Lima.

———. 1945. "Notas y comentarios." November, n.p. Hemeroteca de la Biblioteca Nacional del
Perú, Lima.

———. 1946. "Benjamín Roca Muelle." June, n.p. Hemeroteca de la Biblioteca Nacional del
Perú, Lima.

———. 1948. "Cuzco, Imperial Incaland, the Greatest Goal of Students and Tourists."
October–November, n.p. Hemeroteca de la Biblioteca Nacional del Perú, Lima.

US Department of State. 1937. "Regarding Decree of March 1937 Designating a Special
Commission to Prepare the Draft of a Tourist Law." March 5. Record group 59, decimal file
1930–1939, 823.11/87, United States National Archives, College Park, MD.

US Embassy Lima. 1937. Memorandum to Washington, DC, "Subject: Encouragement of
Tourist Traffic by the Government of Peru." December 20. Record group 59, decimal file
1930–1939, 823.111/102, United States National Archives, College Park, MD.

Valcárcel, Luis E. 1934. *Cuzco: Capital arqueológica de Sud América, 1534–1934*. Lima: Banco
Italiano.

Ventocilla, Elodoro. 1944. "Sentido del Cusco en la peruanidad." *La crónica*, June 24.
Hemeroteca de la Biblioteca Nacional del Perú, Lima.

Von Hagen, Victor W. 1948. "Machu Picchu." *New York Times*, December 5.

Wilson, Tamar Diana. 2008. "The Impacts of Tourism in Latin America." *Latin American
Perspectives* 35, no. 3: 3–20.

Tourists in Uniform

American Empire-Building and the
Defense Department's Cold War Pocket Guide Series

Scott Laderman

Bill was not unlike many Americans. Steeped in Cold War ideology but having never left the United States, he enlisted in the United States Army and was sent abroad in the early 1950s. This excited him. It meant meeting new people, seeing new places, and experiencing new cultures. And his first impressions were positive. The local people welcomed him amiably. But this initial joy turned into frustration. Although he was there to protect their freedom, the locals' attitudes began to change. What had once been warmth became indifference, exasperation, even outright hostility. It got so bad that when Bill took a weekend off from his official duties and headed into town for a bit of fun and recreation, he was met on the bus with the bitter stares of local community members. Warmth was nowhere to be found. This incensed Bill. "These foreigners are beginning to get on my nerves," he seethed. "You'd think they'd show some appreciation of what we're doing for them."

Fortunately, Bill had his American compatriot Joe to help set him straight. Joe, a bit older and wiser, was better versed in the ways of cross-cultural understanding. He was capable of contemplating how he might feel if the roles were reversed. "They're not the foreigners here," Joe corrected Bill. "We are. This is their country and we're here as guests. If the people here don't seem too friendly, maybe we're partly to blame. Maybe we're doing a lot of things that irritate them." Bill's belief that they were in the country on their hosts' behalf concerned Joe. "We're not here

Radical History Review
Issue 129 (October 2017)   DOI 10.1215/01636545-3920691
© 2017 by MARHO: The Radical Historians' Organization, Inc.

to do these people a favor," he said to Bill. "We're here for only one reason. We're here to do a job for the United States. Our government believes that the security of this country we're stationed in is tied up with the security of our own country."

And what was that threat to the security of the United States? The answer in 1953, when this account appeared, was simple: communism. "Any way you look at it this job of holding back Red aggression is just too big for one nation," Joe explained. "The free nations have got to work together. The people in this country right here realize that. That's why they're willing to let us occupy bases and quarter troops on their soil."[1]

In truth, Bill and Joe never engaged in any such exchange. That is because Bill and Joe were not in fact real—or at least not literally so. Bill was an emblem of those millions of Americans in uniform going abroad for the first time in the decades following the Second World War, while Joe was the respectful, empathetic model to which they should all aspire. They were brought to life by the US military in its appropriately named *Pocket Guide to Anywhere*, one of dozens of such pocket guides—though the only one not specific to a particular country or region—disseminated within the ranks of the armed forces beginning in the 1940s. Their purpose was simple. The pocket guides sought to culturally and politically indoctrinate their military readers about the importance of Washington's global mission and their own fundamental role in furthering it. And that mission, the pocket guides insisted, was national security and the defense of democracy, not imperialism or support for authoritarian regimes. Simply put, the United States imagined itself providing what Mimi Thi Nguyen calls "the gift of freedom," with its armed forces serving as freedom's frontline champions.[2]

American cultural diplomacy could only be effective, however, if the nation's representatives shed the arrogance, cultural insensitivity, and socially isolationist tendencies that in the early years of the Cold War so alarmed the military veterans William J. Lederer and Eugene Burdick, prompting their authorship of the scathing 1958 novel *The Ugly American*.[3] That sometimes meant more than just the military authorities encouraging respectful behavior of their troops; it could also mean creating the sort of discursive or memorial frameworks that historians Naoko Shibusawa and Brian C. Etheridge have traced for the ideological transformation of Washington's World War II enemies into the closest of allies.[4] If in 1950 the discursive rehabilitation of Japan was still in its relative infancy, with the Japanese being unfavorably compared in racial terms with the Korean people—the Koreans, according to that country's pocket guide, were a "graceful and proud race" whose "features are more regular and finely chiseled [than those of the Japanese], and they are larger and better muscled"—by 1952 the shift in how the Defense Department viewed Japan was apparent. With its accession to the Treaty of San Francisco on September 8, 1951, and its agreement to a bilateral security treaty with the United States that same day, Japan was now firmly ensconced in the "family of free nations."[5] But there was still work to be done at the grassroots level. The Pentagon implored each member of its armed forces in Japan, whose "individual contacts will mean more than all the speeches of our statesmen in shaping Japanese ideas," to "treat no one as though he belongs to an inferior race or group" and to labor tirelessly as a "salesman of democracy."[6]

Yet the pocket guides did not only encourage humility and cross-cultural solidarity. They also interpreted the geopolitics of the Cold War for their uniformed readers in ways favorable to American imperial ambitions. With narratives justifying US foreign policy as, in essence, an expression of God's will for the human race, the pocket guides gave meaning to those troops who sought it—which, given Americans' generally shallow comprehension of global affairs, was most of them. Cloaking their politics in a literary and referential genre most often associated with pleasure, these peculiar guidebooks performed critical work in reinforcing Cold War ideology while, surprisingly, turning the Pentagon into one of the world's most prolific travel publishers.

. . . . .

One of the more significant developments in twentieth-century US foreign policy was the establishment and expansion of a network of US military bases in dozens of nations around the world. Their strategic purpose was the preservation of the modern American empire, a Washington-dominated, neoliberalism-enhancing system of global influence and control that had to do less with conquest and colonization—though the United States had certainly demonstrated that it was not above these—than with the assertion of political, economic, cultural, and military power. Because this empire was not an empire in the traditional sense—it was more informal than formal—and because US actions were typically framed as instances of benevolence (which is not dissimilar from how other empires have characterized their actions), most Americans did not consider the United States an imperial nation.[7] On the contrary, Americans during the Cold War were wont to think of US foreign policy as decidedly anti-imperialist, with most of the nation's dominant ideological structures, from schools and the news media to Hollywood and religious institutions, reinforcing the belief that Washington was in the business of defending the free world from communist domination. The American military was very much a part of this ideological milieu.

When the United States created its web of military bases abroad, it meant, in practical terms, the stationing of hundreds of thousands of young, inexperienced Americans on the Cold War's frontiers. This presented challenges both political and cultural. Politically, the troops needed to be convinced—and then repeatedly reminded—about their host nation's importance to the defense of the American way. This was not always obvious, particularly in a struggle that was deeply ideological and could at times seem never ending. And culturally, these bases were often located in countries where the troops did not speak the local language or understand the prevalent social norms, with the Americans sometimes carrying with them their feelings of superiority—racial or otherwise—that, if allowed to materialize, could jeopardize the nation's Cold War mission.[8] But these personnel were not only military expatriates. They were also tourists. They interacted with the communities that hosted their bases, of course, but they took advantage of their time off to tour virtually every noncommunist nation on earth, too.

That was, in fact, one of the benefits of their military service touted by the Defense Department. "To travel as a tourist to the Far East is expensive," its *Pocket Guide to Japan* noted, but "as a member of the United States Armed Forces you become a world traveler at no cost to yourself."[9] In framing one's time in uniform as a taxpayer-funded holiday (with, to be sure, a fair bit of national service thrown in), the pocket guides made manifest what to some Americans was difficult to see. From wartime infrastructure developments that have fueled postwar tourism growth to the countless war-related sites, museums, and memorials that have become popular tourist attractions worldwide, there has long been a close relationship between tourism and militarism.[10] The millions of military personnel who moved through the Cold War's contested terrain, at once fulfilling their national duty while partaking in the pleasures afforded by international travel, are but one example. Yet they were an especially important one. They served as the uniformed counterparts to those hundreds of thousands of American civilians who, with the advent of jet travel and the postwar expansion of the middle class, began taking to the world in the years following the Second World War. And like their civilian compatriots, the troops generated a great deal of concern.

Recognizing that their bad behavior or cultural insensitivity could do enormous damage to US foreign policy, the military did everything it could to ideologically condition them. What Washington wanted to avoid were any situations—from public intoxication to sexual harassment or the rape of local women—that brought the United States into disrepute or suggested moral parity with the nation's enemies. The nightmare scenario was one in which an instance of military boorishness might be interpreted as a symbol—and a potent one at that—of broader imperial arrogance. That was what transpired in 1949, for example, when a dozen US sailors on a three-day furlough from the USS *Rodman* and USS *Hobson* managed to outrage virtually the entire Cuban nation. Apparently drunk and wanting a memorable picture, the sailors climbed a statue of Cuban revolutionary José Martí in Havana's Parque Central. While doing so, one of the Americans unzipped his fly and urinated on Martí's face. He then waved defiantly at a gathering, screaming crowd while sitting on the statue's marble shoulders with his crotch pressed against Martí's head. Among those frantically trying to remove the Americans was a twenty-two-year-old law student named Fidel Castro, who would later cite the episode as a pivotal moment in his growing hostility to US domination of the island. A couple of onlookers captured the brazen episode on film, with one particularly shocking photograph in the following day's newspapers making it appear as if Martí was performing fellatio on the visiting sailor. For more than a week massive demonstrations were held outside the US embassy, the Cuban foreign minister demanded formal apologies from both the ambassador and the US secretary of state, and American flags went up in flames across the nation.[11]

In short, this incident was not a model for how US military tourism was supposed to go. The Pentagon recognized that it had its work cut out for it, and, with this and other episodes surely in mind, the military assigned its growing Pocket Guide series an outsize role in both behavioral and political instruction. While there has been growing scholarly attention to the myriad ways that guidebooks from Fodor's, Lonely Planet, and other publishers have constructed "the other," reflected and shaped historical memory, and contributed to the growth of imperial travel cultures, virtually no attention has been afforded to what in fact amounted to one of the largest guidebook publishers of the twentieth century: the US Department of Defense.[12] Unbeknownst to most tourism scholars, the Pentagon published dozens of guidebooks to numerous locales for the use of millions of armed forces personnel. These "pocket guides," as they were called, envisioned American troops as grassroots ambassadors working to further US foreign-policy objectives while simultaneously reaping the pleasures of global travel.

They served a multiplicity of purposes. At the most obvious level, the Pentagon used the publications to present its young charges with an enticing vision of the delightful discoveries that awaited them overseas. This included florid descriptions of countless sites of interest, from architectural ruins and museums to beaches, national parks, and cultural attractions.

In this way the pocket guides mirrored their private-sector counterparts. Indeed, this resemblance to the civilian literature occasionally spurred criticism. One military official in 1956, for instance, questioned the publications' utility, complaining that their information "can be found in any good commercial guidebook."[13] But this narrow objection overlooks one of the pocket guides' most important functions. Even more than their civilian counterparts, they performed essential ideological work, explaining to American troops why they were in a particular area while attempting to inculcate in them a worldview grounded in a pivotal twentieth-century assumption: the United States and its allies are forces for good, defending freedom and democracy on every part of the planet.

Military officials thus came to view the pocket guides as vital instruments of ideological indoctrination. Recognizing, however, that "troops tend to shy away from 'indoctrination' . . . [and] prefer 'information,'" as one US official noted in 1962, the pocket guides proved a brilliant stroke, with their seeming innocuousness masking their insidiousness.[14] What better way to cloak indoctrination than through guidebooks promising endless opportunities for pleasure. As undoubtedly

Dramatic beauty wreaths falls in Dalat hill country.

6

Figure 1. With photographs of waterfalls, temples, and other enticing attractions, the *Pocket Guide to Viet-Nam* presented this Southeast Asian war zone as a beautiful and exotic destination just beckoning to be explored. OAFIE, *Pocket Guide to Viet-Nam* (1963), 6.

ideological instruments, the guidebooks, drawing on both the military and discursive power of the United States, constructed their historical narratives and their attention to contemporary politics in ways that whitewashed American imperialism, celebrated the modernization project (and its often racialized assumptions of Third World backwardness), and elided the authoritarianism of a number of Washington's closest allies. In doing so, they sought to persuade military personnel of the basic goodness and justice of American foreign policy and thus the benevolence of the troops' mission.

Yet they also sought to recruit these personnel into the uniformed diplomatic corps. The Pentagon and its publications stressed the various ways that military tourists should serve as grassroots diplomats or "ambassadors of goodwill" in Washington's ongoing struggle against the putative communist menace. This meant, as one pocket guide put it, building "a solid foundation of mutual respect and admiration" between the United States and the communities hosting its forces.[15] Put simply, American troops' positive interactions with locals could benefit US foreign policy objectives, while negative interactions—from catcalling and sexual violence to alcohol-fueled aggression and urinating on statues of national heroes—could do incalculable harm. Military travel, in other words, was inseparable from American empire-building, with US militarism's agents cloaked as pleasure-seeking tourists negotiating a fraught political world.

Tourism, Orientation, Indoctrination

The pocket guides did not in fact originate with the Cold War. There were a number of volumes published during World War II, with the army's 1944 guidebook to Hawaii in many ways illustrative of the politics that would mark the later Cold War editions. Hawaii, for American personnel passing through the territory during the fight against Japan, must have seemed a perplexing place. On the one hand, the islands featured "some of the most beautiful scenery in the world," these personnel were told by their *Pocket Guide to Hawaii*, from the "snow-capped mountains" of the Big Island to the "astonishing" Waimea Canyon on Kauai. On the other hand, the territory was home to hundreds of thousands of people, and that is where the pocket guide's narrative may have generated some confusion. For young men taught to think of Japanese Americans in the wake of the Pearl Harbor attack as would-be traitors requiring eviction from their West Coast homes, the Japanese community in Hawaii was apparently different. These Japanese were not "just talking patriotism," the military maintained; on the contrary, they were flag-saluting Americans "willing to die" for their country. "Don't sell them short," the Pentagon pleaded.[16]

Similar entreaties were in order for mainlanders reared on "fantastic fiction[s]" about the indigenous Hawaiian population. By 1941 there were "14,246 pure Hawaiians and 52,445 part Hawaiians," according to the colorfully illustrated volume, and they "believe in strong bodies, in clean living, and in democracy." It would thus be a mistake if newcomers to the islands let their misconceptions "throw

[them] off the beam." In addition to Japanese Americans and "pure" and "part" Hawaiians, there were "8,000 Puerto Ricans, 29,000 Chinese, 7,000 Koreans, and 52,000 Filipinos," as well as tens of thousands of mostly white "folks from back home who came over here to live." How this territorial outpost became a domestic residential option for American mainlanders was explained in the guide's antiseptic take on modern history.[17]

American interests in Hawaii dated to 1820, troops learned, when a boatload of missionaries arrived from Boston to create "a bit of New England in the tropical Pacific." What accompanied this penetration of the islands might have been a monumental tragedy to the Hawaiian people, but it evidently failed to elicit any concern in the Pentagon, which over a hundred years later could not be bothered to acknowledge it: the demographic collapse of the native population with the introduction of foreign pathogens.[18] Rather than a scourge that contributed to hundreds of thousands of deaths, the missionary arrival in the Hawaiian Islands in fact proved a great blessing, according to the military, for it produced a highly educated society in which "Western people and Western ideas were taking hold."[19]

The Hawaiians' good fortune persisted through the end of the nineteenth century. Indigenous rulers "were worried about the possible fate of the Islands as long as they remained independent," with "apprehensive looks . . . cast toward Germany and Japan." Fortunately for the Hawaiian royalty—or so the Defense Department assumed—Washington expressed an interest in the kingdom. The reasons were several. Hawaii seemed a "perfect site" for a US naval base, "American economic ties with the Islands were growing stronger," and, by 1898, the United States had come to accept its increasing global responsibilities. Five years after an "internal bloodless revolution"—not a coup—"dethroned Queen Liliuokalani," Washington accepted the invitation by the haole-led Republic of Hawaii to annex the archipelago, and "Hawaii became American soil." This triumphal tale, according to the pocket guide, explains just how the islands found themselves "an integral part of the United States" and, significantly, an experiment in multiracial democracy, one that knit "many people of different races together in a concerted effort to build a better, freer, and happier life for all."[20]

If the American colonization of Hawaii was richly celebrated in 1944, by 1955, when the Defense Department issued a new, Cold War–era edition of its pocket guide, the apologia for American empire-building had reached truly stunning proportions. In this updated narrative, a group remarkably referred to as "the Hawaiians"—that is, the haole elites, not the indigenous population—proclaimed the abolition of the monarchy following Queen Liliuokalani's attempt to remove some of the constitutional restrictions placed on her.[21] The group then formed a provisional government. While this government saw its "hopes of early annexation to the United States" dashed because President Grover Cleveland "wanted time to investigate the Hawaiian situation," a republic was soon formed and, following the 1896 election of William McKinley, negotiations for annexation resumed. By

1898 the marriage had been consummated—Hawaii would now be a territory of the United States, the House and Senate declared in a joint resolution—and two years later Congress passed the Hawaii Organic Act, which established the territorial government. Thus did Hawaii come "into the Union proudly and voluntarily, preferring the American democratic way of life to the many other forms of government she experienced and was offered."[22]

What these consecutive editions of the pocket guide suggest is the extent to which the military's construction of history as a progressive story of America's salvific mission lay at the center of its twentieth-century global project. If today the Hawaiian guidebooks read like an imperial whitewash and hollow celebration of multiculturalism, such narratives were essential to America's exceptionalist sense of itself. Conjoining national duty and the pleasures to be found in overseas travel, the US Defense Department's dozens of pocket guides to countries and territories around the world followed a similar script. American foreign policy always reflected American beneficence. American allies were always defending freedom. And the American people were always exemplars of decency and the democratic spirit. This was because, in a very real sense, the Pentagon's guidebooks were only partially about international travel. Their enticing photographs of the local scenery and their flowery descriptions of the attractions available to American personnel echoed the sort of prose one might encounter in a Fodor's or a Baedeker. But they surpassed their civilian counterparts in quite consciously embracing their political charge. Their consolidated military creator after 1952, the Office of Armed Forces Information and Education (OAFIE), undertook all of its programs, including the Pocket Guide series, with an eye toward countering what President Dwight D. Eisenhower called the Soviet Union's "frequently announced hope and purpose" to destroy freedom everywhere.[23]

Given the innocuous packaging in which the trope of American benevolence unfolded, the pocket guides may have been among the most effective propaganda instruments in the military's ideological arsenal. With US troops typically hostile to materials that suggested spin, the guidebooks' seemingly neutral provision of a contested Cold War narrative in publications that appealed to Americans' touristic desires made them outstanding instructional tools. Their raison d'être, after all, was to provide basic information about the many exciting places where military personnel might find themselves. "Of necessity," Harold Hayes, a Pentagon administrator overseeing their creation, noted in 1955, "they include many facts about history, geography, and economics. But to maintain reader interest, we try to balance these with a certain amount of trivia" while presenting the particulars in "a light, chatty style."[24] At the same time, the pocket guides enticed military personnel with colorful details about shopping, hotels, and restaurants, as well as "suggestions about recreation" and "the most historic and scenic places to visit."[25]

The guidebooks also stressed to military personnel the crucially important role of decorous behavior in waging the Cold War. In the 1950s, US officials began to speak up about the diplomatic significance of foreign travel—whether military or civilian—and the people-to-people encounters it made possible. Well-behaved Americans could reflect positively on the United States; unruly or disrespectful Americans could do serious damage to Cold War objectives. Recognizing that most of its citizens had little experience with the outside world, Washington sought to ensure that their comportment rendered American tourists "ambassadors of good-will."[26] For both civilians and armed forces personnel, this meant, for instance, the provision of a letter to all US passport holders stressing how Americans could emphasize during their journeys abroad that "the United States is a friendly nation and one dedicated to the search for world peace and to the promotion of the well-being and security of the community of nations."[27] And specifically for those in uniform, whose actions could prove exponentially more harmful given their official status as agents of the state, the Pentagon produced Bill and Joe and *A Pocket Guide to Anywhere*, its generic manual on how to negotiate the cultural challenges one might experience while serving abroad.

Not restricted to any country or region, *A Pocket Guide to Anywhere* was first published in 1953; a second edition appeared in 1956. Its narrative conveyed the various experiences of the two fictional men "stationed in a foreign land." Readers do not learn much about Bill and Joe, but they appear to be white and to have no international experience to speak of. Because of their military service, however, Bill and Joe suddenly "find themselves for the first time among alien people, whose ways are not [their] ways, whose language and customs are different from [theirs], whose religion may be different, [and] whose skin may be of a different color." Employing a framework that excludes the possibility of colonial or imperial resentments—the exasperation of these "alien people" appears to be rooted almost entirely in the deprivation caused by the Second World War—the pocket guide provides hypothetical scenarios in which the two Americans must contend with

Don't try to get too friendly with the average Moslem woman.

Foreigners will judge our country by the way you act.

Figures 2a and 2b. *A Pocket Guide to Anywhere* emphasized the importance of cultural sensitivity and what it called "the inborn dignity of *every* individual." It was essential that military personnel behave decorously, the Pentagon emphasized, for that would be a basis on which foreign nations judged the United States. OAFIE, *Pocket Guide to Anywhere*, 17, 34, 39.

Figure 3. The illustrations in the *Pocket Guide to Hawaii* could also convey the colonialist mentality displayed in its text. One startlingly racist drawing, for instance, featured a naked, childlike Hawaiian greeting a much taller, sophisticated white settler. Special Projects Branch, *Pocket Guide to Hawaii*, 15.

their own frustrations and the animosity of the local residents, in the process offering its readers pointers in how to be both culturally sensitive and politically astute.[28]

This was no trifling issue. It was in fact a matter of national security, as the United States was "facing a threat of aggression even worse than the one we got rid of when we and our allies licked the Nazis and the Japanese warlords," Joe told Bill.[29] The Pentagon thus asked its young charges for patience and understanding in working with host communities.

Of course, this entire project connecting US military tourism with grassroots cultural diplomacy was grounded in a specific postwar vision of racial liberalism, one that assumed that American troops, having conquered their own individual prejudices, could somehow overcome the world's complex racial and colonial legacies with a smile, a handshake, or a bow.[30] But as the case of Vietnam grimly illustrated, grinning American faces—most of them white—did not always prove up to the task. And then there were the mixed messages the troops received from their instructional literature. While *A Pocket Guide to Anywhere* criticized the potential for cultural arrogance and stressed the importance of cultural sensitivity, a number of country-specific pocket guides took for granted the superiority of white American civilization while embracing the modernization project of the United States.[31]

Some of this predated the flux in the postwar racial order. In the 1944 *Pocket Guide to Hawaii*, for instance, an illustration of a childlike "native" and a gentlemanly settler cogently symbolized the racist paternalism of white America in the face of the islands' indigenous population.

A year earlier, the Pentagon suggested in its guidebook for Panama that the indigenous people of the San Blas archipelago ("not the Sand Blast Indians"), living on "some deliciously beautiful islands which, like enormous emeralds, are strung along the Atlantic side of the isthmus for a hundred miles," were congenitally incapable of not sleeping with white visitors. This proved to be a problem, according to the military, for the "offspring" of these relationships "have been killed along with the women who produced them."[32]

Yet even by the 1960s, when racial liberalism was ascendant, little seems to have changed. The 1961 *Pocket Guide to the Philippines*, for example, spun the history of American warfare and colonialism in that country into a celebration of the civilizing mission. The Moros of the southern archipelago, the pocket guide explained, were once "piratical and warlike, attacking and plundering passing boats and Christian villages and towns." But "shortly after the turn of this century, American troops, under the command of Captain (later General) John J. Pershing and other Army officers, successfully pacified them in a long and bloody campaign, which was followed by a successful effort to bring the Moros into the 20th century."[33] Modern American civilization had won.

But the pocket guides did more than provide cultural guidance. Perhaps most significantly in a Cold War context, they sought to mediate the history and politics of the broader world that American personnel would encounter. The guidebooks did not of course exist in a discursive bubble; they were complemented by a wide array of official informational and educational programming, from films and radio broadcasts to fact sheets, weekly lectures, and pamphlet series. And these official instruments were themselves complemented by the countless cultural products churned out by Hollywood, the publishing industry, and the various purveyors of mass entertainment and news that Christina Klein and others have so ably explored.[34] The United States was at war with communism, and culture and the arts were part of its arsenal. Whether it was jazz musicians touring the Soviet Union or abstract expressionists demonstrating freedom—artistic or otherwise—culture was marshaled to serve the interests of the state.[35] Even travel literature was not immune from the Cold War's ideological spell. Eugene Fodor, the legendary writer and publisher and a veteran of the Office of Strategic Services, gave Central Intelligence Agency (CIA) operatives cover as writers for his popular guidebook series, while other civilian travel publishers wholeheartedly embraced a benevolent American imperium.[36] The "hardy citizens" of the Republic of Vietnam ("South Vietnam") were "democracy's greatest friends and communism's greatest foes," Harvey S. Olson gushed in his *Olson's Orient Guide* in 1962. And, he pronounced unequivocally at a time of striking growth in the southern Vietnamese insurgency, "they love us."[37]

This was the context in which the pocket guides operated and in which military personnel were coming of age. While it was often complicated and occasionally rejected, there was no escaping Cold War ideology. It was omnipresent in American life. Yet there remained ongoing concerns about the troops. It says something about the nature of the Cold War, with its perennial US interventionism and its seeming contradictions—the self-described leader of the "free world" offering consistent support for military dictatorships and illiberal regimes, for example—that information and education officials felt compelled to essentially envelop US military personnel in an ideological cocoon.[38]

Their well-grounded fear was the potential failure of Americans to accept and commit to their nation's strategic objectives. They needed only to recall the Second World War and its immediate aftermath. World War II may be popularly remembered today as the "good war" for which Americans enthusiastically pulled together to defeat the Axis enemy, but the reality was in fact far more complex. As Michael C. C. Adams reminds us, the American armed forces of the 1940s "may have been one of the least ideologically motivated military machines in American history," one in which a pragmatic sense existed that there was "a job to be done and that the only way through was to get on with it." But the troops' commitment to the larger cause, he notes, remained "limited."[39] In the case of Southeast Asia, their postwar sympathies flummoxed US officials. When France began its efforts to recolonize Vietnam in the months following the end of World War II, for example, the enlisted crewmen of several US troopships tasked with transporting French personnel to Saigon organized a number of protest actions, from petitions and resolutions to calls for a congressional investigation. The crewmen were alarmed by US support for what they called "the imperialist policies of foreign governments" and the French effort "to subjugate the native population."[40]

Less than a decade later, as the Eisenhower administration was contemplating the insertion of US forces to shore up the floundering French campaign, an American Legion division with seventy-eight thousand members demanded that the president refrain from doing so.[41] Eisenhower decided against direct US intervention in 1954, but he and his successors, John F. Kennedy and Lyndon B. Johnson, sent what ultimately would be thousands of military "advisors" to Vietnam to purportedly help "save" Vietnam from the threat of international communism. Yet even in these early years of the American war, which was well before the explosion of GI dissent in the late 1960s and early 1970s, servicemen hardly seemed committed to the cause. In 1962, for instance, US officials reported after a visit to Southeast Asia that American troops were "not entirely sure why they are in Viet Nam or why it is in the U.S. national interest for them to be [there]."[42] This was alarming, both for reasons of military efficacy and because the Cold War was fundamentally an ideological contest. If military personnel were to be effective forces not only in carrying out US military campaigns but as "living, breathing propagandist[s]" for the United States, as the legendary counterinsurgency specialist Edward G. Lansdale would have it, then this lack of anticommunist fervor was unacceptable.[43]

The Pentagon thus waged an extensive "information and education" campaign grounded in Cold War imperatives. This meant, Assistant Secretary of Defense John A. Hannah wrote in 1953, that OAFIE had to provide ideological instruction that underscored America's role "as a world force for honest dealing and fair play." The military, in this formulation, was "fighting for the ideals of freedom," which were quite unlike "those in a totalitarian state." Of course, just three years after Harry S. Truman's administration drafted NSC-68, there was no doubt about the identity and nature of the nation's principal enemy. OAFIE therefore had to make its charges "fully conscious of . . . Soviet Communism, its meaning, its aims, its objectives, and where it is so strongly in conflict with the free world's concept and practical application of decency, integrity, fair play, the worth of the individual, and the rights assured the individual by [the American] form of representative government."[44]

The pocket guides sought to play an instrumental role in this campaign. If in the 1940s their distribution was restricted to military personnel and depository libraries designated by Congress, by the 1950s OAFIE was freely disseminating the publications to countless civilian organizations and individuals, extending the military's ideological reach far beyond the ranks of the armed forces.[45] The recipients ranged from major organizations that trained foreign aid workers and missionaries to university professors, local libraries, and high schools.[46] The reception to OAFIE's materials, at least as registered through the correspondence it received, was almost uniformly positive. Readers in and out of uniform wrote gushing letters about "splendid" and "very fine" articles and a "job well done."[47] As one serviceman described the OAFIE-produced pamphlet series *Armed Forces Talk*, "[It's] the most practical and most informative literature I've ever had the pleasure of reading."[48] Another believed an issue of the same publication to be "the best objective analysis of Communism that [he had] . . . ever read."[49]

The pocket guides were especially popular, according to one army information officer, for they provided "valid, accurate, and authentic information" in a "handy, useful form" that personnel could "take with them." "We have all learned to look for and depend" on the guides, Colonel Clair E. Towne said.[50] Although rare, there were occasional voices of dissent. In 1955 Alvin H. Niemann, a captain in the air force, with some fear of the consequences that might ensue, specifically mentioned being "reported to the F.B.I. [Federal Bureau of Investigation] and fired from [his] job for possessing dangerous ideas"—objected to the fact that "anything labeled 'Communist' is evil [and] anything 'democratic' or 'U.S.A.' is good." "I can't believe that," he wrote.[51]

One veteran of the Vietnam War, pondering the pocket guide to that country decades later, was less certain than Colonel Towne about its overall utility.[52] "There is a very real question," suggested Bruns Grayson, "of how much force such a guidebook could have in forming the behavior of the average American soldier—about twenty years old, not well-educated, not wily enough to avoid the draft in most cases, very often on his first trip away from the United States."

I don't know what the Vietnamese equivalent of "overpaid, oversexed, and over here" was, but there must have been one, and such a phrase would have described almost all of us. We were curious, scared, open, friendly, and preoccupied with how much time we had left before we could go home. We were no more loutish and noisy than any similar collection of young innocents would be, but certainly no less. What the handbook could not convey to any of us is how alien the culture would feel to such American ingénues.[53]

In fact, when Grayson arrived in Vietnam in 1968, the Cold War consensus was crumbling. The widespread resistance that confronted the United States in many of the places it intervened—in Vietnam in the 1960s and elsewhere at other times—suggests that its military personnel likely experienced a sense of cognitive dissonance, with their pocket guides telling them one thing but their eyes and ears suggesting another. Some GIs, in fact, went so far as to forge anticolonial and anti-imperialist solidarities with those challenging American power.[54]

But if, at least prior to the late 1960s, OAFIE's publications appear for the most part to have been warmly received, one reason may have been their accessibility. Written by people "well acquainted with the country and who [were] there recently"—the 1955 volume to Hawaii, for instance, was authored by the Washington representative of the Hawaii Statehood Commission—they consciously attempted to present their information "for the eighth grade level of understanding."[55] In practical terms, that meant eliding complexity for the most simplistic of narratives. In OAFIE's world, American colonialism was never really colonialism. Imperialism was something *they* did, not us. And the Cold War was an uncomplicated story of good versus evil. Examples of such characterizations abound.

Eliding Empire

The elision of American imperialism's brutality can be seen in the 1953 *Pocket Guide to the Philippines*. Like Hawaii, the Philippines was colonized by the United States. (In the case of Hawaii, this colonization is euphemistically referred to as "annexation.") In particular, Washington exercised formal control over the archipelago—with the exception of a brief period during World War II—from 1898 to 1946. With the onset of the Cold War, however, the idea of the United States as an oppressor nation was strictly verboten. The Spanish who colonized the Philippines in the sixteenth century were thus "conquerors" and the Americans "liberat[ors]," according to the pocket guide.[56] In recounting the history of the Spanish-American War that gave rise to the American occupation, OAFIE did acknowledge the disappointment, bitterness, and hatred that followed the 1898 Treaty of Paris, when Filipino nationalists became convinced that the United States had betrayed their desire for independence. But, the guidebook suggested, these sentiments were rooted more in misunderstanding than in reality. The "mutual lack of knowledge among Americans and Filipinos" caused inevitable confusion, the OAFIE publication asserted, but this was "short-lived, especially when it became apparent that the policy of the United States toward the Philippines had at its base the motto of President William Howard Taft, 'the Philippines for the Filipinos.'"[57] The Taft policy, readers learned, was thus directed at promoting the Filipino people's general welfare while preparing the archipelago for self-determination. Americans from all walks of life—teachers, members of the clergy, businesspeople, doctors, lawyers—sought to "acquaint the Filipinos with the broader aspects of democracy," and at the end of World War II, during which Japan subjected the local people "to the full horror of war and occupation by enemy forces"—revealingly, no such "horror" is ascribed to the earlier American war and occupation—the Philippines did finally achieve its independence.[58]

But independence would not mean peace. In a section called "The Philippines Today," the pocket guide touted that nation's armed forces, identifying many of its members as the former United States Army troops of the Philippine Scouts, and highlighted the difficult struggle in which they were then engaged against the "Communist-inspired Hukbalahaps." The history and politics of the Hukbalahap (Hukbong Bayan Laban sa mga Hapon, or People's Army against the Japanese) requires a nuanced telling, but, in the context of the Cold War, the so-called Huk rebellion instead became to OAFIE a simple story of communist aggression. If the peasants of Luzon who organized the movement had legitimate grievances, the pocket guide failed to consider them. In fairness, it did acknowledge that the tenant farmers to whom the Hukbalahap primarily appealed lived "under a system that at times approached serfdom" and that this "landlord-tenant problem is a grave one," but the authors for the Pentagon dismissed the guerrillas and their "Moscow-trained" leaders as mere pretenders. While notably silent on the Philippine government's repression, the pocket guide pointed to the "far from peaceful" methods of the Hukbalahap, writing that they had murdered "hundreds of innocent farmers and their families." Clearly, readers must have concluded, those murdering innocent farmers could not be their champions. The Hukbalahap may have been constituted to resist the Japanese occupation during World War II, and the organization may have since changed its tactics and its name (People's Liberation Army), but, the pocket guide contended, "their aims remain the same: Communist control of the Government."[59]

The Filipino insurgency, in other words, was nothing more than a symptom of the global communist conspiracy. This tendency to summarily dismiss the peasant revolt of the Hukbalahap was echoed in other pocket guides' treatment of revolutionary nationalism. In the 1952 pocket guide to France, for instance, readers might have assumed that China or the Soviet Union had invaded an independent Vietnam. After all, "in Indochina, one of the overseas partners of France in the French Union, French soldiers and natives of French North Africa have been fighting for more than five years, side by side with Indochinese, against a powerful Communist aggressor." The "French are proud" of this military commitment against the unnamed invader of Indochina, and they are "determined to stand beside other free nations, as they have stood before, in resisting aggression." Indeed, the French drank from the same democratic fountain as Americans. "Their stake in the new alliance [i.e., the North Atlantic Treaty Organization (NATO)] is as great as ours," the pocket guide declared, "and the seeds of liberty are sown as deeply in their souls as in ours."[60]

No conflict since the Civil War divided the United States as deeply as did the war in Vietnam. That became apparent by the late 1960s and early 1970s, when mil-

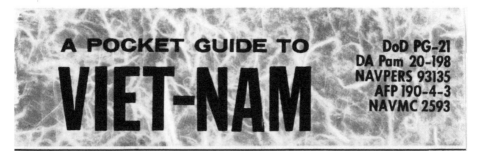

Figure 4. Combining ideological instruction with the pleasures of international travel, *A Pocket Guide to Viet-Nam* almost made military service in Southeast Asia seem more like a working holiday than a plausible threat to life and limb. OAFIE, *Pocket Guide to Viet-Nam* (1963).

lions of Americans, both civilian and military, found themselves participating in anti-war and pro-war activities. When reviewing OAFIE's first pocket guide to Vietnam, however, one would have no sense that the politics of the American campaign might ultimately prove contentious.[61] To be sure, its narrative was deeply ideological—Vietnam was a "brave nation repel[ling] Communist invasion"—but Cold War ideology still retained a firm grip on American society.[62] The liberal consensus had not yet shattered. In fact, in 1963, when OAFIE published its guidebook for the thousands of Americans departing for Southeast Asia, Vietnam sounded more like a holiday destination than a war zone.

Like the *Pocket Guide to the Philippines*, which extolled that archipelago's "fine beaches," historical architecture, and "unusually beautiful" scenery, the *Pocket Guide to Viet-Nam* presented its destination as a site promising untold pleasure.[63] Vietnam, according to OAFIE, was a "lovely country" with "charming" people where personnel enjoyed "opportunity unlimited." "You will certainly have a chance to explore the colorful markets and shops of Saigon and Cho Lon," the pocket guide assured the troops. "You may be able to visit the traditional capital of Hue or cool, hill-encircled Dalat. You may even get in some good swimming or deep-sea fishing from the quiet beaches of the South China Sea or a hunting trip on the high plateaus inland." There was little, it seemed at times, that might constrain the troops' amusement. In language quite startling to those familiar with the escalation that followed, the US military "advisors" were presented with the promise of "fine . . . Eastern architecture," "colorful river communit[ies]," and "dramatic" waterfalls, among other tourist attractions.[64]

Having thus presented military service as a delightful opportunity for those Americans fortunate enough to be sent to Vietnam, the pocket guide did attempt the indoctrination for which the series in large part existed. Amid the country's "invasion" by Communists, the defense of this Free World bastion "is your official job," OAFIE reminded its uniformed readers, "and it is a vital one."[65] But the realities they witnessed on the ground in Vietnam might have confused these personnel. After all, their local reception was often cool, and the invaders they saw were not in fact Chinese or Soviet. OAFIE thus attempted to offer a bit of context. The challenge the publication's author faced was twofold. First, the pocket guide had to explain away the popular support for the Vietnamese revolutionaries who had taken up arms against the Japanese, the French, and now the Americans. And second, it had to establish the legitimacy of the US-backed Republic of Vietnam ("South Vietnam") in the face of widespread opposition to its corrupt and brutal government. How OAFIE approached these objectives is instructive. Whether it in fact succeeded is debatable.

According to OAFIE, the Viet Minh, which was formed during World War II to oppose foreign occupation, only "pretended to be a league for the country's independence." Because, "like many other colonial people, the Vietnamese wanted national independence above all," many "followed Ho Chi Minh and the Communist-directed Viet Minh" in their campaigns against the Japanese and, later, the French. But when Vietnam was divided in 1954 following the French surrender at Dien Bien Phu, it was the "southern part of the country [that] struck out as a free nation—the Republic of Viet-Nam—under [the] leadership of Ngo [D]inh Diem." The "northern part of the country," conversely, remained "Communist-controlled." As for the "legality of the present" Republic of Vietnam government, there could be no question: it was "confirmed in October 1955 by a referendum which offered the people of the nation a choice between Emperor Bao Dai as chief of a state patterned on the old regime, and Ngo [D]inh Diem as chief of state of a republic. The vote was overwhelmingly in favor of the latter, and the Republic was proclaimed with Ngo [D]inh Diem as President."[66]

The narrative seems risible to twenty-first-century readers possessing even a passing familiarity with modern Vietnamese history, but of course most American troops sent to Vietnam in the early 1960s knew nothing about the country and depended on the military for reliable information. They did not receive it. They were instead treated to positive assessments of the "strategic hamlets," unambiguous characterizations of South Vietnamese "progress" and revolutionary "terror," concerted praise for Ngo Dinh Diem's "dedicated leadership," and impassioned pleas to "strike a telling blow for democracy" by "helping the people of this proud new nation repulse the aggression of the Communist Viet Cong."[67] The eventual disintegration of such empirically starved narratives might help to explain the widespread resistance that later emerged among US military veterans and active-duty personnel, with a massive breakdown in morale and discipline by the early 1970s that prompted worried discussion of the armed forces' "collapse."[68] It is difficult to imagine American troops in the early 1970s taking seriously the dubious narrative in the guidebook's third edition.[69]

But in the early decades of the Cold War, with the liberal consensus still intact, there could be no doubt about the United States as a global force for good. Anyone who opposed American policy had to be a Communist and thus ipso facto illegitimate, just as anyone who supported American policy had to be one of freedom's champions. Those cases that proved inconvenient were simply written out of OAFIE's histories for its uniformed tourists. An example of such erasure is that of Mohammad Mosaddeq, the democratically elected prime minister of Iran until his overthrow in a CIA-sponsored coup in 1953. In 1957, in its *Pocket Guide to the Middle East*, the Pentagon touted "ties of friendship and respect in military and civilian circles" between the United States and Iran, noting the significant US assistance in "help[ing] the country resist aggression" and "Soviet-inspired propaganda and other Communist activities."[70] The name Mosaddeq appears nowhere in the guidebook's pages, however. This is a remarkable omission given the premier's enormous contributions to arguably the most significant political development of postwar Iranian history: the nationalization of the British-dominated oil industry in 1951. For this and other reasons, Mosaddeq was not popular with Washington; the *New York Times*, reflecting, as it typically did, the American political establishment, denounced him for going "berserk with fanatical nationalism."[71] The CIA and British intelligence then sponsored the 1953 coup that deposed him. With Mosaddeq's absence from the pocket guide, modern Iranian history appeared to be one continuous string of reformist Pahlavi rule, with the then-current shah distributing "a great many of his extensive acres among landless peasants and encourag[ing] wealthy Iranian landowners to follow his example."[72] But the reality was of course far different—as the shah would learn in the late 1970s.

Similar political inconveniences were largely excised in southern Europe. Greeks, US military personnel were told in their guidebooks in 1954, "take a keen interest in politics and have very strong convictions to air. You would do well to avoid getting drawn into such discussions."[73] OAFIE did its part by almost entirely ignoring the wrenching political violence, including years of bloody civil war, that marked the previous decade in the Aegean nation. This was quite a feat in light of the centrality of that violence to US foreign policy. The Truman Doctrine, which arguably ushered in the Cold War, was of course articulated in large part in response to events in Greece—in particular, to what Truman called "the terrorist activities of several thousand armed men, led by Communists, who defy the government's authority" there; hundreds of American military officers then arrived in the country to participate in what Noam Chomsky identified as "the first major postwar counterinsurgency campaign."[74]

OAFIE did not address the Greek civil war in the pocket guide's history or politics sections. Instead, it devoted two sentences to the conflict—which is two more than it devoted to the Greek royal family's support for the earlier regime of Ioannis Metaxas—in the middle of a seven-page chapter titled "The Greek Soldier and His Army." How OAFIE addressed it, moreover, was deeply problematical, with the conflict framed as little more than a temporary setback to the development of "an entirely new Greek army" after World War II. This army's "problem of getting a start was complicated by the fact that it was forced to fight a full-scale civil war against Red guerrillas. Some 30,000 of these guerrillas, equipped and supported by neighboring Communist states, had to be destroyed in mountain fighting."[75] And that's it. There is nothing about the contribution to the anti-Nazi resistance of those same "Red guerrillas" whom the pocket guide elsewhere denounced as "Red bandits."[76] There is nothing about the persecution by the British-sponsored government of the leftists who had signed a peace treaty in 1945. And there is nothing about the quite legitimate concerns that countless Greeks had with the right-wing regime in Athens, which a US presidential emissary in 1947 privately characterized as "completely reactionary . . . incredibly weak, stupid, and venal."[77]

Perhaps OAFIE's virtual silence on the US- and British-backed repression that claimed tens of thousands of lives was rooted in an uneasiness with Washington's choice of allies: the Greek royalists and Nazi collaborators who drew on American aid to combat the Communists and other leftists that had resisted the wartime Axis occupation. Whatever the reason, the pocket guide was effusive in its praise of the right-wing Greek monarchy. It was King George II, OAFIE remarkably claimed, who was responsible during the Second World War for "lead[ing] his country's struggle against its invaders." (The king, who had endorsed Metaxas's dictatorship in 1936, was in fact exiled in London and exercised virtually no influence over the communist-led resistance.) George II passed away during the civil war in 1947, so his brother Paul and Paul's German-born wife, Frederika, inherited the throne. The "striking couple" were "good" and "popular" rulers, according to OAFIE, and their "sincere interest in the well-being of their people and their active participation in social welfare projects [did] much to endear them to the Greek people."[78] The military guidebook did not identify these "social welfare projects," but it may have been referring to Frederika's well-publicized Queen's Fund, a royalist project in which, argues historian Tasoula Vervenioti, the monarchy "enacted politics through charity" and used the salvation of so-called abducted children as a "method of psychological warfare in the framework of the Cold War."[79]

This apologia for Greek terror was couched in a guidebook that, like others published by OAFIE, extolled the pleasures of military travel, with obligatory references to Greece's "excellent beaches" and "splendid museums," "glorious history," and "fantastic collection of islands and mountains." "All in all," the Pentagon promised its charges, "you should find your visit to Greece most interesting." There would be "lots to do" and "lasting friendships to be made," the pocket guide asserted. "Americans and Greeks have much in common. And today, their two countries have joined hands in the common struggle against Communist aggression. In Greece you aren't really very far from home!"[80] Or so the Pentagon hoped.

. . . . .

Tourism statistics—or, for that matter, the bulk of the scholarly literature—do not typically register military personnel heading abroad among the millions of postwar American tourists. This is a glaring oversight, both because of the considerable number of persons involved but also because these troops' existence starkly illuminates one of the ways that tourism intersected with militarism in the Cold War maintenance of the American empire. The development and preservation of that empire required the dispatch of millions of troops overseas. This was a major undertaking, and one pregnant with the potential for failure. The world of the twentieth century was a messy place, with American power often engendering local frustration. This frustration frequently inspired resistance, and that resistance prompted Washington's sponsorship of innumerable coups, covert operations, wars, and interventions.

How would such militarism be made palatable to the armed forces being sent overseas? The empire's success depended on its safe mediation by those tasked with maintaining it. In a complex global environment in which local political conditions did not always fit the moral simplicities suggested by Cold War ideology—good versus evil, democracy versus communism, freedom versus totalitarianism—political leaders and military officials attempted to flatten complexity and render American policy unassailably virtuous. They were aided by the mass media—daily newspapers, popular magazines, radio and television networks, Hollywood, and travel guidebooks, among others—whose frequent contribution to what Walter Lippmann called "the manufacture of consent" has by now been well established.[81]

For the Pentagon, the mediation assumed a variety of forms. From posters and fact sheets to lectures and pamphlets, military officials sought to instill or reinforce in American troops the belief that their mission was just, moral, and necessary. The Pocket Guide series, which perhaps more than any other collection of materials helps to illustrate the Cold War nexus between militarism and tourism, furthered this campaign while taking it in entirely new and exciting directions. A fascinating mix of tourist information, appeals to transnational amity, and cultural and political orientation, the pocket guides conjoined the imperative of ideological instruction with the pleasures to be found in international travel. Covering dozens of countries over the course of several decades, they created accessible narratives of a world yearning for American power. That the world was not in fact that simple was immaterial. An illusory vision was preferable to a dissonant one. And if the vision could be cloaked in the promise of untold pleasure, all the better. Nothing sells imperial fantasy like hedonistically frolicking through the empire's hinterlands.

Scott Laderman teaches history at the University of Minnesota, Duluth. He is the author of *Empire in Waves: A Political History of Surfing* (2014) and *Tours of Vietnam: War, Travel Guides, and Memory* (2009).

Notes

1. OAFIE, *Pocket Guide to Anywhere*, 1–3.
2. Nguyen, *Gift of Freedom*.
3. Lederer and Burdick, *Ugly American*. Lederer was not in fact a veteran when he cowrote the novel; he resigned from the United States Navy as it was being published in 1958. Weber, "William J. Lederer." While *The Ugly American* focused on the US diplomatic corps and featured a couple of US military personnel (Colonel Edwin B. Hillandale and Major James Wolchek) among the novel's few admirable Americans, Lederer and Burdick did worry in the "factual epilogue" they appended to the novel about the "more than a million servicemen overseas." Lederer and Burdick, *Ugly American*, 274.
4. Shibusawa, *America's Geisha Ally*; Etheridge, *Enemies to Allies*.
5. Armed Forces Information and Education Division, *Pocket Guide to Korea*, 22–23; OAFIE, *Pocket Guide to Japan* (1952), 1. The favorable comparison of the Koreans to the Japanese was replicated in the 1953 *Pocket Guide to Korea*, but by 1956 it had been dropped. See OAFIE, *Pocket Guide to Korea* (1953), 22; OAFIE, *Pocket Guide to Korea* (1956), 22.

6.   OAFIE, *Pocket Guide to Japan* (1952), 3, 61. For Shibusawa's discussion of the pocket guide, see Shibusawa, *America's Geisha Ally*, 18–19.

7.   As Edward W. Said notes, "Every single empire in its official discourse has said that it is not like all others, that its circumstances are special, that it has a mission to enlighten, civilize, bring order and democracy, and that it uses force only as a last resort." Said, *Orientalism*, xxi.

8.   In addition to those stationed on these foreign bases, hundreds of thousands of others would pass through on short-term visits.

9.   OAFIE, *Pocket Guide to Japan* (1952), 6.

10.   See, e.g., Gonzalez, *Securing Paradise*; Imada, *Aloha America*, 213–54; Laderman, *Tours of Vietnam*; and the essays appearing in Gonzalez, Lipman, and Teaiwa, "Tours of Duty and Tours of Leisure," a special issue of *American Quarterly*.

11.   Donoghue, "Between Desire and Protest."

12.   To the best of my knowledge, the sole exception (apart from a few brief references) is Laderman, *Tours of Vietnam*, in which I devote a chapter to the Pentagon's three guidebooks to wartime Vietnam. This article broadens and deepens the analysis I began there.

13.   H. E. L. Zastrow to the Office of Information Services. That may be true, an OAFIE official conceded, but "the remedy lies in revision," not "discontinuance," with the information "geared specifically to the needs of Armed Forces personnel." Ibid.

14.   Office of the Secretary of Defense for the Record.

15.   OAFIE, *Pocket Guide to Viet-Nam* (1963), 1.

16.   Special Projects Branch, *Pocket Guide to Hawaii*, 2–8.

17.   Ibid., 8–9.

18.   This followed the earlier pathogenic incursions of Captain James Cook and other sailors. Precisely how many Hawaiians died is unknown. But even the more conservative estimates, such as those posited by Andrew F. Bushnell, suggest an attrition rate of staggering proportions. For three of the most important works on the issue, see Stannard, *Before the Horror*; Stannard, "Disease and Infertility"; and Bushnell, "'Horror' Reconsidered."

19.   Special Projects Branch, *Pocket Guide to Hawaii*, 13.

20.   Ibid., 14–16.

21.   OAFIE, *Pocket Guide to Hawaii*, 25–26.

22.   Ibid., 26–27. On what in fact was widespread Hawaiian opposition to the American annexation, see Silva, *Aloha Betrayed*. J. Kehaulani Kauanui has argued that annexation through a joint resolution rather than a treaty rendered the entire enterprise illegal. See Kauanui, *Hawaiian Blood*, 28; Kauanui, "Precarious Positions," 3–4.

23.   OAFIE, *Armed Forces Information Pamphlet*, 5; Eisenhower, "Radio Address to the American People on the National Security and Its Costs," 306–7. On the consolidation of the different military branches' information and education programs into OAFIE, see DeRosa, *Political Indoctrination in the U.S. Army*, 91.

24.   Harold Hayes to Egon E. Weck.

25.   "Description and Purpose of Information Materials Supplied by the Office of Armed Forces Information and Education," in OAFIE, *Armed Forces Information Pamphlet*, 8.

26.   Randall, *International Travel*, 4.

27.   *Department of State Bulletin*, "Letter of President to Be Included in U.S. Passports," 276.

28.   "You've got to realize," Joe told Bill, "that other nations have just as fierce a pride in their country as we have in ours. You've got to remember that they've suffered quite a comedown. You've got to remember that they took a terrific pounding in the last war. Remember all the

destruction you've seen over here. Remember that these people once were able to take care of themselves without help from foreigners. Remember they once lived better than they do now." OAFIE, *Pocket Guide to Anywhere*, 1, 5.

29. Ibid., 6.

30. For more on postwar racial liberalism, racial capitalism, and American racial formations in a global context, see Feldman, *Shadow over Palestine*; Melamed, *Represent and Destroy*; and Singh, *Black Is a Country*.

31. On modernization and US foreign policy, see, for several examples, Engerman et al., *Staging Growth*; Gilman, *Mandarins of the Future*; Adas, *Dominance by Design*; and Ekbladh, *Great American Mission*.

32. War and Navy Departments, *Pocket Guide to Panama*, 53–54.

33. OAFIE, *Pocket Guide to the Philippines* (1961), 15.

34. Klein, *Cold War Orientalism*.

35. This is not to suggest, however, that these cultural diplomats did so uncritically. On jazz musicians, see Von Eschen, *Satchmo Blows Up the World*. On abstract expressionists, see Cockcroft, "Abstract Expressionism, Weapon of the Cold War."

36. On Fodor, see Laderman, *Tours of Vietnam*, 32.

37. Olson, *Olson's Orient Guide*, 972–73.

38. On US support for authoritarian regimes, see, e.g., Schmitz, *Thank God They're on Our Side*; and Schmitz, *United States and Right-Wing Dictatorships*.

39. Adams, *Best War Ever*, 88–89.

40. Franklin, *Vietnam and Other American Fantasies*, 50.

41. Ibid., 51.

42. Flint, "Visit of Committee Men to Army Aviation Units [at] Nha Trang, Viet Nam."

43. Edward G. Lansdale to Colonel A. A. Jordan Jr., memorandum, "Instruction for Personnel Assigned to Critical Areas." Lansdale was the likely model for the Colonel Hillandale character in *The Ugly American*.

44. John A. Hannah to the Secretaries of the Army, Navy, and Air Force, July 31, 1953, in OAFIE, *Armed Forces Information Pamphlet*, 4.

45. Walter E. Sewell to R. A. Southworth.

46. On the organization Global Frontiers, see, e.g., M. B. Waldron to OAFIE. On libraries and educators, see the correspondence in Pocket Guides, National Archives II.

47. Fabriano Bertocci to the editor in chief, *Armed Forces Talk*; Fred B. Harrison Jr. to the editor in chief, *Armed Forces Talk*.

48. Joseph J. Mona to OAFIE.

49. William Rehr to the editor in chief, *Armed Forces Talk*.

50. Clair E. Towne to Brilsford P. Flint Jr.

51. Alvin H. Niemann to OAFIE. For an example of a reader's criticism that OAFIE was engaged in precisely the sort of propaganda it denounced when undertaken by the Soviets, see Ivan Ronald Levin to the editors, *Armed Forces Talk*.

52. On Bruns Grayson's arrival in Vietnam in 1968, see Mirsky, "Advice for Soldiers in Vietnam."

53. Grayson, foreword to *Pocket Guide to Vietnam*, vi.

54. See, e.g., Cortright, *Soldiers in Revolt*; Man, "Radicalizing Currents"; Moser, *New Winter Soldiers*; Onishi, *Transpacific Antiracism*.

55. OAFIE, *Armed Forces Information Pamphlet*, 6; H. E. L. Zastrow to Margaret C. Turner; E. W. Maxson to Leland B. Kuhre.

56. OAFIE, *Pocket Guide to the Philippines* (1953), 27, 30.

57. Ibid., 30–31. A later edition of the pocket guide could not have been more blunt about the misunderstanding: After the United States "liberated the Philippines" in 1898, Emilio Aguinaldo and his associates "believed they had been betrayed" when Washington established sovereignty over the islands. "Actually, however, the United States assumed its role of 'occupying power' in the Philippines to forestall any possible attempts by European colonial powers to annex the island country, newly freed from Spanish rule." In fact, the pocket guide maintained, the United States "has nurtured the growth of [the country's] democratic institutions from the turn of the 20th century until the Republic of the Philippines was proclaimed in 1946." OAFIE, *Pocket Guide to the Philippines* (1961), 4, 62–64.

58. OAFIE, *Pocket Guide to the Philippines* (1953), 32–35. The next edition of the guidebook, which was published in 1955, dropped the more vivid descriptions of the Japanese occupation. OAFIE, *Pocket Guide to the Philippines* (1955), 33–34.

59. OAFIE, *Pocket Guide to the Philippines* (1953), 38–39.

60. Armed Forces Information and Education Division, *Pocket Guide to France*, 11–12.

61. For a more extensive analysis of the three pocket guides to Vietnam, see Laderman, *Tours of Vietnam*, 47–85.

62. OAFIE, *Pocket Guide to Viet-Nam* (1963), 1.

63. OAFIE, *Pocket Guide to the Philippines* (1953), 58–62, 64.

64. OAFIE, *Pocket Guide to Viet-Nam* (1963), vi, 1, 4, 6.

65. Ibid., 1.

66. Ibid., 20–21.

67. Ibid., 2, 22–23, 30.

68. Heinl, "Collapse of the Armed Forces."

69. OAFIE, *Pocket Guide to Vietnam* (1971).

70. OAFIE, *Pocket Guide to the Middle East*, 86–87.

71. *New York Times*, "Iranian Accord."

72. OAFIE, *Pocket Guide to the Middle East*, 92–93.

73. OAFIE, *Pocket Guide to Greece* (1954), 34.

74. Truman, "Special Message to the Congress on Greece and Turkey," 177; Chomsky, *World Orders Old and New*, 192.

75. OAFIE, *Pocket Guide to Greece* (1954), 48. This language was excised from the 1960 edition of the pocket guide. Instead, there were several vague references to the "Communist aggression (1946–1949)" and "the Greek soldier . . . fighting and killing Communist bandits" from "1946 until the Korean conflict," as well as more pointed statements about the "civil conflict [that] broke out with Communist guerrillas who, until defeated in 1949, seriously threatened the independence of Greece" and the Greek Communists "direct[ing] guerrilla bands against the country, terrorizing villages and disrupting essential rehabilitation work" with "support . . . from the Soviet satellites." OAFIE, *Pocket Guide to Greece* (1960), 6, 20, 27, 33–34.

76. OAFIE, *Pocket Guide to Greece* (1954), 47.

77. Paul A. Porter quoted in Merrill, "Truman Doctrine," 31.

78. OAFIE, *Pocket Guide to Greece* (1954), 38.

79. Vervenioti, "Charity and Nationalism," 118–19.

80. OAFIE, *Pocket Guide to Greece* (1954), 1, 59, 66–67.

81. Lippmann, *Public Opinion*, 248.

References

Adams, Michael C. C. 1994. *The Best War Ever: America and World War II*. Baltimore: Johns Hopkins University Press.

Adas, Michael. 2006. *Dominance by Design: Technological Imperatives and America's Civilizing Mission*. Cambridge, MA: Belknap Press of Harvard University Press.

Armed Forces Information and Education Division. 1950. *A Pocket Guide to Korea*. Washington, DC: Government Printing Office.

———. 1952. *A Pocket Guide to France*. PG-5. Washington, DC: Government Printing Office.

Bertocci, Fabriano. 1955. Letter to the editor in chief, *Armed Forces Talk*, January 27. General Subject Files, box 21, decimal file 461, record group 330, National Archives II, College Park, MD.

Bushnell, Andrew F. 1993. "'The Horror' Reconsidered: An Evaluation of the Historical Evidence for Population Decline in Hawai'i, 1778–1803." *Pacific Studies* 16, no. 3: 115–61.

Chomsky, Noam. 1996. *World Orders Old and New*. New York: Columbia University Press.

Cockcroft, Eva. 1985. "Abstract Expressionism, Weapon of the Cold War." In *Pollock and After: The Critical Debate*, edited by Francis Frascina, 125–33. New York: Harper and Row.

Cortright, David. (1975) 2005. *Soldiers in Revolt: GI Resistance during the Vietnam War*. Chicago: Haymarket Books.

Department of State Bulletin. 1957. "Letter of President to Be Included in U.S. Passports." Vol. 37, no. 946: 275–76.

DeRosa, Christopher S. 2006. *Political Indoctrination in the U.S. Army from World War II to the Vietnam War*. Lincoln: University of Nebraska Press.

Donoghue, Michael. 2011. "Between Desire and Protest: Prostitution and Concubinage in U.S. Military-Cuban Relations, 1941–1949." Paper presented at the annual meeting of the Society for Historians of American Foreign Relations, Alexandria, VA, June 23.

Eisenhower, Dwight D. 1960. "Radio Address to the American People on the National Security and Its Costs, May 19, 1953." In *Public Papers of the Presidents of the United States: Dwight D. Eisenhower, 1953*, 306–16. Washington, DC: Government Printing Office.

Ekbladh, David. 2010. *The Great American Mission: Modernization and the Construction of an American World Order*. Princeton, NJ: Princeton University Press.

Engerman, David C., Nils Gilman, Mark H. Haefele, and Michael E. Latham, eds. 2003. *Staging Growth: Modernization, Development, and the Global Cold War*. Amherst: University of Massachusetts Press.

Etheridge, Brian C. 2016. *Enemies to Allies: Cold War Germany and American Memory*. Lexington: University Press of Kentucky.

Feldman, Keith. 2015. *A Shadow over Palestine: The Imperial Life of Race in America*. Minneapolis: University of Minnesota Press.

Flint, Brilsford P., Jr. 1962. "Visit of Committee Men to Army Aviation Units [at] Nha Trang, Viet Nam." April 23. Report of Southeast Asia Subcommittee, box 4, record group 330, National Archives II, College Park, MD.

Franklin, H. Bruce. 2000. *Vietnam and Other American Fantasies*. Amherst: University of Massachusetts Press.

Gilman, Nils. 2003. *Mandarins of the Future: Modernization Theory in Cold War America*. Baltimore: Johns Hopkins University Press.

Gonzalez, Vernadette Vicuña. 2013. *Securing Paradise: Tourism and Militarism in Hawai'i and the Philippines*. Durham, NC: Duke University Press.

Gonzalez, Vernadette Vicuña, Jana K. Lipman, and Teresia Teaiwa, eds. 2016. "Tours of Duty and Tours of Leisure." Special issue, *American Quarterly* 68, no. 3.

Grayson, Bruns. 2011. Foreword to *A Pocket Guide to Vietnam*, by Office of Armed Forces Information and Education, v-ix. Oxford, UK: Bodleian Library.

Harrison, Fred B., Jr. 1953. Letter to the editor in chief, *Armed Forces Talk*, June 22. Decimal File, 1953–1954, box 23, decimal file 461, record group 330, National Archives II, College Park, MD.

Hayes, Harold. 1955. Letter to Egon E. Weck, June 29. 461 Pocket Guides / 1 Jan. 55—Section I, box 22, record group 330, National Archives II, College Park, MD.

Heinl, Robert D., Jr. 1971. "The Collapse of the Armed Forces." *Armed Forces Journal* 108, no. 19: 30–38.

Imada, Adria L. 2012. *Aloha America: Hula Circuits through the U.S. Empire*. Durham, NC: Duke University Press.

Kauanui, J. Kehaulani. 2008. *Hawaiian Blood: Colonialism and the Politics of Sovereignty and Indigeneity*. Durham, NC: Duke University Press.

———. 2005. "Precarious Positions: Native Hawaiians and U.S. Federal Recognition." *Contemporary Pacific* 17, no. 1: 1–27.

Klein, Christina. 2003. *Cold War Orientalism: Asia in the Middlebrow Imagination, 1945–1961*. Berkeley: University of California Press.

Laderman, Scott. 2009. *Tours of Vietnam: War, Travel Guides, and Memory*. Durham, NC: Duke University Press.

Lansdale, Edward G. 1962. Memorandum to Colonel A. A. Jordan Jr., "Instruction for Personnel Assigned to Critical Areas," March 27. Report of Southeast Asia Subcommittee, box 4, record group 330, National Archives II, College Park, MD.

Lederer, William J., and Eugene Burdick. 1958. *The Ugly American*. New York: Norton.

Levin, Ivan Ronald. 1953. Letter to the editors, *Armed Forces Talk*, July 8. Decimal File, 1953–1954, box 23, decimal file 461, record group 330, National Archives II, College Park, MD.

Lippmann, Walter. 1922. *Public Opinion*. New York: Harcourt, Brace.

Man, Simeon. 2014. "Radicalizing Currents: The GI Movement in the Third World." In *The Rising Tide of Color: Race, State Violence, and Radical Movements across the Pacific*, edited by Moon-Ho Jung, 266–95. Seattle: University of Washington Press.

Maxson, E. W. 1954. Letter to Leland B. Kuhre, December 29. Decimal File, 1953–1954, box 22, decimal file 461, record group 330, National Archives II, College Park, MD.

Melamed, Jodi. 2011. *Represent and Destroy: Rationalizing Violence in the New Racial Capitalism*. Minneapolis: University of Minnesota Press.

Merrill, Dennis. 2006. "The Truman Doctrine: Containing Communism and Modernity." *Presidential Studies Quarterly* 36, no. 1: 27–37.

Mirsky, Jonathan. 2012. "Advice for Soldiers in Vietnam: 'The Fish Is Good.'" *New York Review of Books*, August 20. www.nybooks.com/daily/2012/08/20/department-defense-guide -vietnam.

Mona, Joseph J. 1953. Letter to OAFIE, February 21. Decimal File, 1953–1954, box 23, decimal file 461, record group 330, National Archives II, College Park, MD.

Moser, Richard R. 1996. *The New Winter Soldiers: GI and Veteran Dissent during the Vietnam Era*. New Brunswick, NJ: Rutgers University Press.

New York Times. 1954. "The Iranian Accord." Editorial, August 6.

Nguyen, Mimi Thi. 2012. *The Gift of Freedom: War, Debt, and Other Refugee Passages*. Durham, NC: Duke University Press.

Niemann, Alvin H. 1955. Letter to OAFIE, February 9. General Subject Files, box 21, decimal file 461, record group 330, National Archives II, College Park, MD.

OAFIE (Office of Armed Forces Information and Education). 1952. *A Pocket Guide to Japan*. PG-2, DA PAM 20-177. Washington, DC: Government Printing Office.

———. 1953. *Armed Forces Information Pamphlet: Information Materials*, no. 1.

———. 1953. *A Pocket Guide to Anywhere*. PG-13, DA PAM 20-184. Washington, DC: Government Printing Office.

———. 1953. *A Pocket Guide to Korea*. PG-3, DA PAM 20–180. Washington, DC: Government Printing Office.

———. 1953. *A Pocket Guide to the Philippines*. PG 16, DA PAM 20-186. Washington, DC: Government Printing Office.

———. 1954. *A Pocket Guide to Greece*. PG-15, DA PAM 20-183, AFP 34-3-5. Washington, DC: Government Printing Office.

———. 1955. *A Pocket Guide to Hawaii*. DOD PAM 2-1, DA PAM 20-190, AFP 34-3-8. Washington, DC: Government Printing Office.

———. 1955. *A Pocket Guide to the Philippines*. DOD PAM 2-3, DA PAM 20-186, AFP 34-3-10. Washington, DC: Government Printing Office.

———. 1956. *A Pocket Guide to Korea*. DOD PAM 2-8, DA PAM 20-180, AFP 34-3-14. Washington, DC: Government Printing Office.

———. 1957. *A Pocket Guide to the Middle East*. DOD PAM 2-13, DA PAM 20-192, NAVPERS 92437, AFP 34-3-16, NAVMC 1149. Washington, DC: Government Printing Office.

———. 1960. *A Pocket Guide to Greece*. DOD PAM 2-20, DA PAM 20-183, NAVPERS 92398, AFP 34-3-5, NAVMC 2529. Washington, DC: Government Printing Office.

———. 1961. *A Pocket Guide to the Philippines*. DOD PAM 2-3A, DA PAM 20-186, NAVPERS 92943, AFP 34-3-10, NAVMC 2578. Washington, DC: Government Printing Office.

———. 1963. *A Pocket Guide to Viet-Nam*. DOD PG-21, DA Pam 20-198, NAVPERS 93135, AFP 190-4-3, NAVMC 2593. Washington, DC: Government Printing Office.

———. 1971. *A Pocket Guide to Vietnam*. DOD PG-21B, DA Pam 360-411, NAVPERS 93135B, AFP 216-4, NAVMC 2593B. Washington, DC: Government Printing Office.

Office of the Secretary of Defense. 1962. Memorandum for the Record, "'OBSERVATIONS' During the Southeast Asia Trip," April 20. Report of Southeast Asia Subcommittee, accession no. 64-A2021, box 4, record group 330, National Archives II, College Park, MD.

Olson, Harvey S. 1962. *Olson's Orient Guide*. Philadelphia: J. B. Lippincott.

Onishi, Yuichiro. 2013. *Transpacific Antiracism: Afro-Asian Solidarity in Twentieth-Century Black America, Japan, and Okinawa*. New York: New York University Press.

Pocket Guides. Section I—General (1 January 1, 1955–December 31, 1956), box 22, General Subject Files, decimal file 461, record group 330, National Archives II, College Park, MD.

Randall, Clarence B. 1958. *International Travel: Report to the President of the United States*. Washington, DC: Government Printing Office.

Rehr, William. 1953. Letter to the editor in chief, *Armed Forces Talk*, November 27. Decimal File, 1953–1954, box 23, decimal file 461, record group 330, National Archives II, College Park, MD.

Said, Edward W. (1994) 2003. *Orientalism*. Twenty-fifth-anniversary edition. New York: Vintage Books.

Schmitz, David F. 1999. *Thank God They're on Our Side: The United States and Right-Wing Dictatorships, 1921–1965*. Chapel Hill: University of North Carolina Press.

———. 2006. *The United States and Right-Wing Dictatorships, 1965–1989*. Cambridge: Cambridge University Press.

Sewell, Walter E. 1946. Letter to R. A. Southworth, June 14. Folder 350.03 / 1 Nov. 43—Section II-E, box 636, decimal file 350.03, record group 330, National Archives II, College Park, MD.

Shibusawa, Naoko. 2006. *America's Geisha Ally: Reimagining the Japanese Enemy*. Cambridge, MA: Harvard University Press.

Silva, Noenoe K. 2004. *Aloha Betrayed: Native Hawaiian Resistance to American Colonialism*. Durham, NC: Duke University Press.

Singh, Nikhil Pal. 2004. *Black Is a Country: Race and the Unfinished Struggle for Democracy*. Cambridge, MA: Harvard University Press.

Special Projects Branch, Morale Services Section, Central Pacific Base Command. 1944. *A Pocket Guide to Hawaii*. Washington, DC: Government Printing Office.

Stannard, David E. 1989. *Before the Horror: The Population of Hawai'i on the Eve of Western Contact*. Honolulu: Social Science Research Institute, University of Hawaii.

———. 1990. "Disease and Infertility: A New Look at the Demographic Collapse of Native Populations in the Wake of Western Contact." *Journal of American Studies* 24, no. 3: 325–50.

Towne, Clair E. 1962. Letter to Brilsford P. Flint Jr., October 23. Chief of Information, General Correspondence, 1960, 1962, folder 260/32(RP) Pamphlets, August, (62), box 23, record group 319, National Archives II, College Park, MD.

Truman, Harry S. 1963. "Special Message to the Congress on Greece and Turkey: The Truman Doctrine, March 12, 1947." In *Public Papers of the Presidents of the United States: Harry S. Truman, 1947*, 176–80. Washington, DC: Government Printing Office.

Vervenioti, Tasoula. 2002. "Charity and Nationalism: The Greek Civil War and the Entrance of Right-Wing Women into Politics." In *Right-Wing Women: From Conservatives to Extremists around the World*, edited by Paola Bacchetta and Margaret Power, 115–26. New York: Routledge.

Von Eschen, Penny M. 2004. *Satchmo Blows Up the World: Jazz Ambassadors Play the Cold War*. Cambridge, MA: Harvard University Press.

Waldron, M. B. 1956. Letter to OAFIE, March 26. 461 Pocket Guides / 1 Jan. 55—Section I, box 22, record group 330, National Archives II, College Park, MD.

War and Navy Departments. 1943. *A Pocket Guide to Panama*. Washington, DC: Government Printing Office.

Weber, Bruce. 2010. "William J. Lederer, Co-author of 'The Ugly American,' Dies at Ninety-Seven." *New York Times*, January 14.

Zastrow, H. E. L. 1955. Letter to Margaret C. Turner, August 3. 461 Pocket Guides / 1 Jan. 55—Section I, box 22, record group 330, National Archives II, College Park, MD.

———. 1956. Memorandum to the Office of Information Services, December 10. 461 Pocket Guides / 1 Jan. 55—Section I, box 22, record group 330, National Archives II, College Park, MD.

"Carrying Our Country to the World"

Cold War Diplomatic Tourism and the Gendered Performance of Turkish National Identity in the United States

Rüstem Ertuğ Altınay

Tarsus is a heaven of pleasure
A floating house of the arts
The power of maturity
Is what makes it a temple
A thousand joys in every corner
A thousand admirations in every face
The beauties are everywhere
They are the voluntary envoys
. . . .
O, the steel lover
Of the sky and the sea
Don't stop, ever move
Toward the victories awaiting
—Sabahat Filmer, "Şiirle çizgiler"

I n excerpts from her poem, Sabahat Filmer, one of Turkey's pioneer filmmakers, celebrates the cruise she embarked on with the ocean liner *Tarsus* in the summer of 1954.[1] The tone of excitement in the poem—published in the ship's newspaper

Radical History Review

Issue 129 (October 2017)   DOI 10.1215/01636545-3920703

© 2017 by MARHO: The Radical Historians' Organization, Inc.

Lâle—reflects the affective experience the organizers wanted to create for all passengers. Visiting nine ports and six countries in three continents over the course
of nine weeks, the cruise was a spectacular tourist event. The passengers included
members of Turkey's political, cultural, and business elite. More importantly, as
implied in Filmer's poem, tourism was not the sole purpose of the cruise. Organized
by the Turkey Tourism Association (Türkiye Turizm Kurumu) with the support of
the government and the New York–based propaganda agency the Turkish Information Office, the trip had a diplomatic aspect as well. Alongside an exhibition on the
ship's deck promoting Turkey's natural resources, industry, military, tourist destinations, folklore, and fine arts, the *Tarsus* also carried fashion models and musicians,
staging performances to introduce the "people of the free world" to the "friendly
nation Turkey."[2]

The main destination of the cruise was the United States, where the ship visited four ports: Miami; Charleston, South Carolina; Baltimore; and New York. There
was also a Washington, DC, tour, which was optional for the tourists. On the way, the
Tarsus also stopped in and was received by officials of Las Palmas, Grand Canary,
Spain; Casablanca; Lisbon; Villefranche-sur-Mer, France; and Havana. Locals in
each harbor then boarded the ship to see the exhibition under the guidance of the
young hostesses, who spoke English fluently. The crew also staged fashion shows at
hotels in collaboration with local charities. There were several prominent bureaucrats and politicians among the passengers, including members of Parliament Lütfi
Kırdar, Suat Bedük, Burhanettin Onat, and Haluk Nihat Pepeyi from the governing
Democrat Party (Demokrat Parti) and Cihad Baban from the opposition Republican People's Party (Cumhuriyet Halk Partisi).[3] Kırdar and Baban were also the
president and the vice president, respectively, of the Turkey Tourism Association. At
the official receptions organized in honor of the *Tarsus*, the Turkish politicians met
members of the US political and bureaucratic elite.

What made the *Tarsus* cruise particularly important as an example of diplomatic tourism was the work of nondiplomats. The organizers believed all the travelers to be representatives of the nation and expected them to play a significant role
in the public negotiations to determine Turkey's place in the Cold War global order
and the future of Turkey–United States relations. They designed a tour program
that would create opportunities for interaction between the tourists and the locals
beyond everyday encounters. In addition to the receptions and public performances,
travelers were invited to attend the Turkey-themed special meetings organized by
local social clubs. The information office on the ship was charged with facilitat-
ing meetings between Turkish and US entrepreneurs.[4] Turkish tourist groups also
visited factories in the United States.[5] The articles published in the association's
monthly *Panorama* and the ship's daily *Lâle* constantly reminded the travelers of
their patriotic duty, making recommendations for appropriate behavior. This diplomatic responsibility was also a privilege that provided the tourists with new experi-

ences and networking opportunities. The accounts of travelers, such as the memoirs of Filmer and the model Lale Belkıs, as well as various essays and interviews published in *Lâle*, reveal that at least some travelers were quite excited about the diplomatic aspect of the tour.[6] The warm and personal welcome they received in the United States, impossible for ordinary tourists, assured the Turkish visitors that Turkey was an important country in the new global order and that they belonged to the "free world." The cruise thus was an event that blurred the lines between tourism and diplomacy.

The *Tarsus* cruise did not simply take Turkish people abroad but ventured to present Turkey to the world. With the exhibition, stage performances, and receptions as well as everyday encounters with the Turkish travelers, the *Tarsus* also provided a visit to Turkey for the people of the United States. This aspect of the cruise was particularly important at a time when the spread of media technologies had not yet made virtual tourism part of the everyday experience for most individuals living in the United States.[7] The amalgamation of tourism and diplomacy elided the difference between "hosts" and "guests," as all parties occupied both positions simultaneously. The travelers representing Turkey, and the locals working to create a specific image of the United States and American capitalism, also both produced and consumed propaganda. Moreover, the journalists, politicians, and bureaucrats working to foster Turkey–United States relations helped disseminate propaganda on behalf of either side. The encounters between the people of Turkey and the United States thus became a stage where individuals performed their national and other identities while constantly negotiating their knowledge about the self and others.

Interpreting tourism through the lens of performance denaturalizes categories on which it relies, such as "host" and "guest" or "home" and "away."[8] As "an interactive and contingent process," performance reveals how the foundational categories of tourism are both reproduced and challenged through everyday interactions.[9] Studying the performative construction of social identities, spaces, and histories in the context of tourism provides insights into broader systems and manifestations of power. These dynamics were made explicit in the *Tarsus* cruise, whose purpose was to make tourism an instrument of diplomacy and diplomacy a key element of the tourist experience.

The performance of national identity on the *Tarsus* took on special significance at a time when the national utopia was being redefined in Turkey. The country's formative years, also known as the Kemalist period (1923–38) after President Mustafa Kemal Atatürk, were characterized by a centralized secular modernization and nation-building program. The national utopia in this period, in the words of Atatürk, was to "rise to the level of the most civilized countries in the world."[10] These norms of civilization reflected Western European, primarily French, bourgeois norms and social practices.[11] Turkey's economy and vision for the future underwent a significant transformation when the 1925 Soviet-Turkish Treaty of Friendship and Neutrality expired in 1945. As the Soviet side chose not to renew the treaty and imposed several heavy demands on Turkey, the Turkish government embarked on cultivating closer relations with the Western bloc. When the United States replaced the Union of Soviet Socialist Republics (USSR) as the cornerstone of Turkish foreign policy, the government took measures to facilitate a shift from the state-controlled and autarkist economy to a liberal, consumerist, and individualist economy that then transformed the hegemonic formulation of the national utopia. While the Western-centric postcolonial desire for modernity persisted, the locus of modernity changed from Western Europe to the United States, reflecting the global reconfiguration of power dynamics in the postwar period. In this shift, the discourse of "civilization" (a defining standard of the West as Europe) was gradually replaced with "democracy" and "free world" (defining standards of the West as the United States).[12] Turkey's postwar political elite wanted the country to become a "little America," and US foreign policy fostered these aspirations.

Imagining Turkey becoming a "little America" gave the trip to the United States a dimension of time travel: the tourists did not just visit another country; they experienced Turkey's possible future. If the tourist experience was a rite of passage, its *liminal* or "out-of-the-ordinary" stage provided the tourists with a new vision for the future of their ordinary lives—which, for many of them, was desirable—and the diplomatic aspect of the cruise enabled the tourists to work toward its realization.[13] However, the travelers' accounts of the cruise suggest that this utopian vision had concerning aspects as well, particularly in terms of social life and gender relations.

As Filmer's poem implies, female tourists and tourism professionals were at the forefront of the cruise's diplomacy efforts. The main reason for this trend was the imaginary relationship between national identity and the female body in patriarchal discourse.[14] This relationship is particularly strong in or with regard to Islamicate societies—not only because of the gendered regulations of embodiment in Islam but also as a consequence of the long history of the fetishization of visibly Muslim women's bodies through various nationalist, imperialist, orientalist, occidentalist, colonial, postcolonial, Islamophobic, and Islamist political projects and discourses around the world.[15] Moreover, in the Western bloc, and especially the United States in the postwar era, stereotypical images of women in media and popular culture presented them as agents of consumer capitalism.[16] Images of the white suburban wife and those of Hollywood stars were also important parts of the idealized image of US capitalism propagated to Turkey's urban population.[17] These cultural products played a significant role in defining the codes of desirable femininity and transforming consumer habits. Hence women's embodied practices, everyday and staged performances, were also signifiers of broader political and economic systems.

The *Tarsus* tour organized by the Turkey Tourism Association in 1954 in which tourism became a site of politics illustrates how Turkish and American tourists and hosts constructed political identities and how established hierarchies that sustained global and local power relations were negotiated—and, at times, contested or subverted. The accounts of the female tourists, performers, and tourism professionals traveling with the *Tarsus* and the news stories about these women demonstrate how the intersecting categories of gender, sexuality, race, ethnicity, and class as well as the discourses of orientalism, Islam, and anticommunism played a central role in these negotiations. The letters and memoirs by women who traveled with the *Tarsus* and the news stories about them also show how the expectations from women were defined at the intersection of conflicting social norms and political desires and how these tensions unfolded in the context of tourism and diplomacy.

The Turkey Tourism Association and the Cold War

Turkey used international tourism as a tool of diplomacy long before the *Tarsus*. The Ottoman Empire's first major international tourist event, the 1863 Ottoman General Exposition (Sergi-i Umumi-î Osmanî), was an early example of world exhibitions that showed the imperial elite's willingness to invest in the Eurocentric conceptualization of modernity and progress.[18] The exposition also led to the establishment of the empire's first travel agencies. The 1923 inception of the Republic of Turkey was quickly followed by the establishment of the nation-state's first tourism organization, the Turkish Travelers' Society (Türk Seyyahin Cemiyeti), upon the request of Atatürk. After 1930, the governments formed several public institutions to regulate tourism, also reflecting their awareness of the significance of tourism for diplomacy. In the Cold War era, as Turkey negotiated its place in a changing global order, the political significance of tourism increased, and new actors and institutions emerged.

Turkey did not actively participate in World War II. Nevertheless, the war strongly affected the young nation-state's fragile economy. Turkey's domestic policies and international alliances underwent a major transformation after 1945 as the country embarked on developing closer relations with the Western bloc. That year, Turkey signed the United Nations Charter. In 1946 a multiparty system was established when the proponents of economic liberalism within the governing Republican People's Party founded the Democrat Party. In 1947 the United States adopted the Truman Doctrine and developed financial aid programs to support the economies and the militaries of Greece and Turkey as a precaution against communism and the political influence of the USSR. This strategy would allow the United States to replace Britain's influence over the region and the broader Middle East, a move that was also important for gaining access to new markets and resources, especially oil. The same year, the Turkish government took measures to facilitate a shift from the strictly controlled and autarkist economy to a liberal free-market economy and became a recipient of US aid under the Marshall Plan.[19] Again in 1947, Turkey joined the World Bank and the International Monetary Fund. In May 1950, the Democrat Party won the elections and stayed in power throughout the decade. In September

1950, Turkey joined the Korean War, a step that also facilitated the country's accession to the North Atlantic Treaty Organization (NATO).

As Turkey adopted a relatively liberal economic program and developed closer relations with the Western bloc, the state established legislation and institutions to support the political and economic significance of tourism. In turn, new nongovernmental organizations to sustain the tourism industry emerged. Founded in 1949 by prominent politicians, journalists, artists, scholars, and businesspeople, the Turkey Tourism Association became a significant actor in this period. The association's purpose was to promote Turkey internationally, to foster the development of local and international tourism as well as the tourist facilities in the country.[20]

The Turkey Tourism Association's vice president, Baban, defined tourism as "the greatest occasion that [brought] nations together"; it united people through sharing history and civilization.[21] Following this approach, the organization's tourism initiatives also aimed to contribute to cultural diplomacy. In 1953 the organization debuted a monthlong Mediterranean tour with the *Tarsus*, a former attack transport that Turkey bought from the United States in 1948. The ship carried an exhibition presenting examples of Turkish fine arts and handicrafts as well as photographs documenting Turkey's politics, economy, and tourist attractions.[22] The Army Film Center also produced a special section for the exhibition, featuring images and information regarding the country's military power.[23] Carrying 353 passengers, the *Tarsus* visited Athens, Palermo, Barcelona, Marseilles, Villefranche-sur-Mer, Genoa, and Naples. At each port, the ship hosted receptions organized by the embassies or travel agencies. The high-profile guests included King Paul I of Greece and his queen consort, Frederica of Hanover.[24] As part of the tour, the Beyoğlu Girls' Maturation Institute (Beyoğlu Kız Olgunlaşma Enstitüsü), a public fashion school, staged fashion shows at various venues, such as Le Pavillon de la Grande Cascade in Paris, Hotel Grande Bretagne in Athens, and Palais de la Méditerranée in Nice.[25] Encouraging telegraphs sent to the organizers by Prime Minister Adnan Menderes, President Celal Bayar, and the minister of economy and commerce, İbrahim Sıtkı Yırcalı, made clear to all concerned the importance of these cultural diplomacy efforts for the Turkish government.[26]

After the success of its Mediterranean tour, the Turkey Tourism Association decided to organize a bigger tour with the *Tarsus* in 1954. The main destination was now to be the United States. From a touristic point of view, this choice was not surprising. In the postwar period, US popular culture began to gain a strong influence in Turkey, raising people's curiosity about the country.[27] Moreover, during the heyday of consumer capitalism, the United States was an ideal destination for shopping tourism. There were also entrepreneurs seeking networking opportunities. Thus, despite the higher cost of tickets in comparison to the Mediterranean tour, the number of passengers increased from 353 to 405. However, 1954 was also a very important year for Turkish politics, and the tour aimed to support the country's diplomatic negotiations at a critical point in Turkey–United States relations.

The year of the tour to the United States was also a time of economic downturn in Turkey. During the early years of the Democrat Party regime, Turkey attained a high economic growth rate. However, the government failed to continue this trend in 1953. Moreover, despite the efforts to facilitate the transition to a liberal free-market economy, private entrepreneurship had remained limited and Turkey's economy was still primarily agrarian. Throughout the 1950s, the country's trade deficit also widened. Largely as a consequence of the liberal economic policy, after 1952 inflation increased while the foreign exchange rate of the Turkish lira fell.[28] The government still insisted on following an overambitious growth-oriented program, which required foreign aid and loans.

In January 1954, President Bayar was invited to the United States, where he was awarded a Legion of Merit—mainly for his anticommunist efforts.[29] However, Bayar could obtain neither more loans from the World Bank nor additional US aid. In June, Prime Minister Menderes paid another visit to the United States, but he could get only 10 percent of the $300 million he requested. In the meantime, the government was also trying to demonstrate its commitment to liberal economic values and attract foreign investment with the aid of legislative measures, such as the Foreign Investment Encouragement Law (Yabancı Sermayeyi Teşvik Kanunu), permitting unlimited conversion of earnings as well as initial invested capital, and the Oil Law (Petrol Kanunu), allowing both foreign and domestic companies to participate in the development of the country's petroleum resources.[30]

The *Tarsus* tour was expected to contribute to Turkey's diplomacy efforts at this critical time. There was again an exhibition, titled *Developing Turkey* (*Kalkınan Türkiye*, after a Democrat election slogan), aimed to demonstrate that Turkey did benefit from the US aid programs. Constructing Turkey's image as a friendly, democratic country with a growing liberal economy and a powerful army, the exhibition presented Turkey as a deserving ally of the United States and the Western bloc, attractive to investors and tourists alike. Given Turkey's rich natural resources and cultural heritage, tourism was anticipated to also bring foreign investment. In fact, Hilton Istanbul was already under construction with help from the Economic Cooperation Administration, which administered the Marshall Plan, and the Turkish Public Pension Fund (Emekli Sandığı). After it opened in 1955, the hotel became a symbol of Americanization in Istanbul.

An essay by the journalist Kerim Kanok, published in *Lâle*, suggests that some members of the Turkish public perceived the *Tarsus* cruise as a test. Kanok presents the views of a friend of his, who had lived in the United States, regarding how Americans would observe the Turkish tourists. According to the friend, Americans would first want to learn about the national identity of the Turks. The ship itself, which was US-built, and the souvenirs or the industrial products, such as the fabrics manufactured by European machines, would be of little interest, he believed. What they would really want to see, however, was the following: "How [do] we live on the ship, the orderliness of our cabins, the insides of our suitcases, our beds, the care and use of the objects in the hall, the number and order of the books in the library, the tablecloths and the napkins, the way we eat, and finally, the most important touchstone of a society—our sinks and toilets."[31]

Kanok's essay reveals how the cruise's amalgamation of tourism and diplomacy defined the experiences and expectations of the Turkish tourists and enabled a unique version of what the tourism scholar John Urry terms the "tourist gaze." For Urry, the tourist gaze is a socially organized and systematized way of looking that shapes the pleasurable experience of tourism. There is no single tourist gaze as such; these practices are formed by the sociohistorical context, reflecting the contrast between what are classified as "tourist" and "non-tourist" social practices.[32] During this long cruise, where the boundaries between tourism and diplomacy as well as hosts and guests blurred, Kanok and his friend encouraged the Turkish tourists, many of whom came from privileged socioeconomic backgrounds, to perceive themselves as objects of observation rather than as observing subjects while in port and as they visited US cities. Like several other pieces published in *Lâle*, the article thus recommends that the tourist gaze should also take on the functions of a post-colonial diplomatic gaze, requiring the tourists to constantly imagine and perform for an American other to whom they should represent the nation. This approach was a consequence of the global hierarchies of power and both Turkish and US fantasies about modernity and civilization.

Kanok's presentation of the tourist encounters as a one-sided observation replicates that of the ever-visible inmate in Michel Foucault's study of the Panopticon: the Turkish tourists are "the object of information, never a subject in communication."[33] The article thus reveals how tourism, like the prison, can also function as a modern disciplinary institution. In his account of surveillance and discipline, Foucault argues that "[he] who is subjected to a field of visibility, and who knows it, assumes responsibility for the constraints of power; he makes them play spontaneously upon himself; he inscribes in himself the power relation in which he simultaneously plays both roles; he becomes the principle of his own subjection."[34] Defining tourism as a practice of surveillance, Kanok (and the organizers who published the article) similarly expected it to make the tourists internalize power hegemonies and approach the ideal of the Westernized and thereby civilized Turkish subject by exercising self-discipline.

Turkey's cruise preparations and its self-imposed priorities highlight interesting perceptions of US social norms and hierarchies. When Baban states, for instance, that a major aim of the tour was to demonstrate that Turks are white, his statement of mission reveals an awareness of racism as a formative feature of US social life.[35]

In Baban's formulation, Turkey–United States relations would improve if the public were to recognize Turks as white. Such racial concerns, however, had a long history in Turkey. Turkish scientists and politicians mounted efforts during the Kemalist period to prove that Turkish people are members of the white race. The 1954 tour's commitment to whiteness could easily resonate for participants on the tour and the audiences in Turkey as well. According to a story published in Charleston's local newspaper the *News and Courier*, before the ship's arrival, a reporter asked a bureaucrat from the Turkish Information Service what a Turk looked like. The bureaucrat responded, "Look at the people in a bus in any American town."[36] Most of the ship's passengers, as upper-class Turks, did not necessarily look like working- or middle-class Americans who took the bus—and surely not like the African American passengers sequestered in the back. Hence this response concealed the privileged class status of the visitors. Of course, it also served as a comment about the racial characteristics of Turks. By suggesting a parallel between the phenotypes of the people on the ship and those of Americans on a bus, the Turkish bureaucrat offered a monoracial image of the United States, which the reporter eagerly accepted. When the ship arrived, he agreed that Turks looked like Americans: there were brunettes, blondes, and even a few redheads—nevertheless, "the dark-haired, swarthy Mediterranean type" was dominant.[37] In US whiteness discourse, where Mediterraneans were often not quite white, that was an important difference, but not one apparent to Turkish visitors who were ready to embrace US racialism and distance themselves from nonwhite people both in and outside the United States. Through the mutual assertion of this similarity (albeit with differences), Turks were recognized as white and a monoracial image of the United States was sustained, as white.

A Nation on the Runway

During the *Tarsus* tour, while the organizers expected all passengers and members of the crew to represent the nation, the imaginary relationship between the female body and national identity put women at the vanguard of the cruise's cultural diplomacy efforts. The stage performances also aimed to serve this purpose. In that regard, a particularly important element of the tour was the "Turkish Fashion Show" prepared by Beyoğlu Girls' Maturation Institute.[38]

The girls' institutes were public vocational schools established in the 1927–28 school year as part of the Kemalist modernization and nation-building program. Also serving as fashion houses, the institutes came to be known for their attempts to create a national style. Their design strategy reflected the broader trends in Kemalist cultural policy, inspired by the Durkheimian sociologist Ziya Gökalp and his distinction between culture (*hars*) and civilization (*medeniyet*). For Gökalp, civilization "refers to modes of action composed of the 'traditions' which are created by different ethnic groups and transmitted from one to another," while culture "is composed of the 'mores' of a particular nation and, consequently, is unique and sui generis."[39] For successful social transformation, Gökalp argued, Turks had to adopt elements from European civilization while preserving an innate national culture.

To amalgamate a constructed Turkish culture and an imaginary European civilization, the students and teachers affiliated with the institutes conducted research across the country, collecting materials and designs. Classifying these diverse sartorial elements and the related handicraft techniques as "Turkish," the institute workshops combined them with popular European dress forms of the time.[40] This design strategy, termed "modernization," aimed to define the sartorial codes of desirable citizenship. These fashions were also intended to legitimize the existence and borders of the nation-state by erasing ethnic and historical differences.

To promote the national style they developed, the institutes organized some of the first major fashion shows in Turkey. In the Cold War era, the shows gained a diplomatic dimension as they were staged in honor of political dignitaries visiting the country. The honored guests included Shah Mohammad Reza Pahlavi of Iran and his queen consorts, Soraya Esfandiary Bakhtiari and Farah Pahlavi; King Abdullah I of Jordan; Yugoslav president Josip Broz Tito; Queen Elizabeth II; and Prince and Princess Mikasa of Japan. At these shows, the models emerged as secular, modern, liberal citizens whose dresses helped to construct an authentic Turkish culture compatible with Western civilization.[41] The fashion show, a genre directly associated with consumer capitalism, was interpreted as a sign of a liberal economy—and thus crucial for diplomatic negotiations with the Western bloc—even if the clothes were produced and often presented at public schools.

While the models represented an idealized Turkish femininity, not all of them were ethnically Turkish or Muslim. Sevim Burak, who later became a prominent literary figure, was a Bulgarian Jew on her mother's side. Semra Dağoğlu had an Armenian grandmother. As noted by the sociologist Mesut Yeğen, legal citizenship has never been the sole maker of citizenship in Turkey, and "there has always been a gap between 'Turkishness as citizenship' and 'Turkishness as such.'"[42] The fashion shows allowed these young women to overcome this ethnic gap and emerge as legitimate representatives of the nation and agents of diplomacy. Their participation in the shows, however, depended on the erasure of the women's ethnic heritage and their embodiment of an idealized femininity that was presumably ethnically Turkish and Muslim. That Dağoğlu performed in the diplomatic fashion shows may seem bitterly ironic given Baban's statement that the aims of the tour included changing US views on Turkey, shaped by Islamophobia and "the forced deportation of Armenians."[43] However, the model denied the Armenian genocide and was happy to serve her country.[44] Dağoğlu's story demonstrates the complexities of ethnic and national identification and how these dynamics unfold in gendered ways in the context of cultural diplomacy.

Although the diplomatic fashion shows were not explicitly sexual performances, sexuality sometimes played a central role in the interactions between the performers and the audiences. In a posthumously published letter to her son, Burak claims that George C. McGhee, the US ambassador to Turkey, was in love with her and that the diplomatic performances served as a venue where he could watch her. Burak was also convinced that the US embassy's support of the *Tarsus* tour was a gift from McGhee, an expression of his love for her.[45] The model's interpretation of the events reflects her prominent role as a fashion model and the expectations placed on her. As a model and a woman, Burak was burdened with representing (which, in effect, meant performatively constructing) the nation. Her embodied performances were signifiers of national identity, both on and off the stage, and they served the broader systems of power by shaping the imaginations concerning Turkish society and the nation-state. By interpreting the ambassador's involvement in an event, which was explicitly implicated in global political dynamics, in terms of her body and sexuality, Burak emphasized her success as a model and a citizen while making her political agency and affective labor visible.

Turkish Import

Dolly Güzelbahar, of Istanbul, is one of the shapelier packages that arrived at New York on the Turkish liner Tarsus. The ship is on a good-will visit and is holding a floating "open house" to exhibit products and natural resources of Turkey. —UP Photo

Figure 1. The story about Dolly Güzelbahar, UP photo, 1954

Sexuality also informed the reception of Turkish women's performances in the United States—where the women were at times objectified quite literally. The *Stars and Stripes*, a newspaper read by members of the United States Armed Forces, published a story about the Turkish-Jewish hostess Dolly (or Doli) Güzelbahar. Titled "Turkish Import," the story described Güzelbahar as "one of the shapelier packages that arrived at New York on the Turkish liner *Tarsus*."[46] The story also featured a photograph of the hostess dancing, wearing a sleeveless top, shorts below the knee, and big hoop earrings. By presenting the hostess as an object of visual pleasure, the story added a sexual dimension to Turkey's diplomacy efforts—or, rather, rendered this already-existing element spectacularly visible. This approach also reflected the longer orientalist tradition that feminized the Middle East.[47] While the reporter defined Güzelbahar as a package, presumably awaiting to be opened by US soldiers, Turkey emerged as a country waiting to be exploited—not only economically but also as a military base.

As Turkish women strove to represent Turkey and a specific mode of Turkish femininity, both with their staged and everyday performances, their hosts in the United States did their best to introduce them to the "American way of life." As Burak reported to her son:

In Baltimore, we were under the attack of housewives; they took us from the ship and carried us to their homes almost on their shoulders and showed us their loos. . . . Scenes from typical American family life . . . For instance, we learned the meaning of "picnic" from the social women of Baltimore. They

kept our ship at the harbor for a week so that we could have picnics. We left
the ship for a week and spent our time eating fried chicken, sandwiches, and
hamburgers in napkins, drinking Coca-Cola on tables in the meadows, singing
anthems.[48]

In the context of the Cold War, in and through such everyday performances, "the
social women," as Burak calls them, presented a particular version of the American
dream to the Turkish performers and tourists, while the visitors demonstrated their
willingness to be drawn into this dream. It remains unclear whether any Americans
observed the toilets on the *Tarsus* to test the Turkish tourists' level of civilization,
but the women of Baltimore did show their toilets as indicators of American civilization and the pleasures of consumer capitalism.

In Washington, DC, Treasurer Ivy Baker Priest and the wives and daughters of prominent politicians, including Cecilia McGhee and Pat Nixon, modeled
in the fashion show. This performance, which served as an act of hospitality and
pleased the Turkish visitors, created great publicity for the show, in both the Turkish and the US press. Images of these women in Turkish fashions were such an
alluring novelty for the American audience that the pictures were even featured
in local newspapers in states the *Tarsus* could not visit. By sartorially embracing the Turkish other, the American women—whom journalist Andrew Tully
described as "real cute and mysterious East-ish"—emerged as political agents,
and their role in diplomacy became visible.[49] Because the models were now white
American women, the "exotic" element in the designs became more prominent,
fostering orientalist imaginations about Turkey and thus informing the reception
of the shows. This element was also visible in the titles US reporters employed
in their stories, such as "Treasurer Wears Harem Pantaloons."[50] It is worth noting, however, that unlike in many other orientalist performances, Turkish women
were actively involved in the creation of this show. Despite (and in part thanks
to) its orientalist dimension, the performance served the diplomatic efforts of the
Tarsus, both by creating publicity and by providing an excellent opportunity for
networking with elite American women, and pleased the Turkish public.

The Turkish models' performance of capitalist femininity emerged as an
especially pleasant spectacle in the face of Cold War fears about communism, associated with other exoticized women. These concerns had erupted in June 1954 at
the Miss Universe contest. First, Miss Greece, Rika Dialina, was denied entry into
the United States because she had once drawn an illustration for a book written by
a Communist. Then, Miss South Korea, Puh Luk Hi, was replaced by the runner-
up, Key Sun Huy, because she had lived in North Korea until 1951.[51] In the twined
contexts of the Miss Universe contest and the Turkish fashion show, Turkish diplomats gave public speeches explaining why Turkey could never become a communist
country.[52]

In the words of Baban, the fashion shows "demonstrated the elegance of the civilized Turkish woman to the elite audiences" and revealed that Turkey was a Western country.[53] The opposition press in Turkey, however, was not so easily assuaged by the organizers' claims. Concerned that the shows could actually affect the country's Western image, aspiring young diplomat and journalist Bülent Ecevit, in an essay published in the daily *Halkçı*, accused the Turkey Tourism Association of reminding Europe and the United States of the image of Turkey described by the orientalist French novelist Pierre Loti.[54] Ecevit criticized the organizers for showing harem clothes in the name of propaganda, arguing that the counterpart of these clothes in contemporary Turkey was shorts or blue jeans. Ecevit's defining blue jeans, the ultimate US garment, as the dress of the modern Turkish woman demonstrated the colonizing power of Americanization not only in the government but also in the main opposition, conducted by the Republican People's Party.

Another essay, in the opposition magazine *Akis*, also claimed that the garments were far from reflecting contemporary fashions.[55] Moreover, the anonymous authors expressed concerns about what they saw as additional problematic diplomatic performances in Turkey. Elite urban women, the authors noted, performed *çiftetelli*—a rhythm and dance of Anatolia and the Balkans that is associated with belly dance—at diplomatic receptions and expressed plans to promote Ottoman fashions in Europe.[56] These criticisms reflected the broader sociopolitical atmosphere during a time of crisis for the Republican People's Party. The story was published in June 1954, only one month after the Democrat Party won the elections for the second time. The Democrat Party had deviated from the secularism of the Republican People's Party and implemented policies to please religious Sunni Muslim voters. The government had also begun to increase its control over the press as well as universities and thus abandon its initial promise of political liberalization.[57] In

The Eyes Have It

Figure 2. The story about Ceylan Ece, *Charleston (SC) News and Courier*, staff photo, 1954

this context, the opposition's concerns regarding the changing political and cultural dynamics in Turkey manifested in the discourses about women, their sartorial practices, and diplomatic and tourist performances that did not satisfy the authors' fantasies about modernity and national identity.

The story "The Eyes Have It," published in Charleston's *News and Courier*, suggests that the pro-opposition journalists' concerns about the gendered politics of representation might have been well founded.[58] The story is about the model Ceylan Ece and features a photograph of her. Reflecting the conventions of lifestyle photography in the 1950s, the image demonstrates an upper-class, cosmopolitan femininity. Ece's makeup, however, deviates from the styles that were popular in the United States at the time and, along with her "Turkish-style" earrings, marks her difference. For the organizers of the shows, in the fashions she presented (which are not visible in the photograph) and in her face, Ece embodied a uniquely Turkish modernity. The newspaper's interpretation was different, though. Not recognizing the elaborate strategies behind the institute's style, the article reports that the models presented "traditional Turkish costumes." It also features an orientalist genealogy of Ece's makeup, arguing that this elaborate eye-makeup style emerged in the days when women wore face veils and persisted as an element of "Turkish woman's gentle art of man-trapping" even though the veil had been outlawed. In the reporter's account, through other embodied signs such as the makeup, the veil not present in the image was brought back into the narrative construction of the body of the exoticized and eroticized other as the marker of an essential difference. The story thus demonstrates that despite their efforts on- and offstage, the models' performance of a cosmopolitan and Turkish modernity was not necessarily interpreted as such. Indeed, the performance of everyday life is always a negotiation among performers, and these negotiations can be shaped by gender and global politics as well as strategic engagements with history.

The Turkish performers and tourists were not only the object of orientalist fantasies; they were also desiring subjects who (re)produced orientalist discourses. A spectacular example of this phenomenon is the story of Jakline, narrated by Belkıs. A group of Turkish tourists from the *Tarsus* met Jakline in Morocco when her eyes charmed Cengiz, a young man among them. Dressed in a black veil, her entire body was covered except for her eyes. On the insistence of Cengiz, she took off her face veil, revealing, according to Belkıs, a huge mouth full of gold teeth. The man lost interest in her, and the group went back to the ship. As the *Tarsus* was leaving Casablanca, however, Jakline was at the port, waving at them.[59] In this story, the face veil indicates Jakline's and, by extension, Morocco's lack of modernity and civilization and renders her an object of orientalist desire. This desire can lead only to disappointment and renunciation. The supposedly unattractive face hidden behind her veil not only affirms the beauty of Turkish women but also attests to Turkey's civilized, Western identity. As Turkish women (and Turkey) continue their journey to the land of civilization, that is, the United States, the visibly Muslim woman (and Morocco) must stay behind. The story reveals how orientalist discourses informed the Turkish tourists' perception of the Middle Eastern other and suggests how such encounters helped them overcome the sense of postcolonial belatedness and inadequacy they experienced vis-à-vis the United States.

The Turkish subjects' negotiations of their identities in the face of global power dynamics were shaped by not only orientalism but also occidentalism—and the latter was also gendered and sexualized. Once the *Tarsus* left the United States, *Lâle* conducted a questionnaire survey among the passengers about their experiences there. The questionnaire reveals that tourist encounters are sites where individuals negotiate and revise not only their history and national identity but also their desires and imaginations regarding the future. The last question, for instance, sought the participants' impressions of the American members of the opposite sex. Ali Rıza Gebzeli, a businessman, thought American women were too skinny; they had no meat on their bones.[60] Doctor Togan Demirağ and farmer Sadun Atığ thought they were "too masculinized." Another farmer, Süreyya Bereket, found them to be too mechanical ("fazla mekanik"). Mizad Aydoslu, a hostess, thought American men were too cold and remote. Sevinç Tevs, the famed jazz singer, found them to be "no different from an object" ("bir eşyadan farksız"). Defining the codes of desirable femininity and masculinity, the passengers constructed gendered conceptualizations of the self vis-à-vis the American other. This was particularly important at a time when the United States defined the hegemonic formulation of the national utopia and the horizons of imagination for Turks. Tevs's comparison of American men to objects, and Bereket's use of the word *mechanical* to describe American women, neither of which are common expressions in Turkish, imply concerns about the possible consequences of processes such as mechanization under way with US economic aid. Overgeneralizations about American men and women thus expressed the travelers' concerns about the future of Turkey and the potential costs of capitalism, especially for social relations.

Turkey's Cold War Economic Policy and Its Gendered Discontents

Ecevit's definition of blue jeans as the attire of the desirable female citizen exemplified how Americanization shaped the material requirements for the embodiment of idealized femininity in Turkey. However, it was difficult to satisfy consumerist desires, which had escalated as a consequence of the cultural influence of the United States as well as the debt-fueled economic growth and the liberal economic discourse. Beginning in 1954, the government took precautions to limit imports in the face of the economic downturn.[61] Smuggling and the black market emerged as serious problems. In this context, many tourists perceived the *Tarsus* tour as an opportunity for shopping tourism, which shaped their experiences in the United States.

At each port, the ship organized tours to local places, such as Parrot Jungle in Miami.[62] The organizers framed participation in these tours as a national duty—as they did with many other things. By seeing new places, the tourists would become more cultured people and, therefore, more beneficial citizens to Turkey. Nevertheless, participation in the tours remained limited. The organizers thought that the tourists were saving money for shopping, which may have been a reason. In addition to the personal budget limits, there was a shortage of foreign currency in Turkey, and the tourists were allowed to take only a limited amount of money with them. Moreover, it was difficult to exchange Turkish liras. Given that some consumer

goods, especially certain types of garments, were either unavailable or very expensive in Turkey, many tourists did prioritize shopping. Aware of these dynamics, some
department stores in the United States even published advertisements in Turkish in
local newspapers.

The ship, according to the pro-opposition press, returned to Turkey carrying
two thousand suitcases. The model Belkıs narrates in her memoir how the elite passengers strategized to avoid paying taxes on the luxury goods they brought back and
even planned to bribe the customs officers. As a nationalist Turkish teenager coming
from a modest background, Belkıs was devastated.[63] The smuggled goods, according
to *Halkçı*, included 65 feet of black silk and 40 feet of nylon fabric, 36 nylon shirts, 39
nylon blouses, 21 chemises, 15 nylon panties, 117 ties, 50 men's nylon shirts, 70 pairs
of women's stockings, and a great amount of cosmetics.[64] The women of the *Tarsus*
were now in the newspapers, carrying mink fur coats in Istanbul's summer heat.
Stuck between consumerist desires and cultural expectations, on the one hand, and
protectionist economic policies, on the other, these women were presented in the
opposition press as the embodiment of the society's and the state elite's corruption.

Conclusion

In the postwar period, as Turkey negotiated its place in the Cold War global order
and sought to develop closer relations with the United States, the diplomatic importance of tourism gained visibility. To create the image of a modern, Western, democratic country with a liberal economy, the Turkish governments not only tried to
attract international visitors to the country but also used the international travels of
elite Turkish tourists as an opportunity for cultural diplomacy. The *Tarsus* cruise in
1954 thus emerged as a spectacular event that amalgamated tourism and diplomacy.
Gender was a fundamental element shaping the politics of the tour. During the
cruise, women played a central role in Turkey's propaganda efforts. Through their
everyday and artistic performances, female tourists, performers, and tourism professionals performatively constructed the history of the nation-state while negotiating
the national and global politics of belonging against a backdrop of established power
hierarchies. As political agents, the women resisted orientalist or Islamophobic discourses, but they also strategically reproduced such discourses to contribute to Turkey's diplomacy efforts or as part of their identity practices.

Despite some orientalist undertones in the press coverage, the cruise did
create great publicity for Turkey. Visitors to the *Developing Turkey* exhibition num-
bered 145,000 people.[65] Media coverage of the *Tarsus* produced 420 news stories,
thirty-four newsreels, and thirty-five television shows—often featuring the models and the hostesses. The international success of the fashion shows secured their
status as a popular genre in Turkish cultural diplomacy. To this day, public fashion
schools and independent designers continue to organize fashion shows around the
world to represent Turkey. Although various agencies have organized tours combin-

ing tourism and diplomacy, however, no other event on the scale of the *Tarsus* cruise has ever been produced.

As a single event embedded in a much wider web of political dynamics, the *Tarsus* cruise's direct impact on Turkey's tourism and diplomacy efforts is difficult to evaluate. However, the political developments after the cruise bore an imprint of the tour's aims. Throughout the 1950s, under the successive governments of the Democrat Party, Turkey–United States relations continued with numerous bilateral agreements—many of them confidential and exempt from parliamentary approval. With these agreements, Turkey irreversibly became a market and a military base for the United States, contributing to the emergence of US imperialism in the Middle East. The Democrat Party also continued to work toward the development of the tourism industry. A particularly important step was the establishment of the Press, Broadcasting, and Tourism Department (Basın-Yayın ve Turizm Vekâleti), the first public body of its kind in the country. As a consequence of these measures and the economic liberalization policy, tourism infrastructure developed and the number of international tourists continued to increase.

Despite the image the passengers of the *Tarsus* tried to produce—or, maybe, as revealed by their strenuous efforts to create this image—Turkey's relationship with democracy, as with the postcolonial conceptualizations of modernity, was characterized by precarity. The Democrat Party government stayed in power throughout the 1950s. As economic growth, sustained largely by foreign aid and loan programs, failed, the political atmosphere took an increasingly oppressive turn. On May 27, 1960, the government was overthrown by a coup d'état. Prime Minister Menderes and two ministers were executed. Kırdar, the former president of the Turkey Tourism Association, which had already disbanded, died of a heart attack during his court trial. In December 1960, the *Tarsus* burned in the Bosporus after a three-ship collision. Turkey never became a little America, but the political influence of the United States was there to stay. Over the years, as local, regional, and global power dynamics were reconfigured, both hegemonic and alternative formulations of the national utopia continued to shift in Turkey, rendering national identity a field of vibrant contestation. Even as the discourses and practices surrounding tourism have changed, it has retained its significance as a political site where these power relations are negotiated and at times subverted.

Rüstem Ertuğ Altınay completed his PhD in the department of performance studies at New York University. He is currently an Ernst Mach Postdoctoral Research Fellow in the department of social and cultural anthropology at the University of Vienna. His primary fields of research are feminist and queer theory and performance, queer historiography and archival practice, cultural history, and the sexual politics of citizenship, with an emphasis on Turkey. He is currently completing his first book manuscript, tentatively titled "Dressing for Utopia: Fashion and the Performance of Citizenship in Turkey (1923–2016)."

Notes

The research for this essay was completed with the generous support of the Pasold Research Fund, the History Project Research Grant, the Orient Institute Istanbul, and NYU Washington, DC. I am grateful for the comments and suggestions of José Esteban Muñoz, Karen Shimakawa, Eugenia Paulicelli, Aslı Iğsız, Deborah Kapchan, Tavia Nyong'o, Diana Taylor, Olivera Jokic, Anthony Alessandrini, Jonathan Shannon, Jale Karabekir, and İlker Hepkaner at various stages of this project. I would also like to thank the editors of this special issue, especially Daniel J. Walkowitz, and the reviewers for their generous and insightful feedback.

1. Filmer, "Şiirle çizgiler." All translations from Turkish are mine.
2. In the Cold War era, the term *Free World* emerged as a propaganda tool to describe the United States and its allies, and it was commonly used in the Turkish press in the 1950s, including the Turkey Tourism Association's magazine *Panorama*. During the tour, various US publications referred to Turkey as "the friendly nation." For an example, see *Charleston (SC) News and Courier*, "Cosmopolitan Turkey."
3. Baban was also previously affiliated with the Democrat Party.
4. *Panorama*, "Tarsusu Amerikada."
5. *Charleston (SC) News and Courier*, "Tarsus, Visited by Eight Thousand Here."
6. Filmer, *Atatürk yolunda büyük adımlar*, 179–96; Belkıs, *İpek çoraplar*, 59–115.
7. For exhibitions as sites of virtual tourism, see Hirsch, "Getting to Know 'The Peoples of the USSR.'" For virtual tourism in the digital age, see Urry and Larsen, *Tourist Gaze 3.0*; Kaelber, "Memorial as Virtual Traumascape."
8. See Coleman and Crang, *Tourism*; Edensor, "Staging Tourism"; Edensor, "Performing Tourism, Staging Tourism"; Rickly-Boyd et al., *Tourism, Performance, and Place*.
9. Edensor, "Staging Tourism," 324.
10. Atatürk, "Onuncu yıl nutku," 267.
11. Çınar, *Modernity, Islam, and Secularism*, 5.
12. Bilgiç, *Turkey, Power, and the West*, 128.
13. Graburn, "Secular Ritual," 28–29.
14. For the relationship between national identity and the female body, see Anthias and Yuval-Davis, "Women and the Nation-State." For the Turkish context, see Çınar, *Modernity, Islam, and Secularism*; Göle, *Forbidden Modern*.
15. I use the term *Islamicate* to refer to social and cultural phenomena that are not directly or specifically about the religion of Islam but rather are historically associated with Muslim people or the regions where they have been culturally dominant. See Hodgson, *Venture of Islam*. On Muslim women and the politics of embodiment, see Çınar, *Modernity, Islam, and Secularism*; Göle, *Forbidden Modern*; Lewis, *Gendering Orientalism*; Scott, *Politics of the Veil*; Yeğenoğlu, *Colonial Fantasies*.
16. For the use of women's image as consumers in the global expansion of Americanization and its version of modernity, see Rosenberg, "Consuming Women." For a critical discussion on the stereotypes about women in the postwar United States and the complexity of their actual experiences, see Meyerowitz, *Not June Cleaver*.
17. Örnek, *Türkiye'nin Soğuk Savaş düşünce hayatı*, 98.
18. For a discussion on the conceptualization of the global progress of history and its representation as the commodity progress of the Family of Man, see McClintock, *Imperial Leather*.
19. Zürcher, *Turkey*, 224.
20. Türkiye Turizm Kurumu, *Türkiye Turizm Kurumu statüsü*, 1.
21. Baban, "Panorama," 7.

22. *Milliyet*, "Türk sanat eserleri Avrupada tanıtılıyor."

23. *Milliyet*, "Tarsus vapurunda ordu için de bir köşe ayrıldı."

24. Akçura, *"Tarsus* ve Amerika," 229.

25. *Lâle*, "Gemide kabul ve ziyaret saatleri."

26. *Lâle*, "Cumhurbaşkanımız'dan Tarsusa selam."

27. For the influence of US popular culture on Turkey during the Cold War, see Bora, "Türkiye'de siyasi ideolojilerde ABD/Amerika imgesi," 152; Erdoğan and Kaya, "Institutional Intervention"; Karademir, "Turkey as a 'Willing Receiver'"; Örnek, *Türkiye'nin Soğuk Savaş düşünce hayatı.*

28. Baytal, "Demokrat Parti dönemi," 551.

29. Erdem, "Türkiye-ABD," 139.

30. McGhee, "Turkey Joins the West," 628.

31. Kanok, "Amerikalılar bizi hangi cepheden tetkik edeceklermiş?"

32. Urry, *Tourist Gaze*, 2–3.

33. Foucault, *Discipline and Punish*, 200.

34. Ibid., 202–3.

35. Baban, "Ters anlayışlara gücenmedik," 5.

36. *Charleston (SC) News and Courier*, "Cosmopolitan Turkey." While the story mentions the "Turkish Information Service" as the bureaucrat's institution of affiliation, it must have been the Turkish Information Office.

37. Ibid.

38. "The power of maturity" mentioned in Filmer's poem is probably a reference to the school, attesting to the importance of the fashion show for the cruise's diplomacy efforts.

39. Berkes, "Sociology in Turkey," 243.

40. For a more detailed analysis of the institute style, see Altınay, "From a Daughter," 116–17.

41. Ibid., 118.

42. Yeğen, "'Prospective-Turks' or 'Pseudo-Citizens,'" 597.

43. Baban, "Ters anlayışlara gücenmedik," 5.

44. Attila, "Ninem Ermeni olmaktan sıkıntı duymadı."

45. Burak, *Mach 1'dan mektuplar*, 25–26.

46. *Stars and Stripes*, "Turkish Import."

47. For the gendered politics of orientalism, see Lewis, *Gendering Orientalism*; Yeğenoğlu, *Colonial Fantasies.*

48. Burak, *Mach 1'dan mektuplar*, 26.

49. Tully, "Treasurer Wears Harem Pantaloons."

50. Ibid.

51. *Cuero (TX) Record*, "Second Beauty Denied U.S. Entry."

52. *Charleston (SC) News and Courier*, "Lions Club Hears Turkish Speaker."

53. Baban, "Ters anlayışlara gücenmedik," 5.

54. Ecevit, "Şarklı mıyız?"

55. *Akis*, "Bu mu Türk kadını," 21–22.

56. Ibid.

57. Zürcher, *Turkey*, 223.

58. *Charleston (SC) News and Courier*, "Eyes Have It."

59. Belkıs, *İpek çoraplar*, 70.

60. *Lâle*, "Okuyucularımız arasında bir anket."

61. Baytal, "Demokrat Parti dönemi," 556.

62. Tanca, "Geziler."

63. Belkıs, *İpek çoraplar,* 112.
64. *Halkçı,* "Tarsus'ta kaçak eşya bulundu."
65. The figures are from *Panorama,* "Türkiye Turizm Kurumu Reisvekili," 43.

References

Akçura, Gökhan. 2012. "*Tarsus* ve Amerika." In *İskeleye yanaşan . . . Denizler, gemiler, denizciler,* edited by Orhan Berent and Murat Koraltürk, 227–44. Istanbul: İletişim Yayınları.

Akis. 1954. "Bu mu Türk kadını." September 4, 21–22.

Altınay, Rüstem Ertuğ. 2013. "From a Daughter of the Republic to a Femme Fatale: The Life and Times of Turkey's First Professional Fashion Model, Lale Belkıs." *Women's Studies Quarterly* 41, nos. 1–2: 113–30.

Anthias, Floya, and Nira Yuval-Davis. 1994. "Women and the Nation-State." In *Nationalism,* edited by John Hutchinson and Anthony D. Smith, 312–16. Oxford: Oxford University Press.

Atatürk, Mustafa Kemal. 2009. "Onuncu yıl nutku." In *Atatürk'ün Bütün Eserleri,* vol. 26, *1932–1934,* 267–69. Istanbul: Kaynak Yayınları.

Attila, Aybars. 2001. "Ninem Ermeni olmaktan sıkıntı duymadı." *Hürriyet,* February 2. www .hurriyet.com.tr/ninem-ermeni-olmaktan-sikinti-duymadi-39222330.

Baban, Cihad. 1954. "Panorama." *Panorama,* no. 1: 7.

———. 1954. "Ters anlayışlara gücenmedik." *Panorama,* no. 4: 5–6.

Baytal, Yaşar. 2007. "Demokrat Parti dönemi ekonomi politikaları (1950–1957)." *Ankara Üniversitesi Türk İnkılâp Tarihi Enstitüsü Atatürk yolu dergisi,* no. 40: 545–67.

Belkıs, Lale. 2006. *İpek çoraplar.* Istanbul: Doğan Kitap.

Berkes, Niyazi. 1936. "Sociology in Turkey." *American Journal of Sociology* 42, no. 2: 238–46.

Bilgiç, Ali. 2016. *Turkey, Power, and the West: Gendered International Relations and Foreign Policy.* London: I. B. Tauris.

Bora, Tanıl. 2002. "Türkiye'de siyasi ideolojilerde ABD/Amerika imgesi." In *Modern Türkiye'de siyasi düşünce,* vol. 3, *Modernleşme ve Batıcılık,* edited by Tanıl Bora and Murat Gültekingil, 147–69. Istanbul: İletişim Yayınları.

Burak, Sevim. 1990. *Mach 1'dan Mektuplar.* Istanbul: Logos.

Charleston (SC) News and Courier. 1954. "Cosmopolitan Turkey: Friendly Nation's Resources, Land and People Vary Widely." July 11.

———. 1954. "The Eyes Have It." July 13.

———. 1954. "Lions Club Hears Turkish Speaker." July 12.

———. 1954. "*Tarsus,* Visited by Eight Thousand Here, Sails for Baltimore." July 13.

Çınar, Alev. 2005. *Modernity, Islam, and Secularism in Turkey: Bodies, Places, and Time.* Minneapolis: University of Minnesota Press.

Coleman, Simon, and Mike Crang, eds. 2002. *Tourism: Between Place and Performance.* New York: Berghahn Books.

Cuero (TX) Record. 1954. "Second Beauty Denied U.S. Entry." July 14.

Ecevit, Bülend. 1954. "Şarklı mıyız? Garplı mıyız?" *Halkçı,* August 5.

Edensor, Tim. 2000. "Staging Tourism: Tourists as Performers." *Annals of Tourism Research* 27, no. 2: 322–44.

———. 2001. "Performing Tourism, Staging Tourism: (Re)producing Tourist Space and Practice." *Tourist Studies* 1, no. 1: 59–81.

Erdem, Erden Eren. 2016. "Türkiye-ABD ilişkilerinin zirve noktası: Celal Bayar'ın ABD ziyareti." In *Türkiye'nin 1950'li yılları*, edited by Mete Kaan Kaynar, 135–50. Istanbul: İletişim Yayınları.

Erdoğan, Nezih, and Dilek Kaya. 2002. "Institutional Intervention in the Distribution and Exhibition of Hollywood Films in Turkey." *Historical Journal of Film, Radio and Television* 22, no. 1: 47–59.

Filmer, Sabahat. 1954. "Şiirle çizgiler." *Lâle*, June 17.

———. 1983. *Atatürk yolunda büyük adımlar*. Istanbul: Gül Matbaası.

Foucault, Michel. 1977. *Discipline and Punish: The Birth of the Prison*. Translated by Alan Sheridan. New York: Vintage Books.

Göle, Nilüfer. 1996. *The Forbidden Modern: Islamist Veiling and Civilization in Turkey*. Ann Arbor: University of Michigan Press.

Graburn, Nelson H. H. 2010. "Secular Ritual: A General Theory of Tourism." In *Tourists and Tourism: A Reader*, edited by Sharon Bon Gmelch, 25–36. Long Grove, IL: Waveland.

Halkçı. 1954. "Tarsus'ta kaçak eşya bulundu." August 18.

Hirsch, Francine. 2003. "Getting to Know 'The Peoples of the USSR': Ethnographic Exhibits as Soviet Virtual Tourism, 1923–1934." *Slavic Review* 62, no. 4: 683–709.

Hodgson, Marshall G. S. 1974. *The Venture of Islam: Conscience and History in a World Civilization*. Chicago: University of Chicago Press.

Kaelber, Lutz. 2007. "A Memorial as Virtual Traumascape: Darkest Tourism in 3D and Cyber-Space to the Gas Chambers of Auschwitz." *e-Review of Tourism Research* 5, no. 2: 24–33. http://ertr.tamu.edu/content/issues/volume-5-issue-1-6-2007/volume-5-issue-2-april-2007 -applied-research-note-1.

Kanok, Kerim. 1954. "Amerikalılar bizi hangi cepheden tetkik edeceklermiş?" *Lâle*, June 28.

Karademir, Burcu Sari. 2012. "Turkey as a 'Willing Receiver' of American Soft Power: Hollywood Movies in Turkey during the Cold War." *Turkish Studies* 13, no. 4: 633–45.

Lâle. 1953. "Cumhurbaşkanımız'dan Tarsusa selam." June 5.

———. 1953. "Gemide kabul ve ziyaret saatleri." June 3.

———. 1954. "Okuyucularımız arasında bir anket." July 28.

Lewis, Reina. 1996. *Gendering Orientalism: Race, Femininity, and Representation*. London: Routledge.

McClintock, Anne. 1995. *Imperial Leather: Race, Gender, and Sexuality in the Colonial Conquest*. New York: Routledge.

McGhee, George C. 1954. "Turkey Joins the West." *Foreign Affairs* 32, no. 4: 617–30.

Meyerowitz, Joanne Jay. 1994. *Not June Cleaver: Women and Gender in Postwar America, 1945–1960*. Philadelphia: Temple University Press.

Milliyet. 1953. "Tarsus vapurunda ordu için de bir köşe ayrıldı." May 16.

———. 1953. "Türk sanat eserleri Avrupada tanıtılıyor." May 24.

Örnek, Cangül. 2015. *Türkiye'nin Soğuk Savaş düşünce hayatı*. Istanbul: Can Yayınları.

Panorama. 1954. "Tarsusu Amerikada Amerikan Hava Filosuna mensup uçaklar ve helikopterler karşılayacak." No. 3: 9.

———. 1955. "Türkiye Turizm Kurumu Reisvekili Cihad Baban'ın kongredeki konuşmaları." No. 9: 43.

Rickly-Boyd, Jillian M., Daniel C. Knudsen, Lisa C. Braverman, and Michelle M. Metro-Roland. 2014. *Tourism, Performance, and Place: A Geographic Perspective*. Burlington, VT: Ashgate.

Rosenberg, Emily S. 1999. "Consuming Women: Images of Americanization in the 'American Century.'" *Diplomatic History* 23, no. 3: 479–97.

Scott, Joan Wallach. 2010. *The Politics of the Veil*. Princeton, NJ: Princeton University Press.

Stars and Stripes. 1954. "Turkish Import." July 25.

Tanca, Semih. 1954. "Geziler." *Lâle*, July 10.

Tully, Andrew. 1954. "Treasurer Wears Harem Pantaloons." *El Paso (TX) Herald-Post*, July 19.

Türkiye Turizm Kurumu. 1949. *Türkiye Turizm Kurumu statüsü*. Istanbul: Doğan Kardeş Yayınları A. Ş. Basımevi.

Urry, John. 2002. *The Tourist Gaze*. 2nd ed. London: Sage.

Urry, John, and Jonas Larsen. 2011. *The Tourist Gaze 3.0*. London: Sage.

Yeğen, Mesut. 2009. "'Prospective-Turks' or 'Pseudo-Citizens': Kurds in Turkey." *Middle East Journal* 63, no. 4: 597–615.

Yeğenoğlu, Meyda. 1998. *Colonial Fantasies: Towards a Feminist Reading of Orientalism*. Cambridge: Cambridge University Press.

Zürcher, Erik Jan. 2005. *Turkey: A Modern History*. London: I. B. Tauris.

Colonization and Resistance
at Bethlehem's Manger Square

Ryvka Barnard

Bethlehem's Nativity Church is an iconic site for Christians around the world, venerated as the birthplace of Jesus Christ. Sections of the church were first built in the fourth century over the grotto where, according to believers, Jesus was born and then placed in the proverbial manger. Depictions of the grotto and manger appear in Christmas songs, paintings, theatrical renditions, figurines, and decorative "nativity scenes" in churchyards, town squares, and private homes globally. The actual site in Bethlehem, the Nativity Church and its surrounding Manger Square, is a major tourism and pilgrimage destination, declared a World Heritage Site by the United Nations Educational, Scientific, and Cultural Organization (UNESCO) in 2012. The church receives over a million visitors each year, most arriving on group pilgrimage tours from Russia, Poland, Italy, South Korea, Brazil, the United States, and other countries.

The Nativity Church / Manger Square is also a site that has been under military occupation since 1967, when Israel seized the West Bank along with other territories known as the Occupied Palestinian Territory (OPT). The military occupation is one element of Israel's broader settler-colonial regime that began with the Zionist settlement movement in the late nineteenth century.[1] The features of settler colonialism in the West Bank since 1967 have included regular landgrabs conducted by the Israeli military and settlers to establish settlement/colonies and accompanying infrastructure; military and settler attacks on Palestinian individuals, villages,

Radical History Review
Issue 129 (October 2017)   DOI 10.1215/01636545-3920715
© 2017 by MARHO: The Radical Historians' Organization, Inc.

towns, and refugee camps; and economic, social, and physical siege manifested in the building of the separation wall and a complex system of military checkpoints and segregated roads that curtail the movement of Palestinian people, while allowing free movement for Israeli settlers. The occupation has affected Palestinian society in the West Bank on every level and permeates every detail of life there.

Bethlehem is not spared the difficulties of the occupation, despite its prominence as a global tourism destination. It is home to three Palestinian refugee camps as well as the separation wall, and the town is regularly invaded by the Israeli military. However, despite the very visible signs of the military occupation and local protest against it, tourist traffic to the Nativity Church / Manger Square, for the most part, has been consistent and has seen increases since 1967.

A historical look at the role of the Nativity Church / Manger Square in the conflict shows that tourism is not simply a side consideration, something taking place against the backdrop or in spite of the occupation. On the contrary, sites such as Nativity Church / Manger Square are codetermined by being international tourism destinations *and* spaces of military occupation. This dynamic becomes obvious by exploring how the Israeli authorities have used tourism as a tactic of colonization and, in turn, how Palestinians have used it in the fight back, making the Nativity Church / Manger Square a stage on which this struggle is enacted.

In this article, I explore the intersection of tourism and colonialism in Palestine, using the Nativity Church / Manger Square in the occupied West Bank as a case study. Looking at the period between 1967 and 1995, I consider the ways Israel strategically used its control over the Palestinian tourism market in the West Bank (1) to colonize and dominate the Palestinian economy; (2) to exert spatial control over the surrounding area; and (3) to surveil and censor the occupied population, repressing local expressions of national identity while promoting for an international audience narratives whitewashing the occupation. Tourism is certainly not the only arena through which these techniques of control were practiced, but it is instructive to view how tourism was strategically used in these three ways and to see the impact that has had on the development of the Nativity Church / Manger Square as a tourist site and central square of the town.

I also survey some of the ways that Palestinians used tourism and tourist spaces, including the Nativity Church, as staging grounds for resistance to Israel's colonial rule, capitalizing on the economic value of tourism and the narrative significance of this space internationally. In particular, I focus on tourism boycotts and other acts of sabotage of Israeli-run tourism operations in the occupied zone.

The historical account I present here is not intended to be a comprehensive account of Bethlehem's history, or the history of the Nativity Church, but rather its focus is to examine some of the less researched elements of it to make a broader point about tourism and colonialism. I use a combination of newspaper archives and on-site research, conducted between 2011 and 2013, to unearth a political history of this tourist site and to draw out reflections on the politics of tourism in occupied Palestine.

For the purposes of this article, I focus on the first three decades of Israeli military occupation (1967–95) before the nominal Israeli military withdrawal from the center of Bethlehem in 1995, following the signing of the Oslo accords. This period of history is largely unwritten in academic and popular accounts of tourism in the West Bank and has heavy bearing on how tourism production is shaped there today. The year 2017 marks half a century of Israeli occupation in the OPT, and while its forms have altered slightly, particularly following the Oslo accords, the occupation today is more embedded than ever before and has as much bearing as it ever did on the shape of tourism in Bethlehem, even if Israeli soldiers are no longer permanently stationed in Manger Square.

Beyond this specific situation, this case study has broader implications for examinations of tourism and colonialism. Useful scholarly research has attended to the "aftereffects" of colonialism in tourist spaces, with particular focus on economic and cultural neocolonialism and tourism. For example, Waleed Hazbun's account of tourism in the Middle East shows how tourism markets are one of the many ways that postcolonial nations have remained tied to, and ultimately in service of, their previous colonial rulers.[2] Others such as Edward M. Bruner and John Hutnyk have looked at the more sociocultural dimensions of the aftereffects of colonialism in travel, in terms of the attitudes brought to host sites in the global South.[3] Other authors such as Jamaica Kincaid have focused on how tourism is received by people in host communities, with an intimate look at some of the bitterness or outright opposition to tourism among people who do not benefit from the visits economically or culturally but are nonetheless expected to be grateful for the business, a theme repeated across the literature.[4]

While studies of tourism and neocolonialism are exceptionally significant, they describe a structurally distinct historical moment: the postcolonial. Fewer critical studies have actually looked at tourism under colonialism and military occupation as in the case of Palestine (an exception must be made to describe Canada, the United States, Australia, and other settler-colonial societies where tourism to indigenous sites may have comparable dynamics, though none of those are also under military occupation). Some useful historical insights are provided by Benedict Anderson, who has looked particularly at the role of museums in colonial South Asia, observing how they were developed to promote "traditional" culture, specifically as a push back to nationalist forces aimed at modernization in the education system.[5]

When it comes to Palestine, and the West Bank specifically, much of the writing on tourism has focused on contemporary tourism and the "conflict" between Palestinians and Israelis. Even while acknowledging or highlighting military occupation, the scholarship for the most part has lacked the historical depth to explore how tourism and colonialism were built hand in hand, with some notable exceptions of texts not specifically about tourism per se, such as Nadia Abu El-Haj's study of Israeli archaeology.[6] Most of the literature also focuses on the post-Oslo period, after 1995, and often implicitly accepts the false framing of the context as "post-conflict" or "postcolonial," which erases present-day colonialism and doesn't allow for attention to continuities, instead focusing on Oslo as a rupture moment.[7]

Finally, existing scholarly accounts of tourism in Palestine tend to focus on Palestinian tourism operators who work against incredible odds to carve out a niche for themselves, but these accounts tend to discount the dynamics within Palestinian society where there is disagreement on the tactical use of engaging with tourism under occupation. We rarely hear the voices of Palestinian dissenters, those who actively boycotted or sabotaged tourism to fight against Israel's normalization. I include them in the story, not as background players, but as coproducers of the dynamics of tourism in Palestine.

Background

In 2016 over a million tourists from around the world reportedly visited Bethlehem. These numbers have increased significantly in the past two decades, after hitting low numbers in 2002 during Operation Defensive Shield, an Israeli military invasion that included the infamous thirty-nine-day siege of the Nativity Church. Dramatic events such as the siege understandably focus attention on issues in contemporary tourism to Palestine, but international travel to Palestine is by no means a new phenomenon. For centuries, religious pilgrims from around the world journeyed to sites holy in Christianity and Islam (and Judaism, to a lesser extent), sometimes on individual journeys, but more often sponsored by religious institutions or on behalf of monarchs.

The nature of these trips began to change in the mid-nineteenth century when European travel to Palestine became directly linked with European empire expansion. Organizations such as the British Palestine Exploration Fund, founded in 1865, sent teams of archaeologists, surveyors, botanists, and photographers on fact-finding missions to explore and document the Holy Land, often using biblical texts and maps devised by religious pilgrims as guides.[8] These "scientific" missions were accompanied by the development of leisure travel to the area, package tours primarily for citizens of England and the United States. In 1869 the British Thomas Cook and Son company offered an escorted Holy Land tour, opening the possibility for upper-class Europeans to see the "exotic Orient" and "Holy Land," parts of which were very soon to come under British control.

European visits to Palestine increased at the turn of the twentieth century, and even more so in the wake of World War I. By the time Palestine was taken under British control in 1920, Zionist settlement was already well under way, and along with it a new tourism market emerged. This development proved difficult for Palestinian tour operators, who found themselves battling not only British colonial control but also an increasingly well-organized Zionist program that used tourism (among other tactics) to push Palestinian tour operators out of the market and, simultaneously, to develop and disseminate propaganda in support of Zionism. The Zionist Information Bureau for Tourists, established in 1925, organized trips and produced guidebooks, tourist maps, films, and advertisements for Zionist trips and tour guides to promote the cause of Zionist dominance of Palestine.[9]

Zionist depictions of Palestine and of Palestinians echoed other colonial tropes of a "barren land" passively waiting to be taken and civilized by Europeans. In reaction, Palestinian tour guides tried to build sympathy and support for the Palestinian cause among their clients, but the structural conditions of colonialism privileged the Zionist establishment (in general and also in tourism), putting the indigenous Palestinians on the double defensive.[10] In 1948 the Zionist "manifest destiny" narrative was actualized when the State of Israel was declared on historic Palestine, and, in the accompanying war, over four hundred Palestinian villages were destroyed and some eight hundred thousand Palestinians expelled or forced to flee in a period of two years, a set of events Palestinians call the Nakba (catastrophe).[11]

The new State of Israel began to expand its tourism industry, largely oriented around what had been Palestinian-run Christian pilgrimage itineraries. Some of the most significant Christian sites, such as Nazareth and the Sea of Galilee, were located there, and the Israeli state benefited from the economic boost that this already-existing tourism market could offer, as well as using the opportunity to market the state as a hub of progress and development. The industry's growth was incomplete though, since many of the accompanying sites on pilgrimage itineraries, including old Jerusalem, Bethlehem, and Jericho, were in the Jordanian-controlled West Bank. This all changed dramatically when Israel occupied the West Bank in 1967.

Today the tourists coming to Bethlehem are rarely exposed to any of this history. They do not hear from their tour guides about the current difficulties facing Palestinians, nor do they learn about the century of colonialism that gave rise to these struggles. The narrative that most tourists are given focuses almost exclusively on the ancient "history" of Palestine as the "Land of the Bible," following closely along the lines of the nineteenth-century colonial narratives that accompanied the first wave of mass tours at that time.

The vast majority of tourists fly into the Israeli airport outside of Tel Aviv, having contracted Israeli tour companies that arrange their flights, buses, guides, and hotels. Palestinian tour guides and bus drivers from the West Bank do not have permits that would allow them to meet groups at the airport. While their West Bank and Gaza counterparts are totally excluded, Palestinian tour companies inside Israel are structurally disadvantaged, reflecting the broader situation of Palestinians in Israel.

That means that the millions of tourists coming to Bethlehem are profitable for Israeli companies and translate into economic loss for Palestinians. The tourists stay in Israeli hotels in Jerusalem, visiting Bethlehem on average for a maximum of two hours on their entire trips. Their buses drive through the checkpoint and straight to a drop-off next to the Nativity Church, where they are whizzed in and out of the church to make room for the next group. Most of them will not even know if they have spoken to a Palestinian, and most would not know or perhaps care to ask. They have been prepared by their churches and tour companies to expect to see the birthplace of Christ, not a complex and dynamic modern society struggling for survival under colonial domination.[12]

While the signs of the military occupation are all around in many ways, they may not be detectable to those who are not explicitly looking for them, especially in Manger Square. At the time of my research in Bethlehem, the only overtly "political" marker in Manger Square was a faded and beat-up exhibition sign with long and small-printed text explaining the occupation, put up sometime after the Israeli military withdrew from the center of town. The rest of the square is dominated by souvenir shops and restaurants, but even those receive few visitors, as most groups are brought to special complexes, some of which are in Jerusalem, and encouraged to buy souvenirs within the "safe" confines of "official" shops with (inflated) set prices. In any event, the battered sign explaining the occupation is the last thing curious tourists would be drawn to in the unlikely event that they would stray from their group.

What is it that makes Bethlehem's Manger Square such a depoliticized space, even when the town itself is a hyperpoliticized environment? Surely, the problem of tourists not seeing the political situation is partly a feature of most contemporary tourism, and, on top of that, the "political" tourist may hold false promise as a lever for social change. That said, Bethlehem's Manger Square was not always such an environment, and to deconstruct the dynamics at play it is important to unpack the history of its construction as a tourist site under military occupation, the topic of this article.

Mapping Bethlehem

Relative to other Palestinian towns in the West Bank, Bethlehem was fairly well-to-do before 1948, with links internationally through churches and family members abroad and higher-than-average rates of education. Over the centuries, the tourism industry in Bethlehem had helped to create a class of merchants, traders, crafts workshop owners, hostel owners, travel agents, and a variety of others who were able to sustain themselves through the constant flow of pilgrims and other tourists.

After the Nakba, during the period of Jordanian rule between 1949 and 1967, other parts of the West Bank were neglected by the Jordanian authorities who favored the East Bank for development projects, but Bethlehem was an exception. It received special attention because of its role as a tourism destination, and some Palestinians were able to prosper through the tourism industry since it was significant to the development of Jordan's modern national profile. A number of the traditional elites ingratiated themselves to the Jordanian regime through their involvement in tourism, and while some objected to the co-optation of Palestinian sites into a "Jordanian" story, ultimately it benefited them to remain involved to retain some control and reap some of the economic benefits of the growing tourism.[13]

On the other end of the spectrum, a large number of Palestinian refugees from the Nakba had sought shelter in the small town of Bethlehem, and the United Nations soon established three refugee camps in the town, Aida, al-Azzeh / Beit Jibrin, and Dheisheh. The camps were home to several thousand Palestinian refugees from over forty different villages in what became Israel, most of which were completely destroyed and depopulated between 1947 and 1949. The refugees made up a large minority of the town's total population, forming a sizable demographic bloc separate from the traditional Bethlehem families.

Palestinian refugees were at the forefront of political organizing around the material conditions in their own camps, but also in the eventual development of the transnational Palestinian revolution. Cut out of the economic, social, and political worlds of the traditional elite, refugees created new realities that ultimately would lead to renewed national political struggle. United Nations schools in refugee camps meant that many more Palestinians gained access to schooling than before. The emergence of a generation of formally educated refugees meant that Palestinian universities, once elite and exclusive institutions, gained waves of new students from the most marginalized classes and were transformed into organizing spaces for young people creating platforms for anticolonial politics. Bethlehem University, for example, eventually became one of the biggest sites in the town for political protest. The university is a significant piece of the story, not only because it became an incubator of protest, but also because it, along with the refugee camps, is a short walking distance from Manger Square.

These dynamics of internal change within Palestinian society were already starting to stir in June 1967, when the Israeli military seized and occupied the West Bank. Palestinian communities in the West Bank, still reeling from the trauma of the Nakba, were hit with a new wave of destruction and expulsions during the war, as well as the further upheaval that came along with a new group of Palestinian refugees forced out of Jerusalem. Israeli soldiers flooded into West Bank towns, and even after the official fighting was over there was still no clear sense among the residents what their status under the new military authority would be, and given that the local community at the time was already split by geographic origin, class, social status, and political priorities, there was not a clear single Palestinian representative through whom the town's interests could be advocated for.

On the one hand were the small numbers of traditional elites, many of whom were linked with the tourism industry and many of whom had been favored under Jordanian rule. Some of these figures, including longtime mayor Elias Freij, would go on to take relatively reconciliatory stances toward the occupation regime to preserve business interests. On the other hand were the refugees, some of whom were active in developing the newest version of Palestinian liberation struggle along with left-wing groups associated with the Communist Party and other left nationalist groups that had agitated against the repressive Jordanian regime, already poised to play a key role in resistance to Israeli colonial rule.

Economic Occupation

The occupation of the West Bank provided an opportunity for Israeli tourism expansion, and while that was surely not a direct reason for Israel to hold on to the territory after the end of the war, no time was lost seizing the opportunity when the smoke cleared in June. Tourism figured seriously into the decision making taking place at high levels of the Israeli government as the fighting came to a close.

The clearest example of this process is the infamous destruction of the Magharbeh neighborhood in Jerusalem. Israeli strategists decided to destroy the Palestinian houses closest to the Western Wall, now one of the most-visited Israeli-controlled tourism sites, not to facilitate a military fight but to create a plaza for Jewish worshippers and tourists who they knew would flood the site in the coming weeks. The operation was put in the hands of the Israeli National Parks Authority, "to give the matter as far as possible an unofficial character," according to then mayor Teddy Kollek.[14] On June 11, 1967, the National Parks Authority oversaw the razing of an entire Palestinian neighborhood, its residents given only a few minutes notice to leave. Several days later the plaza was ready to accommodate an estimated two hundred thousand Israeli and foreign tourists. Kollek then created an $80 million development plan for a new "united Jerusalem," which included settling Jews in the old city and establishing tourism sites in it.[15]

This example shows the interconnection between the economics of tourism development, national/colonial ideology, and military occupation. The economic benefits to Israel from its occupation of the West Bank were significant. At the time, Christian pilgrimage tours accounted for the largest percentage of tourism to the country, a fact that is still true today. However, between 1948 and 1967, important Christian sites were spread between what had become Israel and Jordan, respectively. Nazareth and Galilee fell in Israeli territory, while Bethlehem and East Jerusalem fell under Jordanian control. This divided access was managed clumsily, as tourists wanting to see all the sites located in a very small geographic area would have to cross a cease-fire line and enter into a separate state's territory to do so.

The 1967 war and the resulting occupation allowed Israel to incorporate sites in the West Bank into its national tourism package and expand its marketing efforts to include more focus on the pilgrimage tours that would now be able to visit Nazareth and Bethlehem under the control of the same state power. Israel profited massively from this expansion, boasting an over 56 percent increase in tourism arrivals by 1968.[16] In the first year following the occupation, the Israeli Ministry of Tourism began its collaboration with the military to run tourism events in Bethlehem and other West Bank cities, as well as to develop Dead Sea tourism and tourism revolving around antiquities and ruins in the West Bank.

Until 1967, Israeli state resources for tourism development were focused more on Catholic pilgrimages that had historically made up the larger portion of pilgrimage visits. After the 1967 war, Israel conducted client surveys in the US tourism markets, finding that American evangelical Christians formed a fast-growing market. The Israeli government then established the Department for Encouragement of Pilgrimage and, by the mid-1970s, was actively advertising Holy Land tours in evangelical magazines and other spaces in the United States.[17] This paved the path for an even greater surge in Christian Zionism in the United States, which proved to be a lucrative tourism market for Israel.

In contrast, the Palestinian operators in the tourism industry suffered great losses under occupation. The Palestinian tourism industry stagnated, as development was discouraged and made virtually impossible by the Israeli military to prevent competition with Israeli tourism operators. Palestinians now under military control would have to apply for permits for any new building, a lengthy process requiring money and connections, and even then likely to fail. From 1976 to 1994, the number of Palestinian hotels remained unchanged, as building permits required by the Israeli authorities were not granted. At least fifteen military orders and regulations related to tourism were issued by the Israeli military after 1967, changing the qualifications for tourism development–related permits, creating bureaucratic blocks to tourism development in the Palestinian sector, and adding to the general difficulties of life under military occupation.[18] From 1967, no new Palestinian tour guides from the West Bank were granted tour guide licenses by Israel, meaning that only those licensed under Jordanian rule continued working, around 260 in 1967 and down to 38 in 1984, while in the meantime over 3,300 Israelis held guiding licenses, a booming industry for them after 1967.[19]

The de-development of the Palestinian tourism industry was part of a larger Israeli strategy to cut out Palestinian competition, to create dependency and thereby increase Israeli control over Palestinian life.[20] Undermining Palestinian agriculture and industry forced Palestinians to look to the Israeli labor market for mainly unskilled work, forming a new class of manual laborers inside Israel and even responsible for building Israeli settlement infrastructure in the West Bank.[21] The work was presented by Israel as a benefit to Palestinians, an antidote to high rates of unemployment, but was a direct result of the de-development of indigenous industries.

These transformations in the labor market intersected with tourism directly. While Palestinians were not given permits to work in tourism or expand tourism infrastructure in the West Bank to accommodate the increasing number of tourists, Israel built a highway along the eastern edge of the West Bank through the Jordan valley, which would connect the Israeli tourism sites in the south and the north and along which dozens of new Israeli-run tourism sites were established. The building project employed tens of thousands of Palestinians as laborers, meaning that Palestinians who might have otherwise found work in the Palestinian tourism industry were forced to find work building up the Israeli tourism infrastructure instead.[22]

Over time, this dynamic resulted in a loss of skills and the other factors relevant to keeping an industry going and fostered a high Palestinian dependence on Israeli "benevolence" to ensure continued access to the Israeli labor market. When Palestinian groups or individuals committed acts of resistance or violence against Israel, the laborers were cut off from their ability to travel to their work, as occurred frequently into the 1990s until the OPT was essentially blocked off, and Israel began to import low-skilled workers from abroad. This tactic was deployed to incentivize Palestinian accommodation to the occupation and impose collective punishment on the entire society for any acts of resistance.

Spatial Control

Settler colonialism, and colonialism in general, always has a distinctly spatial element. In the case of Palestine, Israel's spatial control over the OPT in the period at hand manifested most visibly through the stationing of Israeli soldiers in Palestinian towns and through the confiscation of Palestinian land. Control over already-operating tourism sites was another way through which Israel was able to cement and deepen its spatial control over the West Bank. Zooming in on Bethlehem's Manger Square is one way to see how tight control over a tourist space was used to control the entire area, under the pretext of securing the space for tourists in order to impose strict restrictions on local access to public space.

As soon as the Israeli military rolled into Bethlehem in the first days of June 1967, it set up in Manger Square and made its control visible and unavoidable through physical markers. The old British municipal building on the north side of Manger Square was transformed into Israeli military/police headquarters, with a watchtower constructed outside from which Israeli soldiers could survey the area. An Israeli flag flew from the watchtower, directly in front of the Nativity Church. That meant that every tourist would have a visual marker of the space as Israeli, and every Palestinian would be reminded of it constantly.

By mid-June after the war, most of the Palestinian shops around Manger Square had reopened, and Israeli soldiers and civilians came to Bethlehem in numbers to buy souvenirs and to see the conquered territory. While the shops were open, under such surveillance any public politicking or activity by Palestinians was limited, and the square was transformed from the town's most prominent public space into one dominated by the occupation and tourists.

The spatial control used by the Israeli military over touristic spaces was not simply a way to exert control over Palestinians. It was also a carefully choreographed performance to shape the impressions tourists would take away both from the space and about the military occupation. Manger Square was particularly useful and important to manage in this sense, and Christmas 1967 demonstrated the dynamic well.

Upon entry to Bethlehem, visitors were greeted by signs in English, Arabic, and, for the first time, Hebrew. The Jewish National Fund provided the Christmas trees in Manger Square.[23] The Israeli police choir performed outside the church, and Israeli military officials participated in the religious procession. Israeli soldiers checked passes to make sure only the authorized could enter. Special postage stamps were issued for the occasion, so that tourists could mark their postcards and letters abroad with a stamp from the new Israeli authority in Bethlehem.[24] The stamp read "Christmas" and, in Hebrew, "Hag HaMolad," but left out the Arabic words for the holiday. In short, it was made abundantly clear who was controlling the space, and the festivities were specially designed to project a narrative to be repeated in the years to come, positioning Israel as the protector and keeper of Christian holy sites and the securer of access to the sites for Christian pilgrims from around the world.

This controlled management translated into the exclusion of local Palestinians from the space. In 1967, and in many of the years to come, Muslims (the majority faith group in Bethlehem by that time) were completely barred from entering Manger Square on Christmas under the pretext of security (since Palestinian activists were often depicted as "Muslim extremists," even though they came from all faith backgrounds).[25] That meant that the majority of the local Palestinian population was excluded from their town's main square and from participating in a major international tourist event. In other years, Muslims were barred allegedly to make space for Christians. The show of Israeli control and of Israeli religious "tolerance" toward Christians was repeated year after year.

Dividing access between Palestinian Christians and Muslims would become a regular feature of the occupation, a classic colonial tactic to seed sectarian divisions that could be exploited for colonial gain. That was also a part of the public messaging external to the Palestinian community about who belonged and who didn't. The banishment of Palestinian Muslims from the space fit with colonial travel narratives still persisting from decades before, which saw Palestinian Muslims as "out of place" in the Holy Land. This perspective was adopted by Zionist narratives claiming that Palestinians were not indigenous but rather were outsiders who had wandered into Palestine to take the place of the ancient Hebrews who rightfully owned the place. Touristic narratives about entitlement to the space and belonging were mobilized politically in terms of physical exclusion, allowing for the narratives to commingle and reinforce each other.

Exclusion from Manger Square repeated in various forms each year, every time the military decided on who would be allowed where and in what proportions.

The exclusion also affected mobility and space in the rest of the town. On Christmas in several years, nearby Palestinian refugee camps were placed under curfew to make sure that refugees did not try to enter Manger Square to tarnish the Christmas atmosphere. That means that touristic events such as Christmas became synonymous with curfews and other forms of repression for local Palestinians.

Whitewashing and Censorship

Under Israeli control, Palestinians were still technically able to lead tours, but they were under close watch and censorship, governed by the same military orders that prevented any political activity among Palestinians that went as far as prohibiting publishing materials with "any suggestion that West Bank inhabitants are suffering under occupation, any talk of love and loyalty to the homeland, or any representation of national aspirations."[26] Under this type of censorship and surveillance, Palestinian tour guides who were able to maintain their work would not dare trying to bring attention to the Palestinian cause. Tour guides suspected of voicing political opinions to their customers easily risked losing permission to operate or worse.[27]

The new narrative about the sites was produced and disseminated by the Israeli Ministry of Tourism and focused on the ancient history of the sites and their importance to world Christians. Palestinians were able to keep working and participate in tourism insofar as they stuck to this message. In this way, not only were Palestinians historically erased by the heritage discourse produced under Israeli occupation, but also Palestinian tour guides, if they wanted to keep their jobs, were forced to participate. In the meantime, Israeli tour guides openly attempted to sway the positions of tourists and journalists and, as one tour guide described, "to make them Zionists."[28]

The Israeli Bethlehem story highlighted a Judeo-Christian narrative of the place and downplayed or even denigrated the Islamic-Christian influences that had developed over time as a part of the local character.[29] In the Israeli narrative, Muslims are posited as the invading Arab armies that callously looted the church, a renewal of a trope in the nineteenth-century travelogues that represented Muslim sites or Arab/Muslim control over sites as negative layers cluttering up the otherwise pure Christian sites.[30] The Israeli narrative positions Israel as the "protector" or "preserver" of sites holy to Christians around the world, saved from the hands of careless Arabs or antagonistic Muslims. Regulating local use of religious sites and instead reserving them for display to tourists was also a colonial tactic used by the British in South Asia, accompanied by a similar narrative that presented the colonizing power as the benevolent preserver of unique sites otherwise misused by the native population.[31]

Aside from Christmas, the Israeli tourism industry and the occupation administration were eager to develop experiences in Bethlehem specially configured for Israeli Jews. One such event was staged only a year into the Israeli occu-

pation, in the summer of 1968. That July, Israeli president Levi Eshkol hosted the
Israel Philharmonic Orchestra headed by conductor Zubin Mehta in Manger Square
for a concert of Verdi's Requiem, cohosted by Elias Bandak, the Palestinian mayor
of Bethlehem. In Manger Square, the audience of nearly three thousand was made
up mostly of Israelis, and each of the hosts delivered messages about peace and
goodwill, under the watchful eye of Israeli soldiers on top of the Nativity Church.
The music was projected through the town on loudspeakers, making it so that Israel
occupied not only the physical space of the town but the soundscape as well. The
media coverage of the concert in the Israeli and Western press is telling. Israeli and
US news coverage of the concert depicted it as cooperation between "moderate"
Palestinians such as Bandak and the affable Israeli occupiers, bringing culture to
the grateful natives.[32]

The wider political moment gives some context to the concert and particularly Bandak's important role there. A year after the occupation began, Israel was
still developing its strategies of control, and the growth of the Palestine Liberation
Organization (PLO) was one of its main concerns. News coverage of the concert
was juxtaposed with reports of violent terrorists whose actions were thwarted by the
Israeli military. The presence of such a "universal" (read: Western) concert, or more
accurately the imposition of it, demonstrated that Israel was in control and fulfilling
its colonial role as a "bringer of civilization" fighting "radicals."

Figures such as Bandak and his successor, Freij, a major player in the tourism industry, reveal the interconnectedness of the West Bank tourism industry, the
Israeli colonial regime, and the shape that Palestinian tourism was to take after the
Oslo Accords. They demonstrate how Israel strategically engaged traditional power
hierarchies within Palestinian society to carry out an agenda of control. The Palestinian pilgrimage tourism industry and its major players were a significant part of
this plan.

Resistance

In contrast to Freij and Bandak, many Palestinians were increasingly emboldened
in their opposition to the colonial status quo over the years. As long as there was
an Israeli presence in the West Bank, some Palestinians attempted sabotage by
disrupting the charade of normality carefully choreographed by Israeli occupation
forces. Already by the first Christmas under occupation, the Israeli authorities were
concerned about security, indicating that the supposedly pliable occupied population was not so docile as initial Israeli news reports presented. In the weeks before
Christmas in 1967, Israeli forces rounded up tens of Palestinian men who they
claimed were operatives preparing attacks on Christmas.

Media reported that the Palestinian guerrilla organization Fatah had warned
ahead of time that while it would not target tourists, it could not guarantee tourist safety at the event.[33] No attack on people took place, but there were reports

of "saboteurs" cutting telephone and cables necessary for the media coverage that was a crucial element of Israel's projection of normalcy.[34] Calls for boycotts of the Israeli-sponsored Christmas partly contributed to the small number of Palestinians attending the Christmas events.[35] Boycotts and warnings were tactics consistently used by Palestinian activists throughout the years. On the one hand, Israel used that as a way to justify its military presence, but, on the other hand, too much military presence made the experience uncomfortable for tourists.

Demonstrations and strikes in the town became more frequent toward the end of the 1970s, often starting around the camps and the university, only minutes' walk away from Manger Square. As the brutality of the Israeli occupation started making the international news on a regular basis, Bethlehem was associated no longer only with Christmas festivities but now with political unrest as well. Manger Square became a center from which reporters covered unrest among Palestinians.

In 1987 decades of protest came to a head, and the first intifada, or uprising, against the occupation swept through the OPT. Daily general strikes and demonstrations were met by fierce Israeli military repression. Thousands of Palestinians were arrested, injured, or killed, but the popular movement persisted. Local community organizations and committees had over the years built networks and social infrastructure useful during the intifada years. These networks were expanded and mobilized, allowing for schooling to be organized by neighborhood committees during curfew, community gardens for food production, and more. The organizing had active roles for people across generational, gender, class, and religious divides, creating not only resistance toward the Israeli occupation but also a social upheaval through which social categories intentionally manipulated by Israel were overturned.[36]

Different Palestinian political factions united together under the Unified National Leadership of the Uprising (UNLU), which issued communiqués to coordinate resistance strategies, boost morale, and control messaging to the international press and solidarity supporters around the world. While disruptions to tourism spaces were frequent in the years before, they were usually quickly contained and managed by Israel. However, Christmas in Bethlehem was essentially shut down during the years of the intifada, 1987–92, in coordinated boycotts, general strikes, industry-specific strikes, and demonstrations organized by the UNLU, a blow that hit Israel's tourism industry and international reputation hard.

In December 1988, the UNLU called for a general strike on December 24 in a communiqué, describing it as "a day for ringing church bells and calling out *Allah akbar* in the minarets of the mosques, marking the birth of the messenger of peace, the Lord Messiah." It stated, "We extend felicitations to our Palestinian Christian brothers and urge them to make do with observing the religious rituals" (i.e., not to participate in the Israeli-sponsored festivities).[37] Another communiqué called for stores to be open special hours before strikes so that Christians could buy what they needed for the holiday and also called for visiting the families of the martyrs. Despite frequent attempts by Israel to cleave divisions between Palestinian Christians and Muslims, or religious and secular, the sentiments driving the intifada kept hold. The unity also reached Nazareth (in Israel), where Palestinians kept Christmas as a day of solidarity with their countrymen in the West Bank, much to the dismay of Israeli officials.

Palestinian refusal to celebrate publicly on Christmas created a public relations problem for the Israeli Ministry of Tourism, prompting it to issue a press statement attempting to position international tourists and pilgrims as the targets of Palestinian protest, saying that "nothing has changed in the intrinsic meaning of Christmas in Bethlehem, and no secular municipal action will either dampen the religious fervor of the pilgrims or mar their freedom of worship."[38] The Israeli military governor of Bethlehem called on local merchants to put up their Christmas decorations and force them to open their souvenir shops, but to no avail. The international and Arabic press reported that, aside from the religious rites, the streets and Manger Square were full of Israeli soldiers and empty of Palestinian residents.

Shopkeeper strikes were not limited to Christmas and were one of the first types of coordinated mass actions of the intifada, hitting especially hard in Jerusalem and Bethlehem, where the semblance of normalcy was important for the Israeli tourism industry. On several occasions, Israeli soldiers broke the locks on the metal shutters of closed shops participating in strikes, and the UNLU responded by having locksmiths on call to repair or replace the locks of striking shops for free.[39] While certainly not all Palestinian tourism operators cooperated with the resistance happily, a tipping point had been reached. The general atmosphere was transformed into one in which acquiescence to the occupation's status quo was not tolerated by the popular movement, and small gestures such as fixing the locks were an attempt to recognize the sacrifice made by shopkeepers.

During the intifada, Manger Square became a site of frequent clashes between Israeli soldiers and Palestinians, usually armed only with rocks or sometimes with Molotov cocktails. The Israeli army, replete with armor, guns, tear gas, and tanks, faced off with the Palestinian "children of the stones." Dedicated in their mission to chase out the soldiers, they created a major difficulty for the army and were targeted with arrest and violence, often through the use of snipers or undercover agents. Many were already familiar with the Israeli practice of using *must'arabin*, or Israeli undercover agents dressed as Palestinians, to attack or arrest stone-throwers, a new tactic that was used in Manger Square during the intifada. In 1989 undercover Israeli soldiers dressed as tourists shot at Palestinians suspected of throwing rocks in the square, killing one and wounding another.[40]

This tactic was especially upsetting to Palestinians who prided themselves on taking great care not to harm tourists, fearful now that this incident would create mistrust. In one of the few cases in which a tourist was intentionally targeted by a Palestinian at Manger Square, the event was condemned by both the mayor of Bethlehem and the leaders of the resistance, who released a communiqué stating that the resistance "including all its arms and members, condemns the criminal murder of the French tourist in Bethlehem and emphasizes that doubtful actions of this kind are meant to harm the Palestinian national movement and tarnish our people's religious, cultural, and historical image," further stressing that their uprising was against the occupation (and not against tourism).[41]

Conclusion

While this account is by no means comprehensive, it demonstrates how Israel incorporated tourism development into its colonial project, a story that can be developed much further by looking at the wider case of historic Palestine. Tourism was not an afterthought for the Israeli colonial regime but was instead strategically engaged to de-develop Palestinian economies and to deepen control over space by creating an impossible situation for Palestinians, pushing them to take part in the normalization of the violence against them for the benefit of keeping things smooth for the sake of tourism.

It is not surprising that this charade lasted for years before erupting. Given the siege-like conditions in the West Bank, tourism presented a rare opportunity for Palestinians to continue an industry that they had run effectively for decades, if not centuries, and to have some valuable contact with the outside world, perhaps with the fleeting hope that they could convince visitors that they were not the terrorists that Israel painted them to be. However, the conditions of the occupation proved difficult enough that, before long, there was more to lose than to gain from participating in Israeli tourism whitewashing, and it's no surprise that eventually the collective grievances of Palestinians fully disrupted Israeli-run tourism in Bethlehem.

Ryvka Barnard holds a PhD in Middle Eastern and Islamic studies from New York University, where she wrote her thesis on the politics of tourism development in the West Bank.

Notes

1. Salamanca et al., "Past Is Present."
2. Hazbun, *Beaches, Ruins, Resorts.*
3. Bruner, *Culture on Tour*; Hutnyk, *Rumour of Calcutta.*
4. Kincaid, *Small Place.*
5. Anderson, *Imagined Communities.*
6. On tourism and occupation, see, e.g., Isaac, Hall, and Higgins-Desbiolles. On tourism and colonialism, see e.g., *Politics and Power of Tourism.* Abu El-Haj, *Facts on the Ground: Archaeological Practice.*
7. For more on this framing, see Taghdisi-Rad, *Political Economy of Aid.*
8. Moscrop, *Measuring Jerusalem.*
9. Cohen-Hattab, "Zionism, Tourism, and the Battle for Palestine," 62.
10. Smith, *Roots of Separatism.*

11. Pappé, *Ethnic Cleansing of Palestine.*
12. Bowman, "Politics of Tour Guiding."
13. Katz, *Jordanian Jerusalem.*
14. Masalha, *Politics of Denial,* 191.
15. Gorenberg, *Accidental Empire,* 44.
16. Collins-Kreiner, *Christian Tourism to the Holy Land,* 26.
17. Kaell, *Walking Where Jesus Walked,* 46.
18. Hazboun, "Needed: A Modern Infrastructure," 1–9.
19. Bowman, "Politics of Tour Guiding."
20. Gordon, *Israel's Occupation,* 72.
21. Farsakh, *Palestinian Labour Migration.*
22. Eldor, "Military Administration."
23. Feron, "Religion."
24. Lavi, "Frozen Mass in Bethlehem."
25. *Hartford (CT) Courant,* "Israeli Soldiers on Guard."
26. Gordon, *Israel's Occupation,* 37.
27. Bowman, "Politics of Tour Guiding."
28. Crown-Tamir, "O, Little Town of Bethlehem."
29. Feldman, "Constructing a Shared Bible Land," 362.
30. Kattaya, "Writing the 'Real Jerusalem,'" 14.
31. Anderson, *Imagined Communities,* 182.
32. Tzuriel, "Jews, Muslims, and Christians."
33. Jewish Telegraphic Agency, "Arab Terrorists."
34. *Davar,* "Identity of the Terrorists."
35. *Hartford (CT) Courant,* "Israeli Soldiers on Guard."
36. Robinson, *Building a Palestinian State.*
37. Mishal and Aharoni, *Speaking Stones,* 156.
38. Quoted in Kifner, "Pervasive Protest by Palestinians."
39. Hunter, *Palestinian Uprising,* 112.
40. Perera, "Report of the Special Committee to Investigate Israeli Practices."
41. Mishal and Aharoni, *Speaking Stones,* 194.

References

Abu El-Haj, Nadia. 2001. *Facts on the Ground: Archaeological Practice and Territorial Self-Fashioning in Israeli Society.* Chicago: University of Chicago Press.

Anderson, Benedict. 1991. *Imagined Communities: Reflections on the Origin and Spread of Nationalism.* London: Verso.

Bowman, Glenn. 1992. "The Politics of Tour Guiding: Israeli and Palestinian Guides in Israel and the Occupied Territories." In *Tourism and the Less Developed Countries,* edited by David Harrison, 121–34. London: Belhaven.

Bruner, Edward M. 2004. *Culture on Tour: Ethnographies of Travel.* Chicago: University of Chicago Press.

Cohen-Hattab, Kobi. 2004. "Zionism, Tourism, and the Battle for Palestine: Tourism as a Political-Propaganda Tool." *Israel Studies* 9, no. 1: 61–85.

Collins-Kreiner, Noga. 2006. *Christian Tourism to the Holy Land: Pilgrimage during Security Crisis.* Burlington, VT: Ashgate.

Crown-Tamir, Hela. 2008. "O, Little Town of Bethlehem." *Jerusalem Post,* December 25.

Davar. 1967. "Identity of the Terrorists in the Bethlehem Region Not Yet Discovered" [in Hebrew]. December 26.

Eldor, Rafael. 1967. "Military Administration Employs Fifteen Thousand Local Workers in the Held Territories" [in Hebrew]. *Ma'ariv*, August.

Farsakh, Leila. 2005. *Palestinian Labour Migration to Israel: Labour, Land, and Occupation*. London: Routledge.

Feldman, Jackie. 2007. "Constructing a Shared Bible Land: Jewish Israeli Guiding Performances for Protestant Pilgrims." *American Ethnologist* 34, no. 2: 351–74.

Feron, James. 1967. "Religion; Merry Christmas and Shalom." *New York Times*, December 24.

Gordon, Neve. 2008. *Israel's Occupation*. Berkeley: University of California Press.

Gorenberg, Gershom. 2006. *The Accidental Empire: Israel and the Birth of the Settlements, 1967–1977*. New York: Times Books.

Hartford (CT) Courant. 1967. "Israeli Soldiers on Guard at Christ's Birthplace." December 25.

Hazboun, Samir. 1994. "Needed: A Modern Infrastructure." *Palestine-Israel Journal of Politics, Economics and Culture* 1, no. 1: 1–9.

Hazbun, Waleed. 2008. *Beaches, Ruins, Resorts: The Politics of Tourism in the Arab World*. Minneapolis: University of Minnesota Press.

Hunter, F. Robert. 1991. *The Palestinian Uprising: A War by Other Means*. Berkeley: University of California Press.

Hutnyk, John. 1996. *The Rumour of Calcutta: Tourism, Charity, and the Poverty of Representation*. London: Zed Books.

Isaac, Rami K., C. Michael Hall, and Freya Higgins-Desbiolles, eds. 2016. *The Politics and Power of Tourism in Palestine*. New York: Routledge.

Jewish Telegraphic Agency. 1967. "Arab Terrorists Active on West Bank and in Gaza in Preparation for Christmas." *Jewish Telegraphic Agency Daily News Bulletin*, December 25.

Kaell, Hillary. 2014. *Walking Where Jesus Walked: American Christians and Holy Land Pilgrimage*. New York: New York University Press.

Kattaya, Mona. 2010. "Writing the 'Real Jerusalem': British and American Travel Accounts in the Nineteenth Century." *Jerusalem Quarterly*, no. 44: 14–28.

Katz, Kimberly. 2005. *Jordanian Jerusalem: Holy Places and National Spaces*. Gainesville: University Press of Florida.

Kifner, John. 1988. "Pervasive Protest by Palestinians Leaves Bethlehem a Joyless Place." *New York Times*, December 25.

Kincaid, Jamaica. 1988. *A Small Place*. New York: Farrar, Straus and Giroux.

Lavi, Zvi. 1967. "Frozen Mass in Bethlehem but Not Because of the Weather" [in Hebrew]. *Ma'ariv*, December 25.

Masalha, Nur. 2003. *The Politics of Denial: Israel and the Palestinian Refugee Problem*. London: Pluto.

Mishal, Shaul, and Reuben Aharoni. 1994. *Speaking Stones: Communiqués from the Intifada Underground*. Syracuse, NY: Syracuse University Press.

Moscrop, John James. 1999. *Measuring Jerusalem: The Palestine Exploration Fund and British Interests in the Holy Land*. London: Leicester University Press.

Pappé, Ilan. 2006. *The Ethnic Cleansing of Palestine*. Oxford, UK: Oneworld.

Perera, Daya R. 1989. "Report of the Special Committee to Investigate Israeli Practices Affecting the Human Rights of the Population of the Occupied Territories." United Nations General Assembly, 43rd sess., October 12.

Robinson, Glenn E. 1997. *Building a Palestinian State: The Incomplete Revolution*. Bloomington: Indiana University Press.

Salamanca, Omar Jabary, Mezna Qato, Kareem Rabie, and Sobhi Samour. 2012. "Past Is Present: Settler Colonialism in Palestine." *Settler Colonial Studies* 2, no. 1: 1–8.

Smith, Barbara J. 1993. *The Roots of Separatism in Palestine: British Economic Policy, 1920–1929.* Syracuse, NY: Syracuse University Press.

Taghdisi-Rad, Sahar. 2011. *The Political Economy of Aid in Palestine: Relief from Conflict or Development Delayed?* New York: Routledge.

Tzuriel. 1968. "Jews, Muslims, and Christians Listened to the 'Requiem' in Bethlehem" [in Hebrew]. *Ma'ariv*, July 22.

Falling off the Tourism Ladder

Spanish Tourism from Franco
to the Housing Bubble of 2008

Max Holleran

The City of Arts and Sciences is a collection of architecturally daring cultural structures nestled into the bottom of a manicured riverbed park in the Spanish city of Valencia. The science museum, opera house, and IMAX theater, all designed by the internationally acclaimed Valencian architect Santiago Calatrava, were meant to draw high-spending cultural tourists and to distinguish the city from other destinations on the Costa Blanca that specialize only in sand, sangria, and sunshine. The project, started before the 2008 economic crisis, cost over €1 billion of taxpayer money. After that the Spanish economy slowly disintegrated, sending youth unemployment to nearly 50 percent. For Valencians, the project came to represent the Spanish state's obsession with tourism as an economic tool that awarded lavish subsidies for urban development in the lead-up to the 2008 crisis. Rosa, an unemployed mother of three whom I met in the City of Arts and Sciences in 2013, told me that her son enjoys running in the park, but she said: "This kind of park doesn't cost a billion euros . . . and the opera? Who the hell is going to see an opera? . . . We aren't opera people . . . if I have twenty extra euros I try and pay my bills."

The negotiations between labor, the state, and industry, which produced the contemporary postwar welfare state, also factored leisure into the demand-making process: it often conceived of time in terms of health and well-being rather than amusement.[1] As industrial laborers in countries such as France, the United

Radical History Review
Issue 129 (October 2017) DOI 10.1215/01636545-3920727
© 2017 by MARHO: The Radical Historians' Organization, Inc.

Kingdom, and West Germany won wage victories in the 1950s and 1960s, they also pushed for increasingly lengthy summer vacations: enabling a generation of workers to holiday longer and farther from their factories. Spain became a particularly large player in budget coastal tourism. At the very same time as it began to democratize after Francisco Franco's death in 1975, the post-Franco government attracted large crowds to the country's beaches, using tourism to grow regional cities, improve infrastructure, and market "American-style" retirement colonies to wealthier European home buyers.[2] By the 1990s, Spain became a global model of how to transform mass "Fordist"-era tourism into a thriving real estate industry and a variegated cultural economy.

The Spanish economic transformation, accomplished with billions of euros in grants and loans from the European Union (EU), became a trusted economic development model. During the 1980s and 1990s, the Spanish government and the European Community came to see coastal tourism as a means to invigorate a laggard economy, to demonstrate modernity through an economic growth sector that seemed intrinsically future-oriented, and to erase the memories of a dictatorship in which beachfront morality and expressions of sexuality were policed by the state.[3] What's more, Spain's ability to construct entire tourist cities ex nihilo and then to refine those spaces of mass tourism into architectural, culinary, and arts centers became far more than a simple development model. Politicians, from both the socialist party (Partido Socialista Obrero Español, or PSOE) and the conservative party (Partido Popular, or PP), saw tourism as a means to transcend the Southern European history of partial incorporation in the imagined community of modern Europe and to join the actual political community of the EU.

After providing a brief outline of the origins of mass tourism and how leisure came to occupy an important space in the cultural life of postwar Europe as well as how it became an essential part of the global economy, this essay argues that the Mediterranean "edge" of Europe was particularly important to the tourism industry. Using the case study of Spain's Costa Blanca, it examines how the southern periphery of Europe promised relaxation away from Northwestern Europe and its "rational" use of time and Calvinist morals. A Weberian conception of European regionalism, while not fully believed, was not entirely banished from the collective European imaginary. Drawing on historical sources and nearly two years of participant observation with residents, tourism promoters, and real estate developers in and around the cities of Valencia and Alicante, I argue that the beach holiday, while rapidly transforming the Costa Blanca culturally and environmentally, became the emblematic escape and a marker of post-Franco democratization and European integration.[4]

Vacationers also regarded the Mediterranean as the near periphery and sometimes conceived of it as a space for a more ribald approach to sexual experiences and alcohol consumption. Nested orientalism, or the notion that one's neighbor is exoticized through an overemphasis on microcultural differences, was present in the case of Spanish tourism between Spain and Northwestern Europe, and the newly democratic government profitably utilized it to attract tourists.[5] However, while this strategy brought mass tourism and second-home ownership to Spain's coasts, it presented a problem for the post-Franco modernization project because low-budget holidays confirmed a North-South hierarchy.[6] Spain, as we shall see, attempted to dismantle this hierarchy, again using the tourism industry, by revamping tourist cities with cultural projects.[7]

There is a common sentiment that the growth created by this tourism and its attendant urbanization, by the vast swaths of hotels and retirement communities that stretch across Spain's eastern and southern coasts, has been a process of modernization by selective underdevelopment.[8] Mass tourism, while promising economic growth beyond that sector alone, has not delivered on this promise. Instead, it has created numerous new kinds of precarious and seasonal labor highly vulnerable to frequent changes in the global leisure industry. Rather than providing economic uplift to struggling regions, it has reified categories of center and periphery in much the same way that resource extraction versus manufacturing divided colonies and colonizers a generation earlier. Places that are visited are often on the "edges" of development, while centers of economic affluence and political power send visitors. Since the 2008 crisis, Spain's real estate industry has collapsed, leaving millions of unoccupied homes, many in touristic areas. It has also left a quarter of the population unemployed, calling into question the entire project of post-Franco economic modernization.[9] The tourism economy of 1975–2008 was well financed by EU grants and loans, promising the mobility to travel and settle anywhere within the Schengen zone, but as the fortunes of Northern and Southern Europe diverge, the environmental and social sacrifices made to create one of the world's largest tourism economies are increasingly seen as an unrewarding burden.

The Grand Tour No More: Mass Tourism and the European Good Life

In the early twentieth century, there was a widespread view in Northern Europe that coastal vacations were health-promoting excursions that were particularly beneficial to children, who, increasingly, were too cloistered in cities and estranged from nature. Particular attention was given to children's developing bodies, using the physical problems of asthma, fever, and "sickliness" as corporeal manifestations of the moral failings of city life. As travel demand grew at the end of the nineteenth century and in the early twentieth century, coastal tourism became a facet of the summertime in continental Europe for the upper and middle classes. It also became an extensive business based on hotels, resorts, and casinos. The idea of leisure, and particularly beachfront summer vacations, changed quickly from a place of respite to regain one's health to a season and place for personal reinvention and revelry. Resort towns in the French Riviera became known as sites of ribald escape from more conventional daily life. Coastal tourism, while still a family practice, also became associated with a relaxation of social rules, although this occurred only step-by-step and still with the socially beneficial mission of healthful revitalization. Skimpy bathing attire and mixed-gender beaches became seasonal escapes that could be enjoyed in summertime, but would also aid in maintaining the moral rectitude of everyday life for the majority of the year.

Coastal tourism in Europe also had important geopolitical implications, as many anthropologists have demonstrated.[10] Increasingly, tourists from Britain, France, and Germany sought hotter, more "exotic," and cheaper destinations. Tourism in Southern France, Italy, and Spain took wealthier Northern Europeans to the semiperiphery, and visiting enforced the status of Southern Europe as somewhere away from but related to the "center."[11] This tradition began centuries earlier with elite travelers such as the American Washington Irving, who chronicled, with fascination and mild fear, Roma living out-of-door in the ruins of the great Alhambra palace in Andalusia.[12] As depictions of semiperipheral Europe shifted from Byronesque exaltations of nineteenth-century Greece to more consumable versions aimed at a wider tourist market, the southern semiperiphery became economically and politically subordinated to Northern Europe.

Tourists visited Spain, Portugal, and Greece, but those countries rarely produced visitors. For those who enjoyed Southern Europe's beaches, these spaces represented not only the physical but also the conceptual edge of European society. Even the beaches outside of major cities were imaginatively rendered by tourists as sites of "tribal" ritual where people could safely play at a Robinson Crusoe removal from society before reentering the constraints of urban European life.[13] While these associations and any notion of tourism as journey faded over the course of the twentieth century with the inception of mass tourism, they were still a latent force and a cultural subtext that added to the notion of the culture of the Mediterranean periphery as a liminal exotic good to be consumed.[14] During the course of the twentieth century, Southern Europe became a space of even more fetishized European otherness as Portugal, Spain, and Greece failed to economically develop at the same pace as Northern Europe. The Spanish Civil War, 1936–39, only reified the cultural difference between North and South further: first with bloodshed, then with political isolation.

The European postwar generation was the first to embrace international tourism with gusto: after years of immobility, borders were open, safe, and convenient to cross for the purpose of adventure and relaxation, not necessity. Middle-class families, newly equipped with automobiles, were interested in exploring the South of Europe, which had been closed off during the war. The growth of the welfare state gave them the money and time to do so (codified by the widespread adoption of the paid vacation in the mid-1930s). As an elderly Norwegian told me in the Spanish city of Calpe, one of the Costa Blanca's most highly developed hubs, which now sports dozens of high-rise apartments: "You have to understand that this place, in the 1960s, was a completely different world: it felt tropical and away from Europe. It was like an island, almost." Indeed, Southern Europe, with its relative lack of industrial development, represented a contrast to the metropoles of Northwestern Europe. As the cultural theorist Iain Chambers has observed in the case of Naples, much of Mediterranean Europe presented itself to travelers from the European core as spaces of "interrupted modernity."[15] While some anthropologists have followed Immanuel Wallerstein to suggest that the Mediterranean represented a semiperiphery in contrast to the decolonizing actual periphery, Italy, Portugal, Greece, and Spain were also part of a purely regional center-periphery dichotomy.[16] Tourists thought of their postwar visits to Mediterranean Europe in terms of "discovery" and imbibing authentic (i.e., less modern) culture.[17] Places such as Andalusia, Naples, and Cyprus were regarded as hyphenated in their European-ness. European Community policy makers saw North-South holidays as beneficial to those regions visited. They believed the very things that made them interesting to visit, their rural beauty, putative cultural authenticity, and relative poverty, would decline in meaning through successive visits and development. When these qualities eventually faded, the countries would enter a state of "fuller" Europeanness. Thus while Mediterranean countries broadcast an exoticized version of their culture for touristic consumption, including reifications of their peripheral character and connections to the Arab world, this strategy was simultaneously meant to transform the Mediterranean periphery into just another part of Europe.[18]

Spain Reopens Its Doors at Last

In the 1950s, Spain's Costa Blanca emerged as a major tourist destination anchored by the regional capital, Valencia, and the picturesque second city of Alicante. The rest of the region was dominated by over three hundred miles of coast, which enjoys a semitropical microclimate. Following the Spanish Civil War, Valencia continued to produce textiles and engage in Mediterranean trade, while citrus farming and fishing dominated village life. Accounts from European travelers during the 1950s, and even tourists from nearby Madrid, remember a rural existence. One elderly informant in the town of Xàbia reminisced that life in the Costa Blanca during the 1950s was not much changed since her mother's childhood at the turn of the twentieth century: "Men worked in agriculture and women stayed home and did housework. . . . People came to visit for the beaches, but they wore traditional bathing suits and caps over their hair. Sometimes our neighbors would sell sandwiches, because there were hardly any restaurants for out-of-towners to eat in." Yet life in coastal Spain was anything but stable.

By the early 1950s, it was obvious to the Franco government that, without economic reform, Spain would have more in common, economically, with North Africa than with France or Italy. Its economic output was 40 percent of the Euro-

pean average, and black markets thrived because of centralized interventionist policies and lack of economic integration with the rest of Europe.[19] By 1959, the Franco
regime initiated a stabilization and liberalization plan to reinvigorate the economy
before it declined even more and threatened the dictatorship. The plan brought a
new laissez-faire pro-market attitude to Spain, which had been absent in the first
two decades of Franco's reign. It also attempted to mend relationships with the
rest of Europe and the United States (which horse-traded aid money for the placement of military bases in Spain). While free market fiscal reforms helped the United
States begin to regard the Franco regime as an important Cold War anticommunist ally, the late 1950s also brought a large-scale reconfiguration of the national
economy toward externally valued goods and services. One of the most successful
commodities was tourism.

By the 1950s, Franco's government in Madrid was keenly aware of tourism's
place in the European periphery. While other parts of Western Europe had used
and expanded the Marshall Plan to improve infrastructure and modernize industry,
Spain had subsisted on a largely agricultural economy. Indeed, the Franco regime
selectively divested in some cities in Catalonia and the Basque Country that were
industrially advanced, as a form of punishment for their republican sympathies during the Civil War. By the mid-1950s, this underdevelopment was becoming painfully
obvious to the regime. Three key factors aided the liberalization of the Spanish
economy: diminished centralization, a more positive relationship with the United
States because Franco's hardline anticommunist stance opened the floodgates for
American loans, and a thawing of the tense relationship with other Western European economies that culminated with membership in the Organization for Economic Cooperation and Development in 1961. During this period, the Franco government turned its attention to tourism as a major area of potential competition with
the rest of Europe. Unlike the industrial sector, which when held to the standards
of Italy was retrograde and compared to West Germany was hopelessly behind,
Spain had ample beaches and temperate weather. Tourism, as an industry, was also
becoming an economic mainstay of the European semiperiphery: more mobility and
better wages in France and the United Kingdom, for instance, provided a modest
boom of visitors to neighboring countries. While most of these holidays were small-
scale, utilizing campgrounds, pensions, and rented bungalows, entrepreneurs and
economists in the Franco regime had far-reaching ambitions.

Tourism organizations proliferated as French and German tourists began to
arrange for coastal holidays in Valencia. By the early 1960s, the pioneer British firm
Thomas Cook arranged for package tours to the Costa Blanca, offering extremely
cheap deals and beginning a process of internationalizing a tourism business that
had once been dominated by Valencian hoteliers. The tours focused on many hours
of beach time with a splash of culture, such as a flamenco concert or a visit to a citadel or village. Most of the tourism of this era was solidly middle-class and centered

on Spain's ample coastline. Cities such as Calpe, Benidorm, Torrevieja, and Alicante were key destinations, and they began building large apartment blocks to house tourists who wished to rid themselves of middling-quality hotels or rent a flat for the entire summer. A major factor in early tourism was price. Most involved in the Spanish coastal tourism business had no illusions that they were engaged in battle for high-quality vacations or a mission to rejuvenate the international standing of Spain: they were participants in a price war with the French Mediterranean, which they handily won.

Tourism promoters presented the Costa Blanca, along with Andalusia and other locales, as the "other" unknown Europe. Regional governments used a set of stock images of flamenco and bullfighting as well as of the Andalus empire and Roma culture. While many of these images had been Iberian tropes for centuries, they had a new immediacy because they reinvigorated a sense of Spain as a segment of Europe that fascism had sealed off for two decades but had once again become accessible (although not reformed politically). Early tourists in Valencia felt that they were traveling to the edge of Europe. The Spanish Civil War and the triumph of Franco had led Spain to inhabit a semipariah status within the community of European nations, but older geocultural configurations were also present. Dutch tourists saw Spain as the Catholic South, memorialized by their own country's Catholic parts, many of which had been under Spanish rule (in the seventeenth century). As one Dutch woman remembered, Spain was a natural destination for Dutch people: "They took over our country and now we get to have a bit of theirs. . . . I'm Catholic too . . . so maybe I will be meeting in the street with a Spanish 'cousin.'" Still more Europeans categorized Spain as a cultural other for a 500-year-old Moorish past that had severed it from Medieval Europe. These designations, while very tenuous and essentializing, were culturally resonant in the tourism industry, which trafficked in exoticism in order to add a complementary cultural element to good weather and abundant beaches.

The expansion of tourism in the Valencia province was an obvious choice for state grants and increased private investment: its proximity to France allowed for international access by car, and many hoteliers had a tradition of serving elites from Madrid and the city of Valencia who rented homes by the beach in August. These communities were modest collections of homes that were vacant for the rest of the year. But that began to change in the 1960s, when Northern holidaymakers expanded the beach season beyond the Spanish vacation norms and developers bought up vacant lands from fishing families.[20] Preliminary local experiences with foreign tourism in Spain were noncontentious given the glut of underutilized land and the minimal footprint of working-class tourists. Often family holidays were only a step-up from camping, and visitors were forced to learn some Spanish to communicate with their rural hosts. As one Dutch man remembered his trip to Calpe in 1968: "[It was] one of the most memorable experiences of my young life. . . . We played with Spanish kids and they played with us. . . . Now you can find a Dutch menu in every restaurant and sometimes even Dutch music playing." Indeed, the primary image of 1960s Spain for foreign tourists was of European life only slightly touched by modernity. This was a carefully curated experience by local tourism promoters and one that could not last as the number of visitors dramatically increased throughout the 1960s and the visitors' demands for modern comforts grew in turn.[21] The gap between genuine village life and the rural facade created on the sidelines of beach resorts was becoming more and more noticeable as urbanization picked up pace and the simulacra of rurality increasingly did not sustain the suspension of disbelief.

By the 1970s, armed with an influx of foreign capital, many coastal cities in Spain began to remodel themselves in the image of American modernist architecture and to replace the rural charm of "authentic" Europe with the glamour of Palm Beach and a thoroughly internationalized tourism culture. This was a response to the increased demands of tourists, who, as their travel options increased, requested both more comfortable amenities and better services. The change was also a concerted move by the Spanish Ministry of Tourism to represent the Spanish leisure sector as world-class and competitive with the standards of the European core. The professionalization and modernization of the tourism industry exemplified the economic development policies of the late Franco regime, which sought to integrate itself with the rest of Europe through travel and economic cooperation in order to normalize the dictatorship as a political fact. Franco's government attempted to mend its relationship with the rest of Europe by producing a durable sense of nationalism that transcended peripheral nationalisms in Spain (Catalan and Basque and, to a lesser extent, Galician, Valencian, and Andalusian) at the very moment that Basque militants (the Euskadi Ta Askatasuna, or ETA) were taking up arms against the dictatorship.[22] By presenting Spain to the rest of Europe as a coherent and unified block that shared a common past and was destined for a common future, Franco's Ministry of Tourism sought to accomplish a valuable marketing task aimed not only at French and German tourists but also at dissatisfied Spaniards. But this strategy of national symbolism mixed with 1960s advertising was a bit too blatant for many Spaniards. When Manuel Fraga Iribarne, the minister of tourism and a member of the new reformist *falangistas* (Franco's fascist and hyper-religious political party), created the slogan "Spain is different" (often accompanied by photos of *sevillanas* dancers [brightly clad Andalusian folk dance performers]), it quickly became a joke.[23] While the advertising campaign was successful with some Europeans, many Spaniards felt the country was quite *different*: it was still a dictatorship.

Up Goes Benidorm

The most noticeable landscape of Spanish tourism in the 1960s, and perhaps in the entire country, was the town of Benidorm, a fishing village that, within the space of two decades, was transformed into a beachfront strip of high-rise hotels. The city, which would become a symbol of European mass leisure, was little more than a pueblo in the 1950s before being developed by an aggressive state policy to foster tourism. In 1963 the tourism ministry created a list of zones and centers of interest for tourism, which later became set in national law, that helped plan and finance tourism projects. The vast majority were in coastal Valencia and Andalusia.[24] The law (Ley de Zonas y Centros de Interés Turístico) was required not just to stimulate the industry but to control and codify where development could and could not occur. Previously rural lands were quickly bulldozed. The transformed Benidorm changed the romanticized semiorientalist characterization of Spain. All at once, the landscape projected by international tourism agencies was not that of whitewashed pueblos but of ten-story modernist hotels in the style of Miami. Inns (*pensiónes*) were phased out, replaced in the late 1960s by massive and increasingly all-inclusive hotels. The travel culture of wandering through villages in search of a bed and a hot meal procured through interactions with locals in pidgin Spanish was replaced by manicured hotel gardens, multilingual tourism professionals, buffets, and cocktail bars. The vertical ascent of Benidorm, both in profits and in skyline, became an important symbol of Spain's embrace of mass tourism and its commitment to revitalizing the industry through urbanization and modernization. The sociologist Jean-Didier Urbain succinctly describes the commodification of beach regions, such as Valencia, undergoing dramatic social changes in the name of creating a dynamic tourism economy: "What happens with fishermen also happens with seaweed. Rejected, expelled, or eliminated from the shore, these elements are reintroduced into the vacation universe only when they have been transformed into exotic curiosities. . . . They are no longer natural but naturalized, turned folkloric in one case, dried in the other, sweetened in all cases, like the varnished seashell whose inhabitant has been expropriated."[25]

After growing in the 1970s, however, Benidorm did not look like a stereotypical beach town filled with low-slung buildings, bungalows, and motels; rather, its verticality proclaimed the birth of a new city. The surrounding areas of the Valencia region grew with a more sprawling urban logic, but Benidorm was distinctly city-like: it was dense and home to a skyline as tall as downtown Madrid or Barcelona. In Benidorm's urban development plan of 1963, the local government abolished height limitations and permitted the tourism hub to build skyscrapers.[26] By the 1970s, an airport in neighboring Alicante was opened for primarily touristic purposes, bringing visitors year-round from the United Kingdom. Yet the cosmopolitan aesthetics of the tourist city did not always mesh with the cultural politics of Franco's Spain. As a concerted push to increase tourism as a major new sector of the ailing economy occurred, the international appeal of beachfront vacations was an unstable mixture of family rejuvenation and erotic abandon. Moreover, with the growing popularity of places such as Club Med, the image of the area as a bacchanalian playpen ascended in appeal and market pull. Vacationers to the edges of Europe no longer just looked for a family escape from cities in order to spend time together; rather, they sought spaces for discovery and release. As the urban geographer Rob Shields notes, "ludic spaces" were important sites of annual pilgrimage for middle-class Europeans to separate the year into times of work and play.[27] Increasingly, this division was not just a temporal one, for instance, between Mardi Gras and Lent, but a spatial one, such as between Benidorm and Rotterdam or Manchester.

The Franco regime's cultural rubric was deeply influenced by its relationship with the fundamentalist Catholic order of Opus Dei, which directed universities (educating the *franquista* elites) and had tremendous influence over social policy. This closeness to religious fervor gave the fascist government moral cover for some of its abuses, but it complicated its modernization plans. The policing of sexuality in all parts of national life, among its less pernicious effects, had led to a ban on the bikini in coastal Spain.[28] But by the 1950s, foreign tourists were routinely receiving tickets from the Guardia Civil for their improper and "immodest" beach attire. Perhaps no story epitomizes the shift in tourism culture, and the rise of cities such as Benidorm, more than the "bikini legend" of Benidorm's mayor (from 1950 to 1967), Pedro Zaragoza. Zaragoza is said to have rode his motorbike all the way to Madrid in 1953 for a personal audience with Franco to beg for lifting the bikini ban so as not to deter foreign visitors who may not have shared *franquista* (doggedly religious pro-Franco) morals but were helping to revive the economy. Whether the trip to Madrid is mostly fact or fiction, the city of Benidorm was granted special permission to allow tourists to wear bikinis without risk of being ticketed. Indeed, coastal cities, enjoyed mostly by foreign visitors, offered tourists a taste of a more permissive and tolerant Spanish society two decades before Franco's death allowed for the introduction of pop music and drug culture (the countercultural Movida movement in Madrid) to enter Spanish society at large.

Tourism gave the Spanish economy such a boost from the 1960s until 1974 that Franco vigorously petitioned the United Nations to locate its new World Tourism Organization in Madrid, a wish finally granted after Franco's death in 1975. While Franco had wanted the office to legitimate his government to the world, it also ended up accrediting tourism as a profession and a valuable economic sector, as well as establishing Spain as a particularly good practitioner in the field. This signaled a major shift in the European understanding of international travel from a mainly upper-class pursuit dominated by famous hotels and Michelin-starred restaurants to a firmly middle-class industry consisting of local travel agents, all-inclusive packages, and sprawling beach complexes like those that had sprung up near Benidorm. The securing of the UN World Tourism Organization was only the first act in Spain's slow and complex accession to the European Community, a process hindered by incomplete political reforms.[29] The very presence of cities such as Benidorm, along with other hubs in Catalonia and Andalusia that drew 30 million tourists to Spain by 1975, was a form of soft diplomacy. Municipalities and regions that attracted tourists demonstrated a symbolic mixing of Europeans, suggesting a future in which what worked on the level of holidaymakers might be possible at the level of European nations. The "Europeanness" of the sites also served Spain's drive to join the European Community.

As Spain democratized in the late 1970s and 1980s, so did the tourism market on the Costa Blanca in Valencia. Increasingly, throughout Northern Europe Benidorm was thought of as a party city where young people could descend for holiday merriment. The days of risqué (and risky) bikini wearing paled beside the loud bars, discotheques, and, increasingly, drugs and prostitution that packed the city's coastal promenade. By the 1990s, Spain's coasts were urbanized for hundreds of smaller Benidorm-like tourist settlements. The city itself was increasingly maligned by Spaniards, as a place for "low-class" visitors from the United Kingdom more inclined to fight and vomit on the street than to spend money in local businesses. This viewpoint was a reflection both of the genuine ease of European travel and the competitive prices that drew more working-class visitors. The perception also mirrored how Benidorm's own development cycle had reached a point where tourists saw it as a has-been destination marred by too many previous visitors.

By 2007, Benidorm became something of a punch line, ridiculed for its combination of cut-rate retiree trips and alcohol-soaked stag parties. On British TV, the city inspired a comedy series of the same name. The show, a collection of bawdy jibes at working-class manners, satirized British tourists "presumptuous" enough to think that they knew continental Europe yet so dim as to believe that their experiences with Mediterranean culture consisted of mispronouncing the names of cocktails in an all-inclusive resort. Embracing a kind of bawdy slapstick humor, the show depicted tourists to Benidorm as intent on having a good time while losing sobriety and dignity. Yet a growing number of British transplants in Spain, who began buying property in the 1980s and visiting the country regularly, recognized the depiction of a debauched tourism culture but were not amused by it. For many, the democratization of tourism had oversaturated desirable areas, and along with it an ethos of escape had morphed into reckless revelry and abandon. It also undermined the property values of their vacation homes.

Citizens of affluent countries increasingly saw tourism as a universal right for all classes, not a privilege. As the UN World Tourism Organization put it in 1982: "The right to rest, a natural consequence of the right to work, must be affirmed as a fundamental right in terms of human happiness. It implicitly entails the right to the use of leisure time and, in particular, the broadest possible access to holidays."[30] But greater access to leisure in Europe was not seen as a universally good thing by more affluent second home owners. They had been enjoying Mediterranean Spain for years and did not appreciate such boisterous company. As a Norwegian home owner in her midsixties told me after I announced my plans to drive to Benidorm from her luxurious coastal home: "Why are you going there? It's for the shit people. The British tattoo people, who come here on €9 Ryanair flights."

Mass tourism, even with its detractors and problems, did aid in cementing the notion in the European psyche, present since the 1970s, of Spain as a land of vacations, good weather, and parties. This cliché persisted in contemporary associations and pop-culture references in the second decade of the twenty-first century, from the conflation of Ibiza with electronic music and drug-fueled all-night parties to the overstated sensuality of Spanish holidays present in the Woody Allen film *Vicky Cristina Barcelona*. Behind the successful evolution of Spain's post-Franco nation branding lay another more pernicious characterization: that of a national idleness, lack of seriousness, and what travelers or foreign residents casually dubbed the "mañana mentality."[31] As a middle-aged Spanish acquaintance in Madrid remembered: "In the 1980s, everyone loved to come here. They would drink with us, sing with us, spend all summer . . . but doing business with us . . . that was different." Indeed, by the 1980s, as in many places with strong mass tourism economies, Spanish politicians, economists, and business elites had to ask themselves how they could progress beyond "sun and fun" package tourism and how the national economy could move beyond tourism altogether.

From Visiting to Staying: The Rise of Residential Tourism

Despite the fact that Spain was increasingly known for improving its tourism industry by introducing arts and culture as major draws for visitors, that was not the main direction of the market. Nor was it the source of the thriving construction industry associated with coastal tourism. Rather, while Spain was marketing itself to the rest of Europe with images of Sagrada Família, Joan Miró, and the "kitchen science" marvels found in Ferran Adriá's restaurant El Bulli, one of the real growth sectors was the second home and retirement abroad markets. The second home market clearly delineated Northern and Southern Europe because it internationalized the real estate sector while also leaving much of the housing stock empty for long periods of the year. To put this market in perspective, 17 percent of the housing stock in Spain and Portugal was second homes by the early 2000s, compared with just 3.5 percent in the rest of the EU countries.[32] These communities were often very skewed in age and income when compared with nearby Spanish communities (both being much higher). This was particularly true in Valencia, where cities such as Calpe and Torrevieja grew dramatically and shifted from tourism to residential tourism. The latter was a term used to denote the proliferation of second home buyers in warmer coastal regions who spend part of the year in their secondary residence and sometimes transform it into a primary residence for retirement.[33] The trend was facilitated by cheap prices that led Northern Europeans to buy Spanish real estate as investment properties to be rented and sporadically used.

Under the conservative government of José María Aznar, land use laws were significantly reformed in 1998, enabling new developments to be built on virgin and formerly agricultural lands away from existing cities and villages. This allowed for dramatic investment in vast tracts of new homes. Previously, the urban logic in the Costa Blanca had been to keep all development within existing urbanized areas (whether suburbs or densely built villages) to limit sprawl and preserve the country-side. To the displeasure of many urban planners and the elation of developers, who bought land cheap and sold parcels to foreign buyers (sometimes sight unseen), the business-oriented Aznar government eschewed this template. The new law (Ley de Suelo) reversed the burden of proof for rural construction from real estate investors, who previously had to show that a site was developable, to municipalities and conservationists. Those seeking to limit growth now had to contend with a law that proclaimed all land as buildable unless proved otherwise. As expected, many cities were more than happy to receive the jobs and tax revenue from new and significantly wealthier foreign inhabitants. UK residents, in particular, spurred by low prices and an existing relationship with the Costa Blanca from frequent visits, began buying property in the booming Spanish property market as an investment to "cash in on" the future. That contributed to the phenomenon, popular from 2000 until 2008, called "buying on plan," in which developers would propose a project and various investors would sell each unit several times before the first resident owner turned the key in the lock. This selling on plan was particularly popular for Spanish buyers who wished to enter the market before residential tourists and who often operated on systems of local contacts: apartments passed from builders to their friends to residential tourism agencies to foreign buyers themselves.

While Spanish laws facilitated vast amounts of growth for residential tourism, the social transformation of local villages did not necessarily follow. To be sure, as residential tourism grew, mixed communities of new *urbanizaciónes* emerged in which previously rural Spanish village residents were surrounded by suburbs of Northern European retirees. International political economic circumstances helped boost this trend: the EU's cohesion policy normalized property ownership laws across borders and minimized legal procedures for purchasing property in other EU member states. The introduction of the euro in 2001 also allowed for a dramatic uptick in foreign home ownership and lower lending rates for mortgages. Additionally, the rhetoric of EU policy proclaimed a "single Europe," which helped to mitigate some of the more pernicious aspects of residential tourism. While locals continued to regard residential tourists in coastal Spain as wealthy *guiris* (a colloquial and slightly derogatory term referring to foreigners and often bringing to mind the image of a sunburned tourist in flip-flops), they were increasingly accepted as a part of life. What's more, with the increase in salaries in Spain during the 1990s, many Spaniards had joined the tourist community, themselves visiting wealthier Northern countries. The experience of being tourists helped to counteract the feeling that some places are visited and others places produce visitors. The sense of unidirectional travel was particularly eroded by the Erasmus study abroad programs, operated through the EU, which sent many Spanish students abroad, often to acquire linguistic skills to be used for jobs in the flourishing tourism industry at home.

Finally, residential tourism did not represent the new face of a "greener" and more sophisticated Spanish cultural tourism. Rather, it had deleterious environmental effects implicit in tearing up formerly rural lands. The settlement of foreigners, however, did help to cast the tourism economy as an essential component of European cosmopolitanism.[34] The international mixing that occurred in real estate markets, while transactional, was seen by EU policy makers as a positive sign of more people living transnational lives in the EU, never mind that many resident tourists lived in special enclaves and never learned Spanish.[35] For Abelardo, a former urban planner turned real estate developer in Valencia, second homes were a cutting-edge economic maturation of the tourism market as well as a sign of Spain's successful opening to the rest of Europe since Franco's death in 1975. According to Abelardo: "We couldn't keep this place just for ourselves; some people wanted to. . . . No one would just grow oranges with these beautiful lands today. We used to, but now, that's just ridiculous." He continued, saying that he thought foreign residents had transformed the Valencia region by making things more international and a bit more cosmopolitan: "People are here from all over Europe today. Say 'Alicante' to someone in Dubai and they will know where that is." Yet others were not so sure about the evolution of tourism, particularly after the devastating crash in property markets in 2008, which left millions of homes in Spain empty and stripped away years of increases in the value of lands and homes. Teresa, a worker in a hair salon in Valencia, was less positive about the long-term benefits of tourism: "I see a lot of foreigners here when times are good, and they built all those houses for them. . . . But these people have a lot of money, and they have seen how things are going. They can leave whenever they want, and those houses will be empty. . . . Most of them already are."

The Tourism Ladder

The reputational decline of Benidorm demonstrates the vicissitudes of coastal tourism. Some locations are eventual victims of their own popularity through global trends and, more importantly, due to environmental degradation. But it also shows the maturation of Valencia and Spain's overall coastal tourism market into a more variegated sector. Spain's tourism industry grew to the third largest in the world in the 1980s (after France and the United States), thanks mostly to a surge in "fly and flop" tourism that marketed low-cost beach vacations to Northern Europeans. While those in the tourism industry increasingly saw this type of vacation as a working-class holiday, in contrast to more individuated middle-class and upper-class vacations, it was profitable and did not lead to major social conflict between visitors and locals. Many people in the region benefited, even those who simply sold agricultural lands. Juan Fernando and his son Miguel, natives of a small town near Alicante, explain the cultural change succinctly. As Juan Fernando says, "There was one major occupation in this region before tourism, and that was farming; that's what I did and what every man in my family did . . . since forever." He explains how he and Miguel eventually decided to sell their land to real estate developers from Valencia in the early 1990s. They discussed the change as a family, and Miguel, who was the youngest son, agreed to go to school for tourism management, something his family could better support with the sale of their land. Juan Fernando smiles at me and points to Miguel: "And you can ask him if that was the right choice, or if he would rather be a farmer today. . . . Go ahead, ask him. . . . You can ask him in English, French, or German."

By the early 1990s, the tourism market in Spain had become a major part of the national economy and had followed two distinct trajectories from its origins in budget package tourism. Cultural tourism aimed at wealthier and older travelers was pursued by municipalities seeking more revenue from fewer visitors. Residential tourism of both second and retirement homes was invested in by more rural municipalities where Northern Europeans went in search of cheap property deals and abundant sunshine. The regional governments of Catalonia, Valencia, Andalusia, and the Basque Country aggressively experimented with these two new "rungs" on the tourism ladder, using special marketing campaigns, tax breaks, and infrastructure funds. Now that Spain's economy had become synonymous with tourism, politicians and entrepreneurs hoped to demonstrate that this industry both was robust and could innovate and create new markets. One of the key goals of the Valencia region was to harness the income from beach tourism and direct some of the cash flow toward more sustainable tourism such as heritage, culinary, or arts tourism. That had long been the ideal progression of tourism-oriented regional economies. Often the model did not function in practice though, because developers focused on the bottom line and increased capacity, while natural resources were degraded by improper infrastructure and pollution. The country's tourism industry, in its second great boom during the 1990s, did not want Spain to end up a has-been destination, marred by ecological oversights and uncreative resort operators. Global tourism firms hailed the era from the Barcelona Olympics of 1992 to the completion of Calatrava's City of Arts and Sciences in Valencia (just before the 2008 financial crisis), as one of the all-time tourism success stories and a model of economic development. The reality is quite a bit more complex.

The announcement that Barcelona would host the 1992 summer Olympics was made in October 1986, just ten months after Spain was admitted to the European Community. The next ten years of tourism development would radically change the image of the country to the European Community from an inexpensive haven of sun and cheap drinks to a cultural powerhouse for arts, architecture, and cuisine.

Barcelona's urban renewal program, which centered on the Olympics, became the gold standard of mega-events, enlivening the competition among host cities for a generation.[36] That same year, Seville hosted the World Expo. Five years later, King Juan Carlos I opened the doors to the Guggenheim Museum in Bilbao. The museum became the first franchise of the New York brand and a paradigmatic example of postindustrial rebirth for a city and a region that had suffered divestment in its manufacturing industry for decades. Spain's embrace of cultural tourism, including the success of the kitchen science gastronomy movement, new art museums, and heritage tourism, signified the country's economic and cultural ascent during the period of democratization. It was additionally a sign that the redistributive North-South programs of the EU were helping to integrate Europe and alleviate regional economic disparities. Sara, a middle-aged tourism promoter, noted in English: "[The image of Spain was] dramatically aided by culture . . . not necessarily our classical culture but new things that were made possible by a different attitude toward cultural production after Franco. . . . It was no accident that this happened after 1975; before, it would have been impossible, almost subversive."

In the realm of urban development, both the "Bilbao effect" of remedying deindustrialization and the "Barcelona phenomenon" of bringing tourists for cultural trips promised a lighter ecological footprint despite their emphases on mega-events and new constructions. Yet that was not the case. The popularity of cultural tourism actually helped spur even more construction, and the two went hand in hand. Culture, heritage, and gastronomic tours were the public face of a world-renowned economic transformation, while resorts and suburban enclaves of second homes were the perpetually important economic engine behind an economy that, by 2000, relied on tourism for 15 percent of the gross domestic product.[37] By the early 2000s, the "Spanish model" of development was a mixture of highbrow architectural projects often funded by EU and Spanish development grants. They helped keep a massive property market centered in major cities and coastal tourism regions afloat. Yet many critics of the tremendous urbanization that occurred in the aught years argue that cultural projects, such as opera houses, museums, and rail infrastructure, were often not needed by locals. Rather, while incurring millions of euros in debt, these projects represented the state's attempt to spend in order to sustain an overheated property market and postpone a crash.[38]

In just a decade (1997–2007), Spain built 5.3 million new homes. While construction started on 210,000 new homes in 1997, in 2006 almost 700,000 home constructions were initiated.[39] Yet, before the 2008 crisis, few Spaniards feared overdevelopment as an environmental or economic danger. Tourism professionals around the world regarded Spanish tourism, along with the booming construction industry, as the industry standout. The beautiful structures erected in the early 2000s, such as Calatrava's dramatic riverbed park in Valencia, resonated with many in other regions who were looking for development plans that stressed tourism and leisure. Development advocates saw large amounts of public funding as a governmental commitment to the maturation of the tourism industry and a sign that the industry, with proper stewardship, could transcend some of the more nefarious aspects of mass tourism. During the same years that the city of Valencia built Calatrava's arts-focused tourism project, it also invested billions in a Formula 1 track and a yacht-racing port for the America's Cup. Such developments entered the city firmly into the global competition to attract mega-events, but did so at great public cost and debatable long-term public gain.

In the years following the 2008 crisis, Valencia fell off the tourism ladder: while the number of visitors did not diminish, the city developed one of the worst debt ratings in Spain, and between 2010 and 2016 youth unemployment stubbornly remained at 50 percent. The ability of tourism to provide a means to attract other useful economic sectors seemed, to many in the city, chimerical. The only industry that the tourism economy stimulated in the Costa Blanca was construction, but it too stalled with hundreds of thousands of empty homes and an unused airport in the nearby city of Castellón de la Plana (which cost almost €1 billion). Even more infuriating for Spaniards suffering from continued economic crisis and austerity were political revelations about the construction industry after 2008: the entire regional government of Valencia was implicated in widespread corruption, and Spain's former national treasurer, Luís Bárcenas, was tried for distributing envelopes of cash from construction companies to top-level politicians (including the former mayor of Valencia).[40] These outrages, however, affected local political culture and tourism: support rose for new and populist political parties, most notably the left-wing Podemos movement, but with widespread anger over the real estate industry's role in the 2008 financial crisis, public support for tourism as a major way forward for an entire region plummeted.

While visitors once signified the end of the Franco era and the unification of Europe, Spaniards began to question the emphasis on construction and tourism within the Spanish economy. In the 1990s, tourism seemed to herald a new, more connected Europe in which those from the EU core would first visit the Mediterranean South, but the financial benefits of these visits would also enable those in Spain, Portugal, and Greece to vacation in Amsterdam or London. But after the 2008 collapse, increasing numbers of people blamed the political economy of EU integration as milking poorer countries while using public loans to lavishly fund private construction companies building infrastructure. Since the 2008 crisis, the distance between those working in the tourism industry and foreign guests seemed greater than ever, especially as South-North labor migration reached its highest volume in a generation. More dramatically, the cultural distance between hosts and guests was exacerbated by the replacement of the Mediterranean ideal of "relaxation" and "pleasure" (as in the days of Club Med) with the new geographical denomination of the "PIGS" (Portugal, Ireland, Greece, and Spain) countries. This turned the romanticized image of the Mediterranean into a cultural barb that divided Europe between debtors and creditors and, in many people's minds, between "serious and industrious" Northern Europe and the perpetually vacationing South, where it is assumed that people shirk their debts and lack a proper work ethic. The intensification of North-South regionalism may not have actually affected the bottom line of Costa Blanca tourism, but it irrevocably changed the notion of that industry as a means of social and economic betterment that symbolized democratization and European cohesion. In its wake, it left behind—much like the entire EU project of "social Europe"—only the hangover of grand hopes.

Max Holleran is lecturer in sociology at the University of Melbourne. His work focuses on European Union politics, urban planning, and postsocialist Eastern Europe. His essays have appeared in academic journals as well as in *Dissent, Public Books, Boston Review*, and *New Republic*.

Notes

All translations from Spanish to English are my own.

1.   Rojek, *Decentring Leisure.*
2.   Hoffman, Fainstein, and Judd, *Cities and Visitors.*
3.   Pavlović, *Despotic Bodies and Transgressive Bodies.*
4.   Greenpeace España, "Destrucción a toda costa 2013."
5.   Bakić-Hayden, "Nesting Orientalisms."
6.   Urry and Larsen, *Tourist Gaze 3.0.*
7.   Degen and García, "Transformation of the 'Barcelona Model.'"
8.   Anderson, *New Old World.*
9.   López and Rodríguez, "Spanish Model."
10. Salazar and Graburn, *Tourism Imaginaries.*
11. Christaller, "Some Considerations of Tourism Location."
12. Charnon-Deutsch, *Spanish Gypsy.*
13. Urbain, *At the Beach.*
14. Nunez, "Tourism, Tradition, and Acculturation."
15. Chambers, *Mediterranean Crossings.*
16. Wallerstein, *Modern World-System I.*
17. Urry and Larsen, *Tourist Gaze 3.0.*
18. Said, *Culture and Imperialism.*
19. Prados de la Escosura, Rosés, and Sanz-Villarroya, "Economic Reforms and Growth."
20. Pellejero Martínez, *Historia de la economía de turismo en España.*
21. Ibid.
22. Moreno, *Federalization of Spain.*
23. Gracia and Carnicer, *España de Franco.*
24. Martín García, *Explosión urbana del litoral.*
25. Urbain, *At the Beach,* 138.
26. Ivars i Baidal, Sánchez, and Rebollo, "Evolution of Mass Tourism Destinations,"
27. Shields, *Places on the Margin.*
28. Pavlović, *Despotic Bodies and Transgressive Bodies.*
29. Linz and Stepan, *Problems of Democratic Transition and Consolidation.*
30. U.N. World Tourism Organization. 1982. Acapulco Document. www.e-unwto.org/content

/q140770m63621034/fulltext.pdf
31. Aronczyk, *Branding the Nation.*
32. Allen et al., *Housing and Welfare in Southern Europe.*
33. O'Reilly, *British on the Costa del Sol.*
34. Beck and Grande, *Cosmopolitan Europe.*
35. O'Reilly, *British on the Costa del Sol.*
36. González, "Bilbao and Barcelona."
37. World Travel and Tourism Council, *Travel and Tourism.*
38. García, "Breakdown of the Spanish Urban Growth Model."
39. Meliveo, "Tax Incentives and the Housing Bubble: the Spanish Case."
40. Garzón, *Fango.*

References

Allen, Judith, James Barlow, Jesús Leal, Thomas Maloutas, and Liliana Padovani. 2004. *Housing and Welfare in Southern Europe.* Oxford, UK: Blackwell.

Anderson, Perry. 2009. *The New Old World.* London: Verso.

Aronczyk, Melissa. 2013. *Branding the Nation: The Global Business of National Identity.* New York: Oxford University Press.

Bakić-Hayden, Milica. 1995. "Nesting Orientalisms: The Case of Former Yugoslavia." *Slavic Review* 54, no. 4: 917–31.

Beck, Ulrich, and Edgar Grande. 2007. *Cosmopolitan Europe.* Cambridge, UK: Polity.

Chambers, Iain. 2008. *Mediterranean Crossings: The Politics of an Interrupted Modernity.* Durham, NC: Duke University Press.

Charnon-Deutsch, Lou. 2004. *The Spanish Gypsy: The History of a European Obsession.* University Park: Pennsylvania State University Press.

Christaller, Walter. 1964. "Some Considerations of Tourism Location in Europe: The Peripheral Regions—Underdeveloped Countries—Recreation Areas." *Papers in Regional Science* 12, no. 1: 95–105.

Degen, Mónica, and Marisol García. 2012. "The Transformation of the 'Barcelona Model': An Analysis of Culture, Urban Regeneration, and Governance." *International Journal of Urban and Regional Research* 36, no. 5: 1022–38.

García, Marisol. 2010. "The Breakdown of the Spanish Urban Growth Model: Social and Territorial Effects of the Global Crisis." *International Journal of Urban and Regional Research* 34, no. 4: 967–80.

Garzón, Baltasar. 2015. *El fango: Cuarenta años de corrupción en España.* Barcelona: Debate.

González, Sara. 2011. "Bilbao and Barcelona 'in Motion': How Urban Regeneration 'Models' Travel and Mutate in the Global Flows of Policy Tourism." *Urban Studies* 48, no. 7: 1397–1418.

Gracia, Jordi, and Miguel Ángel Ruiz Carnicer. 2001. *La España de Franco.* Madrid: Sintesis.

Greenpeace España. 2013. "Destrucción a toda costa 2013: Análisis del litoral a escala municipal." Madrid: Greenpeace España. www.greenpeace.org/espana/Global/espana/report/costas/DTC%202013.pdf.

Hoffman, Lily M., Susan S. Fainstein, and Dennis R. Judd. 2003. *Cities and Visitors: Regulating People, Markets, and City Space.* Malden, MA: Blackwell.

Ivars i Baidal, Josep A., Isabel Rodríguez Sánchez, and José Fernando Vera Rebollo. 2013. "The Evolution of Mass Tourism Destinations: New Approaches beyond Deterministic Models in Benidorm (Spain)." *Tourism Management* 34: 184–95.

Linz, Juan J., and Alfred Stepan. 1996. *Problems of Democratic Transition and Consolidation:*

Southern Europe, South America, and Post-Communist Europe. Baltimore: Johns Hopkins University Press.

López, Isidro, and Emmanuel Rodríguez. 2011. "The Spanish Model." *New Left Review*, no. 69: 5–29.

Martín García, Juan. 2010. *La explosión urbana del litoral*. Valencia, Spain: Publicacions de la Universitat de València.

Meliveo, Jorge. 2014. "Tax Incentives and the housing bubble: the Spanish Case. Universidad Complutense de Madrid Working Paper. https://www.ucm.es/data/cont/docs/518-2014-09 -25-TFG%20final%20Jorge%20Meliveo.pdf.

Moreno, Luis. 2013. *The Federalization of Spain*. New York: Routledge.

Nunez, Theron A., Jr. 1963. "Tourism, Tradition, and Acculturation: Weekendismo in a Mexican Village." *Ethnology* 2, no. 3: 347–52.

O'Reilly, Karen. 2000. *The British on the Costa del Sol*. New York: Routledge.

Pavlović, Tatjana. 2002. *Despotic Bodies and Transgressive Bodies: Spanish Culture from Francisco Franco to Jesús Franco*. Albany: State University of New York Press.

Pellejero Martínez, Carmelo. 1999. *Historia de la economía del turismo en España*. Madrid: Civitas Ediciones.

Prados de la Escosura, Leandro, Joan R. Rosés, and Isabel Sanz-Villarroya. 2012. "Economic Reforms and Growth in Franco's Spain." *Revista de historia económica* 30, no. 1: 45–89.

Rojek, Chris. 1995. *Decentring Leisure: Rethinking Leisure Theory*. London: Sage.

Said, Edward W. 1994. *Culture and Imperialism*. New York: Vintage Books.

Salazar, Noel B., and Nelson H. H. Graburn, eds. 2016. *Tourism Imaginaries: Anthropological Approaches*. New York: Berghahn Books.

Shields, Rob. 2013. *Places on the Margin: Alternative Geographies of Modernity*. New York: Routledge.

United Nations World Tourism Organization 1982 Acapulco Conference Document. http://www.e-unwto.org/doi/pdf/10.18111/unwtodeclarations.1982.8.4.1. Accessed April 19, 2017.

Urbain, Jean-Didier. 2003. *At the Beach*. Minneapolis: University of Minnesota Press.

Wallerstein, Immanuel. 2011. *The Modern World-System I: Capitalist Agriculture and the Origins of the European World-Economy in the Sixteenth Century*. Berkeley: University of California Press.

World Travel and Tourism Council. 2014. *Travel and Tourism Economic Impact 2015: Spain*. London: World Travel and Tourism Council. www.wttc.org/-/media/files/reports/economic %20impact%20research/country%20reports/spain2014.pdf.

Detroit Is Closer than You Think

Rebecca J. Kinney

Every time I walk into the Shinola Detroit flagship store, in the heart of the city's rebranded "Midtown" neighborhood, my first ritual is trying on the watch that I find so lovely but cannot conceive of purchasing.[1] I then scan the shelves for whatever new book on Detroit's architecture is featured in the revolving and evolving collection of art books. I have been known to buy a beautifully crafted latte from the café and tuck into the comfortable couches to page through Albert Kahn's and Minoru Yamasaki's Detroit or Mies van der Rohe's Lafayette Park—escaping into the vision of twentieth-century Detroit crafted by these architects of the modern city. It is from this same vantage point that I have noted the unmarked luxury tour buses dropping off tourist groups on West Canfield Street and idling along Cass Avenue until the appointed pickup time. As tourist consumers, who come in groups via tour bus, or, like myself, singly, and by car from Metro Detroit, where exactly are we arriving? More than a coffee shop, a lifestyle store, or a staged production tour, Shinola is selling Detroit. Which begs the question: When Shinola sells us Detroit, what are we buying?

You Don't Know Shit from Shinola or Detroit from Texas

In 2011 the Bedrock Manufacturing Company, a Texas-based investment firm headed by the founder of Fossil, opened a watch-building facility in Detroit. The announcement by Shinola Detroit of this new venture leaned heavily on the narrative of bringing jobs back to a city historically motored by its workers. Fast-forward five years and the corporate brand has gone global. As of this writing, its products are featured in 998 stores throughout North America and Europe. One of the

Radical History Review
Issue 129 (October 2017)   DOI 10.1215/01636545-3920739
© 2017 by MARHO: The Radical Historians' Organization, Inc.

conversations I have most often with people interested in Shinola Detroit is about the significance of its name. People ask: Is Shinola a reference to a specific Detroit-based location or neighborhood? What are the company's local ties to the city? In truth: there are none. Numerous articles in the business press have outlined the brief history of Shinola's move to Detroit. The parent company of luxury goods producer and watchmaker Shinola Detroit, Bedrock Corporations, chose to relocate from Texas to Detroit because of the resonance of the brand in the city.[2] Shinola's creative director, Daniel Caudill, commented in a 2013 *Fortune* article: "We wanted people to respond to the integrity of the

Figure 1. Shinola Detroit, Midtown Detroit flagship store, September 2016. Photo by the author

brand. 'Made in America' is a little generic, it's overused."[3] But Detroit, as the company plays up in its personal story, evokes the storied past of the industrial worker in a once-great American city, and it insists that Detroit, and American manufacturing, is not just a part of history but part of the future.[4] For the founder, Made in Detroit evokes a rich industrial past and history, much more compelling and specific than Made in America. Shinola is not the first to use this nostalgic notion of Detroit in a successful branding campaign; most notably, Chrysler used it in its award-winning 2011–14 Imported from Detroit campaign.

As for the name Shinola itself, the company purchased the corporate naming rights from a defunct twentieth-century shoe polish company in 2011. Along with the name, Shinola Detroit was also cashing in on the colloquialism "You don't know shit from Shinola."[5] The saying entered American vernacular, according to popular lore, when a World War II–era GI polishing his commander's boots commented that the officer "wouldn't know shit from Shinola." In this way, the name itself suggests an antiauthoritarian and down-to-earth type of knowledge—the gritty and working-class know-how that this phrase's origin story suggests. It should not be lost that this authentically American phrase gestures back to both a time and a place of imagined and idealized American "greatness."

By focusing on Shinola Detroit's corporate narrative, I offer a way to see the links between the tourist gaze, city branding, and development in the neoliberal city. The experiences that Shinola Detroit provides for its tourist consumers rely on framings of history, location, and labor as key pieces of the brand. This echoes the experience of Dean MacCannell's postindustrial "tourist" who makes "a fetish of the work of others" as a way to understand a shift in class and labor practices. For MacCannell, as the "dirty" jobs of industry become further removed from "modern" society, the sightseeing practices of the tourist are a way to understand the differentiation of social structure.[6] While at first glance Shinola Detroit may not appear to be part of a "tourist" experience, the September 2016 announcement that the "Shinola Hotel"—a joint venture between the eponymous company and billionaire Detroit developer Dan Gilbert's Bedrock Real Estate—will open in fall 2018 crystallizes the relationship between branding, real estate development, and tourism as key features in the development of the neoliberal city. This essay situates corporations such as Shinola Detroit as essential to doing the work of selling the neoliberal city, setting up Detroit as desirable by a reliance on a "tourist gaze." John Urry and Jonas Larsen suggest that the "tourist gaze," while not static over time and not universal because it is bound up in class, gender, ethnicity, and age, relies on the idea of "a departure," a "limited breaking with established routines and practices of everyday life."[7] By focusing on Shinola Detroit, I argue that the evocative branding of its products as an extension of Detroit relies on a tourist gaze, a way for tourist consumers to experience the city through local stores, via virtual factory tours, and, of course, by purchasing the luxury watches, bicycles, leather goods, turntables, and jewelry that Shinola "makes."[8] Centrally, I explore how the luxury goods that Shinola offers for sale are less about the product and more about their association with a nostalgic vision of Detroit—a space of "authentic" blackness, working-class credibility, and grittiness—beautifully produced and captured through an Instagrammable filter.

"Detroit Is Closer than You Think": Branding and Selling Detroit

I spent most of summer 2016 in Chicago, approximately three hundred miles west of Canfield and Cass. However, Shinola, in its store and product e-mails, would close its weekly communication with a friendly reminder that "Detroit is closer than you think" and point me to its Chicago store in Wicker Park / Bucktown.[9] As someone for whom Metro Detroit is "home," this suggestion that "Detroit is closer than you think" elicited in me a brief emotional response. What part and piece of Detroit could I experience if I headed to the Wicker Park / Bucktown store?

As these tidbits of latest and greatest products and employee features were digitally dropped into my in-box, I couldn't help but see the connections between Shinola Detroit's marketing and the Pure Michigan tourism ad, "Detroit Soul," that also ran during summer 2016 throughout the region. Although the award-winning state-funded Pure Michigan campaign has existed for ten years, the "Detroit Soul" ad was the first time in a decade that there was a dedicated Detroit commercial. Not only that, it has been decades since Detroit was a central feature in the state's tourism advertising. My archival research has not yet unearthed a "smoking gun" letter that talks about a formal policy of ignoring Detroit. However, by reading the archive of tourism ephemera, such as brochures, tourist maps, and even the locations of rental car agencies, it is abundantly clear that from the 1970s through the 1990s most of the promotional material steered tourists out of Detroit and into destinations in the western and northern suburbs.[10] As a scholar of Detroit familiar with the well-documented division between the city and its metropolitan suburbs predicated on racially exclusive suburban development, wherein white suburbanization was subsidized by public funding in the form of federally and state-subsidized development of roads, sewerage systems, and highways as an intentional strategy of *distancing* Metro Detroit from the city itself, and as someone who grew up in Metro Detroit during the 1980s and 1990s where this division between Metro Detroit and Detroit was palpable, this shift in suggesting that Detroit is *closer* represents a complete 180-degree turn in the ideological narrative of Detroit. After decades of intentionally distancing Detroit from the rest of the region, the state, and the nation, the emphasis on the "closeness" of Detroit is a radical shift for both Pure Michigan and the branding of the city as a whole. Although the end goals of Shinola Detroit and Pure Michigan are different—buy our stuff versus visit our city (and buy our stuff)—the rhetorical strategy of selling a version of Detroit is similar. As I suggest elsewhere, this narrative of Detroit on the rise is part of the longer cycle of the standard Detroit narrative of rise, fall, rise, where the moments of rise, although tied to population logics of whiteness, are deemed "not about race" and the moment of fall, deeply linked to black population growth, is narrated as "about race."[11]

Increasingly, the tourism narrative of Detroit, which is sold as earnestly to metropolitan Detroiters as it is to regional, national, and international travelers, is coded by both the placement of the articles and the accompanying imagery—that Detroit is "safe" to visit and hip and happening, most frequently rendered by accompanying images of white hipsters and middle-class black people partaking in the life of the city.[12] Indeed, this story is so readily familiar that there are likely very few people who have not seen a travel article on the resurgent city or clicked through a photo gallery of Detroit's "top ten things to do."[13] In this way, whether from ten miles outside the city or from a computer screen half a world away, the visual understanding of "looking" at Detroit through a tourist gaze is one that is readily comprehended. As a Metro Detroiter—and given that so many of the actual on-the-ground "tourists" at places such as Shinola Detroit are indeed Metro Detroiters—I am careful to point to this difference in geographical origin. When, for so long, the metro region has purposefully distanced itself spatially and psychically from the city of Detroit, the resurgent claiming of "Detroit on the rise" by Metro Detroiters without acknowledging the racial logics of capitalism and uneven development that created the twenty-first-century context of development in Detroit reproduces the invisibility of institutional racism in the city's twentieth- and twenty-first-century growth. For me, this is the palpable tension that arises when I'm both tourist and researcher in the "work display" that Shinola has created.

Shinola Detroit's flagship store is located on West Canfield Street between Cass and Second Avenues in the heart of the newly branded Midtown neighborhood. Before the rebranding of place, this neighborhood was widely known as the Cass Corridor throughout the 1970s, 1980s, and 1990s. During the last quarter of the twentieth century, the Cass Corridor was intentionally developed as a neighborhood of last resort, with treatment facilities and homeless shelters for the addicted and transient. The history of this location as a place of willful disinvestment by local government and property owners cannot be lost here, as that is the historical context for the massive amounts of development ushered in by the rebranding of the neighborhood in the late 2000s and early 2010s. Jason Hackworth argues that the gentrification of the neoliberal city relies less on the "hearty individual," as corporate participation is no longer the sign of the completion of gentrification but is increasingly the first sign of development.[14] In this model of gentrification, the changes are happening in areas of "second-wave" gentrification, post-1990s, where in many cases these are the neighborhoods that were considered, as Hackworth suggests, "ungentrifiable." And here I push the language and framework to clearly state that these locations deemed immune to gentrification were often the poorest and the blackest neighborhoods in a city. By pointing to this explicitly, I suggest that the very neighborhoods that emerged as the poorest and the most segregated in cities such as Detroit were created through the racially uneven process of capitalism. As this process of neoliberal gentrification takes hold, outsiders, whether from ten miles or half a world away, "discover" these locations that for decades were willfully underdeveloped— Cass Corridor, Detroit; Downtown Los Angeles (DTLA); Oakland, Brooklyn—these rebranded locations serve as a nod of "authentic" experience through reference as historical locations of working-class communities of color, at the same time these neighborhoods are being transformed by neoliberal gentrification.

Not lost on anyone paying attention, Midtown is a hinge neighborhood in the imagined unified makeover of Detroit stretching through Gilbert's billion-dollar takeover of downtown, Mike Ilitch's multimillion-dollar development of a hockey arena and "arena district," up through Midtown into the cultural centers of the Detroit Institute of Arts and Wayne State University, culminating in the speculative development well under way in Detroit's North End. It is not a coincidence that the highly anticipated M-1 Detroit streetcar line, which opened in May 2017, runs a 3.3-mile route that connects all of these locations. The M-1, now known as the QLine, is a perfect example of investment in the neoliberal city, wherein this streetcar, which takes up space in the public street and received a portion of its funding from public money, was primarily funded by private investors and, indeed, will primarily serve the business interests of those private investors.[15] The M-1 streetcar, rather than a public transportation option to serve a chunk of Detroit's massive 139-square-mile footprint, is intended for local and nonlocal Detroit tourist consumers—those frequenting the 5 percent area of Detroit that the line will serve. It is in this culture of investment and development of the 7.2-square-mile Greater Downtown Detroit neighborhoods that Shinola Detroit is right at home—contributing to and benefiting from the privatization, increasing property values, and skyrocketing rents.[16] Midtown is considered the "hottest" place in Detroit to live, work, and play.

Shinola fulfills the touristic desire for both experience and consumption in its flagship storeroom. Beyond its showroom space featuring its well-curated products are staged production areas for its bicycles and a glassed-off space that, in fall 2016, was adapted to feature the assembly of Shinola's new line of turntables. It is in these spaces that performances of work are staged for the tourist consumers' pleasure of experience. As MacCannell suggests in *The Tourist*, at the same time that tourists seek out an authentic experience, they do so in the context that the experience has been staged and performed for their gaze. As I weave my way through the Detroit flagship store, the showroom fills most of the space where bicycles and watches, leather goods and jewelry are tastefully displayed in island kiosks and attractive shelving (fig. 1). I leisurely finger the products, contemplate taking one of the bikes for a trial ride along West Canfield, and try on watches and leather purses, latte in hand. The backdrop to, or perhaps the main event of, this scene of leisurely consumption is the experience of a live in-store factory tour. The store full of beautiful objects is framed on either side by two distinct work areas—one for bicycle manufacturing and, as of October 30, 2016, one for turntable production.

Sealed behind an entire wall of glass, I watch alongside the other tourist consumers as a group of Shinola workers assemble the new Runwell Turntable (figs. 2 and 3). As we stand on one side of the glassed wall, the production area is fully visible. Workers sit at their uniform work stations, each assembling a turntable. On their side of the glass are shelves full of parts and finished turntables stacked up on metal bakery racks. On their side, a finished turntable sits in the middle of a glassed-off wall display. On our side, other objects that their unseen coworkers have assembled—leather goods, watches, jewelry—bump up directly to the glassed-off wall. As we watch workers assemble a product in full view—the staging of factory production as spectacle—this performance demands the question of what it means to labor under the gaze, both touristic and otherwise. For the tourist consumer, the question is not only what is the cost to those who labor, but what is the desire to "see" the backstage of production? An answer is found in Shinola's curated experience, as the company is able to literally suggest that the tourist consumer's purchase of a $2,500 turntable translates to jobs "on the line" for these workers.

Figures 2 and 3. Shinola Detroit, Midtown Detroit flagship store, November 2016. Photos by the author

Laboring under the gaze is something that has long been a part of working the line in Detroit. Early and mid-twentieth-century workers on the line were regularly surveilled by supervisors, company goons, and tourists. Among the most famous artistic representations of life on the line, Diego Rivera's *Detroit Industry* murals, completed in 1932–33, contain a representation of a factory tour in progress. The practice of "opening" the process of automobile manufacturing for tourists lives on today in the Ford Rouge Factory tour.[17] It is one of Metro Detroit's most popular tours, wherein visitors watch from elevated catwalks as workers complete final assembly of the Ford F-150 truck.[18] MacCannell situates the factory tour as "an attraction," a cultural production he calls a "work display," noting that "labor transforms raw materials into useful objects" and "modernity is transforming labor into cultural productions attended by tourists and sightseers."[19] What I find personally so uncomfortable about the "work displays" at both Ford and Shinola (I have participated in both as tourist and researcher) is how the labor of work is featured as part of the tourist consumer experience. For the price of entry, that is, a $17 ticket for the Ford Rouge tour, or a $5 latte, a $500 Shinola watch, or a $2,500 turntable for the Shinola experience, the labor of one person serves as another's spectacle and leisure. As a working-class Asian American woman who has been employed in a number of service jobs, including one where I made "twisted" pretzels in a Metro Detroit storefront window for a summer, the spectacle of work is definitely part of my discomfort, coupled with the firsthand knowledge that to labor under the tourist gaze means that some of those watching will throw things, knock on the glass, and shout disparaging comments while those who labor perform for their leisure. But what is most troubling is the way that Shinola uses this labor, and the idea of the ethical consumption of work, as its primary brand selling point.

Most of Shinola Detroit's consumers will never visit the Detroit flagship location. Rather, they will purchase products online, in one of a handful of its dedicated store locations throughout the country or in a retailer that features Shinola Detroit

Figure 4. Shinola website, October 2016, shinola.com

products. Therefore, I suggest that the tourist gaze that operates in the Detroit showroom extends to Shinola's online marketing and promotion. On Twitter, part of its prerelease of the Runwell Turntable was an announcement that the very production featured in figures 2 and 3 was up and running in advance of purchase. Potential tourist consumers who were unable to visit Detroit were invited to gaze upon the work and workers in an October 30, 2016, tweet that proclaimed that the turntable was "now being assembled in full view of the public," alongside an image of the production.[20]

Here the relationship between the produced consumable good and the consumption of the labor of production is rendered one and the same. This same narrative flows through "Shinola Detroit's Virtual Reality Tour with Luke Wilson," which allows any viewer with an Internet connection to take a four-minute "360 tour" through the company's production factory in New Center led by goofy guide Wilson.[21] For those who might not have a broadband connection, the splash pages on the company's website provide a static and stunningly clear view of what Shinola Detroit is selling (fig. 4).

Shinola's marketing campaign relies not on testimonials of products but on testimonials of a benevolent company providing jobs. Shinola sells their workers to sell their products. Figure 4 shows a website where page space is devoted not to Shinola products but to its corporate branding narrative: "There's a funny thing that happens when you build factories in this country. It's called jobs." As Shinola markets its products, it does so on the back of a narrative of ethical consumption. The consumption is not only about the purchase of a product—bicycle, watch, turntable—

but it is also an opportunity to consume identity. As Michael Serazio suggests, lifestyle chains "offer the consumer the chance to be simultaneously radical and bourgeois; to be absolved of moral ambivalence about personal wealth and elite status."[22] In the case of Shinola, the consumption is not only about "jobs" and creating a narrative of putting American workers to work (i.e., American Apparel) but also about putting specifically black Detroit workers to work, as is readily apparent in all of the company's marketing and promotion. In this way, the consumption can be read as ethical and also antiracist. In its heavy-handed emphasis on putting black Detroiters back to work, Shinola can rely on its narrative as being both an ethical company and, in particular, a racially benevolent company.

Shinola, with its savvy marketing, positions its products as secondary to its ethical model of selling life on the line. In its advertising copy, the company writes: "We're starting with the reinvigoration of a storied American brand, and a storied American city. Because we believe in the beauty of industry. The glory of manufacturing."[23] The selling of Detroit relies on narratives of the past retooled for the present that resolves the historic and forgets the continuing role of racism in creating racially uneven access to work, education, and housing in Detroit.[24] In the landscape of Detroit-branded tourism and marketing, Shinola is not alone in putting forth this narrative of Detroit—a return to a storied past, an imagined time of equal access to work on the line and access to the American dream.

Shinola Detroit is part of a larger trend of selling products by claiming place, an idea that Oliver Wang and I conceptualize as *neolocal* branding.[25] This term consciously recalls and updates Hal Rothman's notion of the *neonative*—"those who are attracted to the places that have become tourist towns because of the traits of these transformed places."[26] As Rothman suggests, the neonative creates an economic shift, one that is part of the "devil's bargain" of the tourism industry—as businesses and people seek to develop a tourism economy in a location precisely because of its "authenticity," this development in turn has a deleterious impact on existing local communities. Neolocal is intended to emphasize the movement of formerly nonlocal businesses and people into a community, where they establish themselves as "local" in order to position their services and products as part of an authentic local economy. The term *neolocal* echoes *neoliberal* in sound and significance: what is rendered as particular to a hip location (Detroit, DTLA, Oakland, Brooklyn, etc.) is actually part and parcel of the model of neoliberal gentrification that, as Hackworth suggests, is a process that is enacted at multiple scales.[27] Locations where the local coffee roaster, the neighborhood whisky distiller, and the community bike shop all coexist as prime examples of neolocal branding are also unsurprisingly the hallmarks of the redevelopment of the neoliberal city. In neolocal, we suggest that the overemphasis on the "local" in effect obscures the larger processes of capital in the neoliberal city. The suggestion that development by local companies—whether longtime residents or neolocals—is unilaterally positive reproduces a narrative of local authenticity as undisputedly "good" without considering the complex actors and capital in the "local" development of the neoliberal city.[28] Suggesting that a multinational corporation such as Shinola is "local" makes invisible the global capital and production that underwrites the neoliberal city.

As Shinola opens stores across the globe, the brand becomes a proxy location for the nostalgic ideal of Detroit work and workers. In thinking through the idea of the neolocal and Shinola's claim of neolocal credibility, that it is putting Detroit back to work through the creation of Detroit manufacturing jobs, one can see the continuing logic of MacCannell's notion in *The Tourist* that part of the desire of tourism is to escape from the banality of everyday life (work) by consuming another's labor as leisure. While the tourist consumers who purchase Shinola Detroit watches online or Shinola Detroit bicycles at the Tribeca flagship store in New York may never actually visit Detroit, they participate in the tourist consumption of the city. Thanks to Shinola Detroit's impeccably crafted marketing and branding narrative, these tourist consumers escape the bourgeois banality of everyday life by consuming the *idea* of black Detroit at work. In this, tourist consumers can experience Detroit, without ever leaving their homes.

As of this writing, beyond its flagship store in Midtown and its production location in New Center, Shinola's physical presence in Detroit is rather small in comparison to the holdings of real estate developers such as Dan Gilbert's Bedrock Real Estate and the Ilitch Family's Olympia Development, the two high-profile investors behind what John Gallagher, a veteran *Detroit Free Press* urban development and architecture reporter, considers the "peaceful" splitting of "one downtown, two empires" between these two local billionaires.[29] Yet Shinola's impact on crafting a global narrative of Detroit as a resurgent city is undisputable. Which brings us back to the opening question: When Shinola sells us Detroit, what are we buying? Shinola's own marketing narrative answers this question directly in a page devoted to "why open a watch factory in Detroit?": "The question isn't why you'd build a watch factory in Detroit, it's why you'd want to see American jobs go anywhere else. Through four Detroit winters, we've been working to bring manufacturing jobs back to Detroit and back to this country. We build our goods to last, but of all the things we make, American jobs might just be the thing we're most proud of."[30]

Shinola uses "Detroit" as proxy for an imagined return back to a time and place—one that was simultaneously simpler and more abundant. Yet Shinola, like others, comes to Detroit and relies on its primarily black population as a backdrop for selling its story of "putting workers back to work." As evidenced by the company's narrative, Shinola is creating no less than a resurgent community of American work and workers. In so many ways, this is the same populist narrative of American exceptionalism wherein America will be made great once again through corporate benevolence. In this way, Shinola is not selling us consumer goods but rather is selling us the chance to be part of a larger experience—it is letting us buy into the neoliberal city. When Shinola is selling us Detroit, it is selling us permission to be ethical consumers and partial owners of the revitalized black city, even as our consumption is pushing out these very same residents. This suggests, then, as a warning, that in neighborhoods in cities around the world, indeed, Detroit is closer than you think.

Rebecca J. Kinney is assistant professor in the School of Cultural and Critical Studies at Bowling Green State University. Her first book, *Beautiful Wasteland: The Rise of Detroit as America's Postindustrial Frontier* (2016), analyzes the centrality of race making in the contemporary narratives of urban decline and revitalization. As a scholar and teacher of ethnic studies and urban studies, she illuminates in her work the centrality of place, popular narratives, and culture as key sites of racial formation.

Notes

Thank you to Tania Jabour, Clayton Rosati, and the editors of this special issue for insightful comments and critiques on drafts of this essay.

1.   The Birdy, blue face in rose gold with the oxblood leather strap, $525, October 2016 pricing.
2.   Bedrock Corporations, also referred to as Bedrock Manufacturing, is a privately held company, founded by Tom Kartsotis. Kartsotis is also the founder of Fossil, known primarily for its namesake line of fashion watches. Shinola's parent company, Bedrock, is not to be confused with Dan Gilbert's subsidiary, Bedrock Real Estate.
3.   Quoted in VanderMey, "Think You Know Shinola?"
4.   Shinola, "Why Open a Watch Factory in Detroit?"
5.   Green, "Real Story behind the Detroit-Made Watch"; Klara, "How Shinola Went from Shoe Polish to the Coolest Brand."
6.   MacCannell, *Tourist*, 6–11.
7.   Urry and Larsen, *Tourist Gaze 3.0*, 3.
8.   Importantly, the company is careful to note that Shinola products are "built" rather than "made" in Detroit. Their Detroit production locations are for final assembly rather than manufacturing.
9.   During summer 2016, I lived in Chicago, and the closest store was always listed as Chicago's Damen Avenue location. By fall 2016, I was back in Bowling Green, Ohio, and the closest store was always listed as the Detroit flagship.
10. Kinney, "(Re)Branding Detroit."
11. Kinney, *Beautiful Wasteland*.
12. For a local version, see After 5 Detroit, "Our Story." The website's newsletter describes it as a place to get "young professionals" "more excited about living, working and playing in and around Detroit." For a national look, see Krigbaum, "Soul Food for a Hungry City." For an international look, see Baur, "Cycling Detroit."
13. See, e.g., Gray, "Detroit: Ten Things to Do"; Atlas Obscura, "Guide to Hidden Detroit"; *Detroit Metro Times*, "One Hundred Things All Detroiters Should Do."
14. Hackworth, *Neoliberal City*, 128.
15. The QLine was so named by major funder Quicken Loans, whose founder and chairman is none other than Gilbert. On the line's financing, see Shea, "Complex Funding."
16. See 7.2 SQ MI, "About."
17. For an excellent discussion of the historical role of the Ford tour from the twentieth century to the present, see Michael, "Labor on Display."

18. The Henry Ford, "Ford Rouge Factory Tour"; TripAdvisor, "Ford Rouge Factory Tour."
19. MacCannell, *Tourist*, 6, 36.
20. Shinola Audio, "Step 5: The Runwell Turntable."
21. Shinola, "Shinola Detroit's Virtual Reality Tour."
22. Serazio, "Ethos Groceries and Countercultural Appetites," 166.
23. Shinola, "Why Open a Watch Factory in Detroit?"
24. Kinney, *Beautiful Wasteland*.
25. This term owes intellectual debt to a conversation that Wang and I had about Hal Rothman via e-mail, September 28–29, 2016.
26. Rothman, *Devil's Bargains*, 11, 26–27.
27. Hackworth, *Neoliberal City*, 123–49.
28. This narrative of local authenticity can be seen most starkly in the playing up of the hometown roots of Detroit's two biggest developers—Gilbert and Ilitch.
29. Gallagher, "One Downtown, Two Empires."
30. Shinola, "Why Open a Watch Factory in Detroit?"

References

After 5 Detroit. 2016. "Our Story." http://after5detroit.com/about (accessed December 10, 2016).

Atlas Obscura. 2016. "The Atlas Obscura Guide to Hidden Detroit." www.atlasobscura.com /things-to-do/detroit-michigan (accessed December 10, 2016).

Baur, Joe. 2014. "Cycling Detroit Makes Too Much Sense to Ignore." BBC Travel, August 26. www.bbc.com/travel/story/20140821-cycling-detroit-makes-too-much-sense-to-ignore.

Detroit Metro Times. 2014. "One Hundred Things All Detroiters Should Do before They Die." January 28. www.metrotimes.com/detroit/100-things-all-detroiters-should-do-before-they -die/Content?oid=2144181.

Gallagher, John. 2014. "One Downtown, Two Empires." *Detroit Free Press*, July 27.

Gray, Steven. 2016. "Detroit: Ten Things to Do." *Time*, December 10, 2016. http://content.time .com/time/travel/cityguide/article/0,31489,1994456_1994357_1994238,00.html.

Green, Dennis. 2016. "The Real Story behind the Detroit-Made Watch Obama Just Gave to David Cameron." *Business Insider*, May 17. www.businessinsider.com/the-real-story -behind-shinola-detroit-2016-5.

Hackworth, Jason. 2013. *The Neoliberal City: Governance, Ideology, and Development in American Urbanism*. Ithaca, NY: Cornell University Press.

The Henry Ford. 2016. "Ford Rouge Factory Tour." www.thehenryford.org/visit/ford-rouge -factory-tour (accessed Decemmmber 10, 2016).

Kinney, Rebecca J. 2016. *Beautiful Wasteland: The Rise of Detroit as America's Postindustrial Frontier*. Minneapolis: University of Minnesota Press.

———. 2017. "(Re)Branding Detroit: Race and the New Frontier of Urban Tourism." Unpublished article.

Klara, Robert. 2015. "How Shinola Went from Shoe Polish to the Coolest Brand in America: Nobody's Confusing Shit with Shinola." *Adweek*, June 22. www.adweek.com/news /advertising-branding/how-shinola-went-shoe-polish-coolest-brand-america-165459.

Krigbaum, Megan. 2012. "Soul Food for a Hungry City." *Food and Wine*, June, 94–101.

MacCannell, Dean. 1999. *The Tourist: A New Theory of the Leisure Class*. Berkeley: University of California Press.

Michael, Wendy Lynette. 2014. "Labor on Display: Ford Factory Tours and the Romance of Globalized Deindustrialization." PhD diss., University of Michigan.

Rothman, Hal. 1998. *Devil's Bargains: Tourism in the Twentieth-Century American West*. Lawrence: University Press of Kansas.

Serazio, Michael. 2011. "Ethos Groceries and Countercultural Appetites: Consuming Memory in Whole Foods' Brand Utopia." *Journal of Popular Culture* 44, no. 1: 158–77.

7.2 SQ MI. 2013. "About." http://detroitsevenpointtwo.com (accessed July 1, 2014).

Shea, Bill. 2014. "Complex Funding Puts M-1 Rail on Right Track." *Crain's Detroit Business*, October 26, www.crainsdetroit.com/article/20141026/NEWS/310269949/complex-funding -puts-m-1-rail-on-right-track.

Shinola. 2016. "Why Open a Watch Factory in Detroit?" www.shinola.com/our-story/about -shinola (accessed November 1, 2016).

———. 2016. "Shinola Detroit's Virtual Reality Tour with Luke Wilson." Video, 4:32. www .shinola.com/vr-factory-tour (accessed November 1, 2016).

Shinola Audio. 2016. "Step 5: The Runwell Turntable." Twitter, October 30. https://twitter.com /ShinolaAudio/status/792800964285702144.

TripAdvisor. 2016. "Ford Rouge Factory Tour." www.tripadvisor.com/Attraction_Review -g42130-d534632-Reviews-Ford_Rouge_Factory_Tour-Dearborn_Michigan.html (accessed December 1, 2016).

Urry, John, and Jonas Larsen. 2011. *The Tourist Gaze 3.0*. London: Sage.

VanderMey, Anne. 2013. "Think You Know Shinola? Think Again." *Fortune*, July 9, http:// fortune.com/2013/07/09/think-you-know-shinola-think-again/ (accessed August 1, 2013).

Wars of Memory at Puʻuloa / Pearl Harbor

Vernadette Vicuña Gonzalez

The collaboration of two longtime demilitarization activists, Terri Kekoʻolani and Kyle Kajihiro, produced Detours, which provides alternative narratives of US military geographies on Oʻahu. The two first met in the mid-1990s, at the height of a resurgent Native Hawaiian sovereignty movement that had shifted its attention to the US military occupation of Hawaiʻi. Kekoʻolani first became actively involved in Hawaiʻi sovereignty politics through protests in the mid-1970s to demilitarize the island of Kahoʻolawe, which had been used by the United States Navy for live-fire exercises since World War II. She participated in one of the "landings" of Kānaka Maoli activists, timed to coincide with active bombing runs. As she puts it, that was a very different kind of "tour" of Hawaiʻi from the mass tourism that was ramping up in places like Waikīkī : "And then I saw all of the projectiles and all of . . . the devastation of bombing, sixty years of bombing the island, yeah . . . big tar pits and stuff like that. And so on the top of Moaʻula, Moaʻula, that's where the bombing practice was, right, I stood right there, and then I started bawling."[1] Naming this moment as a kind of initial detour that profoundly informed her subsequent activism, Kekoʻolani points out how Native Hawaiian political activism was profoundly geographical and inseparable from the land: "We started to make the linkages between Kahoʻolawe and Mākua [a military reservation on Oʻahu]." That is, while Mākua and other places occupied by the US military were not subject to the kind of dramatic bombing practices at work in Kahoʻolawe, the fact that, on Oʻahu, close to a quarter of the land was also under military control became a key sovereignty issue and continued to be so, even as the Kahoʻolawe protests registered success.[2] Doing work on Mākua and

Radical History Review
Issue 129 (October 2017) DOI 10.1215/01636545-3920751

other Oʻahu sites in the wake of Kahoʻolawe, Kekoʻolani and Kajihiro drew from the kind of educational "tour" that Kekoʻolani had participated in and merged it with similar efforts typified by solidarity tours elsewhere in the Pacific that they had both experienced.

In the two decades since their meeting, Kekoʻolani and Kajihiro have designed and offered an array of Detours tours, ranging from shorter visits focused on the overthrow of the Hawaiian monarchy at ʻIolani Palace and Pearl Harbor, on the leeward side of the island, to longer trips that encompass the windward side (where Bellows Air Force Station and Kaneohe Marine Corps Base are located); the center of the island (Schofield Barracks, Wheeler Army Airfield); and the far-west side (Mākua Military Reservation). While the vast landscape of militarization on Oʻahu has received Kekoʻolani's and Kajihiro's attention, Pearl Harbor, home to the United States Pacific Command, which oversees just over half the world's surface, garners special attention, primarily because it is the fulcrum of militarism in Hawaiʻi, as well as the central attraction of militourism on the islands. Kekoʻolani and Kajihiro recognized exactly just how powerful the mythology of Pearl Harbor is to the militarization of Hawaiʻi and its occupation by the United States, which operates to reframe this long history as one of protection and liberation. As Kajihiro puts it: "At one point we decided that at the heart of the issue is Puʻuloa, Pearl Harbor . . . and that we had to unlock that story and . . . explain how it has a grip on Hawaiʻi and our imagination of this place."[3]

The tour I take one sunny and warm Saturday morning illustrates the analytic power of the Detours tour. I arrive at the meeting place—a bus stop near the University of Hawaiʻi at Mānoa campus—to meet Kajihiro and Kekoʻolani. They gather the dozen or so people who have been milling around together and do introductions. Many are students at the university who are participating in the tour as part of a Native Hawaiian mentoring initiative. I am the lone professor, invited by the guides through activist and research networks around demilitarization. A few months earlier, I had participated in another Detours tour focused on the windward side of the island, sponsored by a local feminist organization. Because 22.4 percent of Oʻahu is militarized, there are many configurations for the Detours tours. The version of the tour planned for today is the most common and streamlined of the tours—encompassing four stops on the Honolulu side of the island: ʻIolani Palace, the residence of the former Kingdom of Hawaiʻi's monarchy and also the site of its overthrow; an overlook at Hālawa Heights, which hosts the headquarters of the United States Pacific Command and affords a view of Pearl Harbor; Pearl Harbor itself; and a small farm adjacent to the base. The group composition is typical for the Detours tours: it is geared as an educational tour with an eye to delving into the geography of militarization on Oʻahu.

I am most interested in how this Detours tour navigates the heavily ideological and nationalist narratives at Pearl Harbor. On the one hand, the narration of Pearl Harbor history—as both a national and a local wound—has become the foundation of the islands' matter-of-fact interpellation into the United States: in 1959 Hawai'i became the fiftieth state. The legacies of World War II are ubiquitous in Hawai'i: its economic dependence on military spending is perhaps the most obvious link to Pearl Harbor's tragedy. On the other hand, given that the history of the Hawaiian overthrow simmers just below the surface of everyday life in the islands, most recently erupting in the early 1990s with the reemergence of the Native Hawaiian sovereignty movement, Pearl Harbor is also understood to be a linchpin of American occupation, past and present. In other words, Pearl Harbor remains a vital site for history wars, and more so because it has been framed as a place of national historical importance. While there might be sympathy among the Detours participants regarding the project's aim to educate about the militarization of Hawai'i, such desires are at cross purposes with a profoundly emotional investment that the majority of tourists and many Hawai'i residents have in Pearl Harbor's World War II narratives. The sunken battleship in the harbor, its sacralization as an underwater tomb, and the ritualization of remembrance around it have produced a memorial that generates and responds to unabashed patriotism, leaving little room for other kinds of narratives.[4] Today, after renovation in 2010, the USS *Arizona* Memorial, the centerpiece of the Pearl Harbor military tourism complex, is more inclusive of Hawaii's multicultural history (which had been excluded, for the most part, in the previous memorial) and attentive to the state's Japanese tourist demographic (clearly delineating between Japanese people and Japanese military rule in the museum) and pays lip service to Native Hawaiian history (definitively characterized as safely long ago). Despite these concessions to inclusiveness, Pearl Harbor's identity as a place—as a military base and tourism destination—remains firmly tied to an affective narrative arc of innocence, betrayal, sacrifice, and triumph.

The Detours tours stand starkly against this narrative, problematizing the ideological foundations that give it coherence and unsettling its justification for the occupation of Hawaiian land. I am interested in how this small effort sets itself up against the behemoth that I have characterized elsewhere as a military-tourism industrial complex.[5] Most of the 1.8 million tourists who come to Pearl Harbor plan their visit around the immersive and nostalgic experience of World War II history at the USS *Arizona* Memorial and its auxiliary sites (the USS *Bowfin*, the USS *Missouri*, and the Pacific Aviation Memorial). For them, the visit is a moment of pilgrimage on a holiday that otherwise typically features sun and sand. How does a Detours tour navigate the currents of a modern indigenous sovereignty politics in the islands alongside the weight of American imperialism that profoundly shaped the landscape of O'ahu in the previous century? How will it position participants of this Detours tour vis-à-vis the majority of tourists at the USS *Arizona* Memorial? What are its expectations of its participants over the course of the tour and after, and how do these differ from the expected reactions to the naked nationalism on display at Pearl Harbor?

The Detours program upends the kind of tourism engendered at Pearl Harbor: Kajihiro and Keko'olani are interested not in the commemoration of World War II tragedy but rather in its unsettling. For the most part, the "tourists" on the Detours tours are not among the millions of visitors who come to enjoy a tropical holiday. They are either local or visiting students, teachers, scholars, and activists. Some already have a deeper knowledge of Hawai'i's history that involves US empire, or are in the process of learning about the islands' complex history, while others bring parallel histories of occupation and colonialism from elsewhere. The tours are offered upon request, typically by word of mouth and recommendation, to small numbers (thousands) compared to the millions who visit the USS *Arizona* Memorial. By the time our small group arrives at the USS *Arizona* Memorial, the guides have made more expansive the historical framework to approach the site. A stop at 'Iolani Palace has emphasized the active role played by the US military in the illegal overthrow of the monarchy. Standing just outside of the Pacific Command headquarters, with its view of the coastal area where Pearl Harbor is located, the guides relate how militarism has contoured the land and water for its needs. In short, at the point the Detours trip brings visitors to Pearl Harbor, they bear ways of understanding the site that are markedly different from those of other tourists.

I should emphasize that Detours' aim is not to refuse World War II history at Pearl Harbor or even to work toward a revisionist version that is more inclusive. Rather, the Detours tour includes the war as only one of many historical moments that are mapped onto this site. For Kajihiro and Keko'olani, Pearl Harbor encompasses and exceeds December 7, 1941, temporally and spatially, and this historiographical framing is unsettling, given the overdetermined American nationalistic narrative that pervades this place. As visitors on the tour enter the Pearl Harbor base territory, Keko'olani insists on the participants learning the name of the land on which they stand—"Pu'uloa"—she invokes the genealogical power of Hawaiian place-names in a kind of "performance cartography" that remembers the connection through land and language.[6] We repeat after her, the unfamiliar name tripping off our tongues. Kajihiro explains that "by saying these stories in places, it brings power to them in some way, it brings them to life in certain ways."[7] Refusing American military nomenclature is a powerful thing here: it invokes a different relationship to the land and a much longer historical framing than the site's insistent focus on World War II.

Upon our arrival, Kajihiro and Keko'olani start by lingering over the map of Hawai'i and the Pacific on the floor of the USS *Arizona* Memorial entrance. The map, which is meant to help tourists visualize the Pacific theater during World War II, is instead used to illustrate the geography of US empire in the Pacific, one that hinged on Hawai'i as a critical fueling station for military and colonial expansion. Kajihiro has the tour participants walk across the map, to understand how Hawai'i became a key node for the US military. He describes this map exercise as the founda-

tion for a "critical discussion about why . . . World War II was an inter-imperialist . . .
rivalry and how these complex forces . . . collided."[8] This reframing of the United
States as an empire rather than a rescuer or protector is at odds with the dominant narrative of the USS *Arizona* Memorial, which portrays Japan as the imperial
aggressor. From the first encounter with Pearl Harbor, then, the Detours tour takes
issue with the simplistic nationalist historical account established by the memorial.
When the tour moves through the two museums on the grounds of the memorial,
the reframing rubs up against the historical narrative on display.

Rather than allow the nostalgic arc of wartime sacrifice to gloss over the
genealogy of Pearl Harbor, the guides instead offer a narrative of how the military
base came to be established and under what conditions. As the tour moves through
the two museums, it observes the more inclusive, multicultural, and transnational
stories that are the result of the 2010 renovation. The experience is immersive, sen-
sorial, and steeped in World War II nostalgia: visitors encounter paraphernalia, uni-
forms, video oral histories, and sound effects of zooming planes, bombs, and radio
communications. Afterward, the tour pauses in the small outdoor walkway / sitting
area between the two museums, where a token Hawaiian story has been inserted.
As participants of the Detours tour sit with other resting tourists, the guides identify the military presence at Pearl Harbor as crucial to the erosion and theft of the
sovereignty of the Hawaiian kingdom, a history evaded by the passive voice narration of the Hawaiian monarchy's overthrow depicted on the metal panels on the
side of the walkway. Kajihiro and Kekoʻolani point out how the USS *Boston* was
the military muscle that forced Queen Liliuokalani to surrender her kingdom to the
United States in 1893 and that the ship was easily called to linger offshore Honolulu because Pearl Harbor was conveniently nearby. They then point out that Pearl
Harbor was nearby in 1893 because a covetous military, mindful of other European
imperial powers in the Pacific and protective of its own imperial ambitions, had laid
claim to the area known as Puʻuloa through an 1875 free trade agreement, which
had been negotiated by American businesspeople to clear tariffs for Hawaiʻi-grown
sugar.[9] Establishing a naval base at Puʻuloa further reinforced an American claim
to the islands and shored up a desire and dependence for a continued military presence in the Kingdom of Hawaiʻi and, ultimately, for Hawaiʻi itself. Bringing the
tour full circle to the beginning of the trip at ʻIolani Palace, where the overthrow
of Queen Liliʻuokalani took place, the Detours guides map Pearl Harbor not as a
graveyard of ships and souls but as a crucial factor in the end of the Hawaiian monarchy. I am struck that people outside the Detours group overhear this detailed history, with mixed reactions. A few look affronted that a site devoted to Pearl Harbor's
World War II history has been reclaimed for other means. Others look interested
and listen.

This active reclaiming of the space and its longer history sometimes rubs
other tourists or National Park Service Rangers the wrong way. Over the course of

bringing multiple groups to the USS *Arizona* Memorial, Kajihiro has noticed that the park rangers have become more alert to groups that approach the site outside the mode of deference and nostalgia, asking them to move along and, more recently, roping off the floor map so that tourists cannot step on it. Whether this is in response to Detours' efforts or not, he believes that it may be part of a broader resistance to the kind of work they do and how the Detours tours are not about paying homage to the nationalist history at hand. Other tourists often notice or overhear the Detours guides' script as the group moves through the memorial grounds. Kajihiro observes that people have different reactions to the Detours tours: Some people linger, others move away, and others are visibly offended. Yet as he also notes: "We've been pretty good . . . about just . . . laying some historical facts, and in a way that just decenters the Pearl Harbor hegemonic narrative and . . . centers it on a Hawaiian geography. So when you're talking about the fishponds that were destroyed or sacred sites, there's nothing there that they can really get upset about us conveying; it's just that it doesn't privilege their story that they wanted to hear, right?"[10] Kekoʻolani's own approach to Pearl Harbor draws on her Native Hawaiian lineage and World War II family history. Sometimes she shares this history. Her grandfather, John A. Gilman, served as a fireman during the bombing of Pearl Harbor and received a Purple Heart for injuries sustained as part of the Honolulu Fire Department's service to Hickam Air Force Base.[11] His is a story that could easily be folded into the almost celebratory multiculturalism in the museum exhibits, but Kekoʻolani resists this. Instead, she contends that her close relationship with him as a child, during which he communicated to her the trauma of the attack, led her to ask, "As Kānaka, what was it like before it was taken over by the military?"[12] A genealogy of Pearl Harbor's present is thus a demand for a radically different version of history that must take into account indigenous life and history. The tour decenters World War II as a conflict that is generally perceived as an American (read: white, male) and Japanese national conflict and insists on a sincere consideration of the land on which the attack took place. Indeed, if one pays attention to history, the Pearl Harbor attack, the seventy-fifth anniversary of which was commemorated in 2016, took place not on American land but on occupied territory. The Detours tour underscores the frailty of settler colonialism, something that otherwise escapes notice with the nationalism of Pearl Harbor narratives. This decentering unsettles the participants of the Detours tours: like most tourists, they, too, come to the USS *Arizona* Memorial prepared to experience it in one particular way, such that Detours' counternarratives leave them unanchored.

Next the tour moves to the manicured grounds of the memorial overlooking the bay. Across the water, a military base features enormous battleships, an aircraft carrier, and launches zipping around the water. From the grounds, tour participants can see the small boat carrying other tourists to the white span straddling the sunken USS *Arizona*. The guides take the opportunity at this point to briefly reflect on the pedagogical intent of the museum and how a focus on World War II displaces and deflects other historical narratives of the US military in this place. Attentive to the disheartening mood the tour thus far has engendered, the Detours guides share their research on the area. Looking out over the harbor, the guides ask participants to replace Pearl Harbor with Puʻuloa, its polluted waters with a fertile estuary. The tour guides describe an intricate ecology of taro fields and fishponds that the lands and waters of Puʻuloa sustained. Instead of the metal and concrete of the base architecture, the participants are asked to visualize an organized and organic system designed to support and feed a community. Kekoʻolani states that this knowledge did not come easily: finding the original Hawaiian names for the landscape and the historical uses of the land and water took work because this traditional historical knowledge was subject to colonial erasure. Depicting the land and water as resources that were responsibly stewarded by Kānaka Maoli, who paid attention to "the rhythm of the growing of the fish" and the organization of life in the harbor and in its connected territories, the guides establish historical claim to Puʻuloa and forge "another way of relating to . . . their homeland and to their history, and to each other as people."[13]

This way of relating is something that surfaces in the Detours tour and is part of the guides' rootedness and devotion to Hawaiʻi. Unlike the National Park Service Rangers and the occasional veterans groups that have interpretive authority at the USS *Arizona* Memorial, Kajihiro and Kekoʻolani have deep roots in Hawaii, and this rootedness informs the shape and intention of the Detours tour. This detour through indigenous history—occasionally fragmented as it is—is simultaneously a reterritorialization of occupied lands, removing it from the kind of heroic narration that operates as a defense of US militarism, and the signaling of another historical arc that gestures to a decolonial futurity. Rooted in an indigenous sense of place and indigenous genealogies, the Detours tour circles back to the future to imagine a radically different occupation of Puʻuloa. The group is quiet as the tour leaves the memorial grounds: it is all a lot to process, even for those familiar with the story. There is something to the presentness of the military base that drives home the stakes of the kind of historical and political work Kajihiro and Kekoʻolani are doing.

The tour leaves the military reservation and proceeds across the bay to Hanekehau Learning Farm, where a thriving grassroots effort led by Native Hawaiians to reclaim land and establish traditional cultural practices has been developed. It stands in incongruous juxtaposition to the overwhelmingly militarized place the group has just left. Here the tour's participants talk with the farm's leaders about the reclamation and restoration of the land in an area they mark out as "heavily impacted by a long history of military misuse, illegal dumping, and pollution."[14] Participants wander through the farm itself, gaining a deeper understanding of one of many efforts to restore the larger Hawaiian nation. The hosts are welcoming, and, around a shared meal, visitors sit on the ground and "talk story" about the mission of the farm, the kind of work they are doing, and how it is small compared to the vast territorial scale of Pearl Harbor and the militarized land on Oʻahu but also important in relation to the multiple kinds of efforts being led by Native Hawaiian sovereignty activists throughout the islands. The tour ends here, and the drive back to the morning's meeting place is full of quiet reflection.

To take a detour means to take a longer or more roundabout route, one that is not always the easiest or most direct. The Detours tour hosted by Kekoʻolani and Kajihiro deviates from the historical narratives of Pearl Harbor, rejecting the claims engineered through the harbor's emphasis on World War II sacrifice, instead proffering an alternate historical trauma of which World War II is only a component. In doing so, this counter-tour contributes to a long and varied tradition of decolonizing efforts that continue to address crucial issues of land, militarization, and sovereignty in a much longer "war" of memory and occupation. Doing so through the genre of a tour, in a place where tourism has partnered intimately with militarism, illuminates the creative methods such wars engender.

Vernadette Vicuña Gonzalez is associate professor of American studies at the University of Hawaiʻi at Mānoa and director of the university's Honors Program. She is the author of *Securing Paradise: Tourism and Militarism in Hawaiʻi and the Philippines* (2013) and is currently working on a book on imperial intimacies as seen through the life of performer Isabel Rosario Cooper and editing a decolonial guide to Hawaiʻi with Hōkūlani Aikau.

Notes

1. Kekoʻolani, interview. A note on terminology: I use *Kānaka Maoli* (true or real people) interchangeably with *Native Hawaiians*.
2. Thanks to the persistence of the protests, which ranged from occupations to legal maneuvers, bombing on Kahoʻolawe ended in 1990. Shortly after, the island was turned over to the state and funding was set aside to remove ordnance. To this day, the island has unexploded ordnance on 25 percent of its landmass.
3. Quoted in Grandinetti, "In the Shadow of the Beast," 39.
4. The film that visitors view before visiting the actual memorial in the bay was once denigrated as too sympathetic to Japan. In 2010 a Fox News program depicted a teacher-training program run by several history professors as unpatriotic and disrespectful to veterans, because it did not clearly valorize the American perspective of the war. See the discussion in White, *Memorializing Pearl Harbor*, chap. 6.
5. Gonzalez, *Securing Paradise*.
6. Kapāʻanaokalākeloa Nakoa Oliveira, *Ancestral Places*.
7. Kajihiro, interview.
8. Ibid.
9. The Reciprocity Treaty of 1875 was renewed in 1887 under King David Kālakaua's reign.
10. Kajihiro, interview.
11. Kekoʻolani, interview. See also Firehouse World, "Fire Response to Pearl Harbor Remembered."
12. Kekoʻolani interview. See also Osorio, "Memorializing Puʻuloa."
13. Kekoʻolani interview.
14. Hanekehau Learning Farm, "About Us."

References

Firehouse World. 2011. "Fire Response to Pearl Harbor Remembered Seventy Years Later." December 7. www.firehouse.com/news/10475965/fire-response-to-pearl-harbor -remembered-70-years-later.

Gonzalez, Vernadette Vicuña. 2013. *Securing Paradise: Tourism and Militarism in Hawai'i and the Philippines*. Durham, NC: Duke University Press.

Grandinetti, Tina. 2014. "In the Shadow of the Beast." *FLUX Hawaii*, Spring, 35–40.

Hanekehau Learning Farm. 2016. "About Us." http://hanekehau.com/about (accessed September 20, 2016).

Kajihiro, Kyle. 2016. Author interview. May 13, Honolulu, HI.

Kapā'anaokalākeloa Nakoa Oliveira, Katrina-Ann R. 2014. *Ancestral Places: Understanding Kanaka Geographies*. Corvallis: Oregon State University Press..

Keko'olani, Terri. 2016. Author interview, May 17, Honolulu, HI.

Osorio, Jon Kamakawiwo'ole. 2010. "Memorializing Pu'uloa and Remembering Pearl Harbor." In *Militarized Currents: Toward a Decolonized Future in Asia and the Pacific*, edited by Setsu Shigematsu and Keith L. Camacho, 3–14. Minneapolis: University of Minnesota Press.

White, Geoffrey M. 2016. *Memorializing Pearl Harbor: Unfinished Histories and the Work of Remembrance*. Durham, NC: Duke University Press.

Tales from a New, Mythic, and Activist South

Kim Cary Warren

Tiya Miles, *Tales from the Haunted South: Dark Tourism and Memories of Slavery from the Civil War Era*. Chapel Hill: University of North Carolina Press, 2015.

Reiko Hillyer, *Designing Dixie: Tourism, Memory, and Urban Space in the New South*. Charlottesville: University of Virginia Press, 2014.

Chanelle N. Rose, *The Struggle for Black Freedom in Miami: Civil Rights and America's Tourist Paradise, 1896–1968*. Baton Rouge: Louisiana State University Press, 2015.

Gregory W. Bush, *White Sand, Black Beach: Civil Rights, Public Space, and Miami's Virginia Key*. Gainesville: University Press of Florida, 2016.

I remember touring the South as a child. During a driving trip, my family experienced a special kind of heat and humidity unfamiliar in our native Kansas City. Deeper accents and richer food enhanced the social and physical landscape of the South. We saw the rolling hills of the Ozark Mountains in Arkansas, the Juliette Gordon Low house in Georgia, and countless Civil War battle sites where tourists could buy antique bullets and touch authentic cannons. My expectation of the South as grand and elegant was met with restored plantation houses. In Florida, we wit-

Radical History Review

Issue 129 (October 2017)   DOI 10.1215/01636545-3921482

© 2017 by MARHO: The Radical Historians' Organization, Inc.

nessed the spectacular, predawn launch of the Space Shuttle mission STS-7 on June 18, 1983, with America's first female astronaut, Sally K. Ride. A few days at the Gulf of Mexico and then at Disney World and Epcot Center sealed the South, and especially Florida, as a region particularly suited as a premier tourist destination. However, even as a kid, I realized that tourism in the South is complicated. At Monticello and Mount Vernon, sites that celebrated American democracy, tour guides struggled to answer questions about the contradictions between a new nation's freedom and its dependency on enslaved labor. Confederate memorials reminded tourists of a time when bold leadership rested on ideals of secession rather than union. The South boasted incredibly detailed civil rights museums celebrating achievements toward racial equality, but also reminded tourists of the sites in the South where leaders had lost their lives in the fight. The South was both a luxurious region promising leisure and nostalgia and a seemingly foreign territory unable to escape its inherent connection with slavery, secession, and racial violence.

This kind of duality embedded in Southern tourism is represented in four recently published books detailing histories of the American South. These new historical studies confirm that Southern states have depended on creating an attractive historical past in order to generate tourists' and investors' interest. At the same time, such states have struggled with the racial violence that is fundamentally rooted to a distant past that included slavery and a more recent past that included legal segregation and racial tensions. Scholarship on the South joins a larger body of scholarship that explores the role of tourism as a mechanism for constructing identities of different regions in the United States. While mythmaking in the American West and Southwest has been widely explored, mythmaking in the New South poses a particular challenge as the region cannot escape its historical position in defense of slavery and the longer challenges regarding race relations. Scholars have shown that the South is not the only region plagued by segregation and residual tensions between residents of different racial groups, but what these four books show is that the South might be the region with the most difficulty reforming its own identity separate from that violent past.

Tiya Miles's brilliantly written *Tales from the Haunted South* demonstrates that a certain aspect of tourism—"ghost tours" or "dark tourism"—has specific characteristics, including sensational stories made more dramatic when told at night. This category of tourism, however, is not limited to a niche area of Southern sightseeing. The industry of ghost tours reveals a larger complication about Southern history, specifically, and American history, generally: "Many of us sense that we live in a haunted country, a land of injured spirits," Miles writes (16). "This is a metaphorical truth that creeps to the surface again and again in our national literature and popular culture. As much as we long to idealize this nation as the birthplace of freedom (and it was, on paper for a privileged few), we are also a country founded on the practice of indigenous erasure, illegal land seizure, and racial slavery," she adds (16).

The South, in particular, cannot escape its relationship with a history made on the bodies of African American men and women. "Without slavery there is no South," Miles reminds readers, "as a region or an idea" (17–18). The message of tourism in the South, then, is about "the destruction of black lives as well as white families by the unfettered beast of sexual slavery" (36).

Stories that include enslaved women and their white mistresses—Molly and Matilda of the Sorrel-Weed House, for example—place sexual jealousy and domestic strife at the core of antebellum history. In her detailed analysis of the Sorrel-Weed House, the most infamous historical home in Savannah, Georgia, Miles shows that nothing is what it seems. For example, the patriarch, Francis Sorrel, appeared to be white but was actually a light-skinned emigrant of Afro-Haitian descent. Sorrel's practice of the occult voodoo religion "betray[ed] his wedding vows and dr[ove] his Christian wife to suicide" (37). He was likely the murderer of Molly, but he went unprosecuted and, in fact, lived an unusually long life for that time. Despite such contradictions, tours in Savannah, New Orleans, and other cities insist that their ghost, vampire, and cemetery tours offer "REAL hauntings" and, therefore, lay a claim to "REAL history" (50).

The notion of authentic history at these Southern sites is problematic, Miles points out. For example, at the Myrtles Plantation in St. Francisville, Louisiana, Miles realizes that an enslaved woman, Chloe, who is a main subject in the ghost tour, actually has no historical record. There are, however, Chloe dolls displayed in the gift shop. Chloe, the person, was not real, but her story and representation as a souvenir doll, are available for purchase. The repeated purchase of enslaved women like Chloe—first their bodies, then their stories, and then their souvenir representatives— cautions readers about the historical injustices that will persist if narratives of tours and of history books continue to "trivialize the experience of African American women by ignoring the bleakness of the plantation setting for slaves, caricaturing social relations between male masters and female slaves, and rendering vigilante murders as spectacle" (104).

Tourists at Southern sites do have some knowledge about the complicated relationship that the region has with violence toward African American men and women. They are willing, however, to remain attracted to the region if tours allow for "a safe emotional distance" (18). Ghost tours might include harsh historical themes of enslavement, sexual coercion, murder, or bodies improperly buried, but stories are presented "with a playful fight and wink" for tourists (18). And, in some cases, stories are simply fabricated, as in the case of the Chloe narrative.

Miles challenges readers to take ghost tours seriously, if for no other reason than to learn that "African American spirits are not gullibly friendly, delightfully cartoonish, or controllably mainstream" (132). Instead, the experiences and voices of African American Southerners "are serious messengers from another time that compel us to wrestle with the past, a past chained to colonialism, slavery, and patriarchy, but a past that can nevertheless challenge and commission us to fight for justice in the present" (132).

The role of storytelling is not only at the heart of tourism in the South, but it is also at the heart of the twentieth-century project of constructing a "New South" identity. The New South was constructed between 1877 to 1913, or the period between the Civil War and World War I, according to Reiko Hillyer in *Designing Dixie*. Promoters of the New South focused on modernism, including industrialization and architecture, and on urban design. Rather than centering on nostalgic stories of large plantations, pastoral agrarian landscapes, aristocratic leisure, valiant war stories, and a romantic version of enslaved labor, promoters built and celebrated new hotels, skyscrapers, expositions, and homes in suburban neighborhoods. These new physical spaces not only symbolized the South's embrace of modernity, but they also provided practical solutions to the needs of elite Northern tourists who sought pleasure and leisure when they traveled to the South. Newer, bigger, first-class hotels were required to attract the kind of elite tourists who would also financially invest in future building projects. Southern cities had to demonstrate their desire to grow by looking forward, by providing links between tourism and investment, and by focusing on luxury and comfort to keep Northerners returning to the South. Therefore, the image of the "leisurely world of the Old South" was pushed aside in exchange for boosters' hyperbolic version of the past (8). This strategy had the larger intention of leading to a more hopeful future than maintaining a concern about representing a realistic present. Modernism, rather than nostalgia, would rebuild the South and attract necessary economic investment from Northern businesses and tourists. Rebuilding the South would require economic investment in Southern industries, and postwar developers realized early that investment would only come if Northerners visited the South to see the economic possibilities tied up in the abundance of raw materials and of cheap labor that both African American and white workers could provide.

Why did it matter to Southerners what Northerners thought of their region? Simply put: Southerners wanted Northerners' money. Hillyer explains to readers: "In the New South, the fate of the southern economy was in the hands of northern capitalists—'empire builders'—who, with the help of a new entrepreneurial leadership class in the South, exploited the South's raw materials and cheap labor and maintained control of the region's profits" (2). To stimulate Northern investment in the South, Northern tourism in the Southern cities had to increase first. Somehow, though, Southerners had to lure tourists to the region by foregrounding symbols of progressive, economic change despite a significant rise in Jim Crow legislation and violence. With opportunity, on the one hand, and deepening racial divisions, on the other, the South attempted to move beyond its difficult historical past linked to slavery, the Civil War, and Reconstruction. Hillyer argues that a strategy employing "selective memory" proved productive during this period (2). Another way to put it is that engineers of the New South "created usable historical pasts in locally varying ways" (5). Just as ghost tours vacillated between historical accuracy and complete fabrication, Hillyer explains that not only were fairy tales told in the Old South, but they were critical to the fabric of the New South as well. In St. Augustine, Florida; Richmond, Virginia; and Atlanta, Georgia—all cities that have a relationship to the Old South but whose past "civic leaders, boosters, and architects edited, ignored, or revised . . . to attract northern visitors and investors"—modern features became the core of new Southern identities (6). Collectively, these cities boasted links to European imperial expansion, industrial development as part of the South's destiny, and Northern architecture as language to situate a modern identity. To prove their modern identities, St. Augustine promoted its Spanish rather than its Southern roots; Richmond pointed to its roles in the American Revolution and in recent industry rather than in the Civil War; and Atlanta pointed to its own destruction as an opportunity to rebuild in the image of the North rather than as a tragedy of the Confederacy. All these efforts were meant to distinguish them from other Southern cities by "rejecting the plantation past to highlight their openness to the future" (6). Tours of tobacco factories, for example, highlighted technological advances and harmony between labor and capital. Workers, if seen at all, were cast as docile; owners of factories were cast as intelligent and experienced, leading their industry into modernity just like Northerners. Hillyer argues that these new identities worked so well that by "World War I, through guidebooks, promotional pamphlets, and architecture, these cities succeeded in promoting an image of a modern South in step with Yankee entrepreneurialism" (6).

In addition to business development as part of the Southern industrial landscape, technology played a role as well. In particular, railroads were critical to Southern growth because they provided both access to the South and insulation from undesirable tourists. In other words, "railroads and package tours promised exclusivity and protection from the disconcerting presence of unrefined people, both on and off the train" (33). The introduction of Pullman dining and sleeping cars in the 1870s dramatically changed train travel, reducing the need for frequent stops en route and allowing "wealthy white passengers to avoid the idiosyncrasies of local southern life" (34). By the 1890s, railroad travel was much more luxurious than the notoriously unpleasant train travel of previous decades. Pullman dining cars provided fresh linen, courteous service, and copious bills of fare. Hillyer adds that "the railroad helped to indoctrinate northern travelers in the creed of Jim Crow" (34). The railroad of the 1880s was contested terrain, a place where Jim Crow laws were challenged, and yet the railroad still firmly segregated white travelers and African American laborers. African American porters hauled luggage, made beds, shined shoes, and babysat children and reportedly did so on little sleep, providing a visual reminder of racially segregated labor in the South. At the same time, the railroad, a symbol of progress in the western territories and a technological tool that facilitated the meeting of cultures on the frontier, metaphorically and literally linked the South and the West with its tracks. Trains ultimately displayed Southern contradictions between technological progress and segregated backwardness, but so did the building of modern, Southern cities. For example, Atlanta, in its concerted efforts to rebuild after Major General William T. Sherman burned it to the ground in 1864, promoted its fashionable boulevards with paved streets and electric lighting a few decades later. However, no amount of modern architecture could completely hide the city's poor and working-class residents who lived without access to clean water and in whose neighborhoods the city failed to install its new gas lines.

Access to modern utilities and to new municipal amenities for working-class and minority residents has historically been at the center of campaigns for desegregation and equal rights. Chanelle Rose and Gregory Bush show that this was particularly true for residents of Miami, Florida, in the twentieth century. Florida is a most Southern of Southern states, but it has also experienced its own version of a complicated, Southern past. In *The Struggle for Black Freedom in Miami*, Rose explains that the state traditionally enjoys a reputation as being more moderate than other Southern states with regard to race relations, but she also claims that efforts to deemphasize its "unique attributes can obscure its complicated racial past, especially in urban communities" (7). Florida's reputation is enhanced by a "tourist progressive mystique," or rather a focus on the ways that Florida's warm climate, sandy beaches, and civil interracial relations have made the state the "premier vacation destination" (7). However, Florida, specifically Miami, has experienced as much racial tension and demand for civil rights as it has experienced influxes of immigrants from a variety of backgrounds. In Rose's Miami, "the convergence of people from the American South, North, and Midwest; the Caribbean; and Latin America created a border culture in a southern metropolis where the influx of Bahamian-born blacks and Latin American tourists, along with Spanish-speaking immigrants from the Caribbean, had begun to alter the racial landscape decades earlier" (9). Miami became an international city in the second half of the twentieth century, but its multicultural residents had transformed Miami long before then. An influx of Latin cultures, specifically, left an indelible mark on the modern civil rights struggle.

Equally important to Latin culture in Rose's book is the activism of various Jewish organizations connected to social action, labor organizing, and civil rights. Rose points out that "even though liberal black and Jewish activists had a history of working together to confront racial bigotry, they intensified their fight for civil rights" after events related to race-based violence (105). For example, in response to a set of bombings, "various mainstream Jewish leaders took a more conservative position that cautioned against a reactionary response to the wave of bombings [and] others joined black leaders in openly criticizing the police department's inaction and demanding racial justice" (105). Red-baiting scared activists in Florida, as well as throughout the country, but Jewish involvement in civil rights persisted, and African American organizations prominently took charge of local and national campaigns.

The National Association for the Advancement of Colored People (NAACP) organized legal battles and gathered support through local organizations and churches. In 1957, when a federal court judge ruled that Miami and Florida bus segregation laws were unconstitutional in light of the decision in Montgomery, Alabama, the NAACP cheered with the judge's statement: "I have no hesitation in saying that these segregation laws are unconstitutional and hence unenforceable" (127). The NAACP followed up with instructions to African American residents to immediately ride buses "without fear" and to "assert their constitutional rights as equal citizens" (127). In a press release, the Miami NAACP issued an order to African American citizens: "We now not only instruct you to sit where you please, but we urge you to do so. Remember that these civil rights which were obtained at a great expense should not be made nullities because of indifference and unfounded fear" (127). The legal triumph allowed the Miami NAACP to be perceived as one of the most active branches in the state. Such victories came with increased risk, however. After the bus desegregation victory, an African American musician moved into an all-white neighborhood, prompting white citizens to visibly and vocally object, even targeting NAACP leaders for assassination.

The Reverend Martin Luther King Jr. shows up in Rose's narrative, just as he does in Hillyer's *Designing Dixie*. Like so many others in Florida, King was a tourist, resting there while en route to the Bahamas. However, even as a tourist, King gave political speeches, and in 1964 he reminded listeners that Miami was not exempt from Southern problems afflicting African Americans. He stated, "The Negro does not get a square deal in Mississippi, but he doesn't get a square deal in Miami either" (231). Two years later, King would also include Miami among the cities that had failed to provide freedom for its black citizens: "In Chicago and New York, Atlanta and Jackson, and Miami, the Negro is freer in 1966, but not yet free" (231–32). Just as in other Southern cities, Miami's mid-twentieth-century history is filled with student sit-ins, school desegregation campaigns, and demands for racial justice.

The activism of Miami's black middle-class leadership figures prominently in Rose's book, especially with its campaign to hire black patrol officers, but also regarding its struggle for Virginia Key Beach. It is the specific history of Virginia Key that Bush picks up to explain the intersections of "jurisdictional fights, competing development visions, and changing cultural values" in a delicate ecosystem that also happens to be the country's first legally recognized bathing beach for African Americans (5). In *White Sand, Black Beach*, Bush explains that the beach was, in accordance with the segregation laws of 1945, an all-black beach. However, the beach was not just a contested place for African Americans to fight against segregation, nor was it simply a place to cool off. Bush demonstrates that this particular site of segregation also became a locus point for "black pride and fellowship and an important link to nature" (5). Access to the beach meant that African Americans had a physical place for inviting nonlocal family and friends to gather with them in fellowship. Yet the segregated beach also reminded locals and tourists of an oppressive past, and eventually white leaders decreased funding for public spaces.

Four types of African American beaches in the United States existed before the civil rights era. First, there were places that were invisible to whites because they were physically isolated or undesirable for other reasons. Second, there was a type of beach that emerged through private ownership, either through African American entrepreneurial endeavors or through access allowed by white beach owners. The third type developed through negotiations with local officials and resulted in formally segregated African American summer homes and beaches. The fourth type were the all-black public beaches that emerged throughout Miami, and elsewhere in the South, and remained sites of contention with the "changing nature of land use, politics, and commercial pressures or by competing visions of public purposes for land" (25). Beaches, therefore, were not simply sites of leisure for African Americans. Rather, they were physical spaces that doubly functioned as expanded public accommodations resulting from campaigns of civil disobedience in places such as Miami, one of the South's fastest-growing cities.

De jure and de facto segregation in Miami functioned similarly to segregation in other Southern cities. Miami simultaneously excluded African Americans from local beaches designated for white tourists, "while containing them in segregated neighborhoods and exploiting their labor in construction" as well as in housework and yard work (73). Bush explains how both leisure and labor were segregated in Miami and that both categories required African American activism to foster change. Initially many African American civil rights activists thought that they should handle their own struggles using local strategies. Therefore, a Miami chapter of the NAACP was established in 1937. However, national events continued to galvanize African American activism, including the 1938 boxing match between American Joe Louis and German Max Schmeling and the 1939 Marian Anderson concert that was famously relocated to the Lincoln Memorial after the Daughters of the American Revolution denied her permission to sing at Constitution Hall. African American activism continued locally, and eventually, in 1964, King became involved in protests in Florida at the same time that white mobs attacked African Americans attempting to desegregate pools. This was the same time that Congress debated the Civil Rights Act that would become national law. Riots continued in Florida cities through 1965, and King maintained a presence in Miami through 1966, addressing the danger of job competition between African Americans and Cubans, along with issues of segregation.

These four books help readers understand that tourism in the South has its own historiography, just as the New South has its historiography, narrating its rapid growth from the 1950s onward. These books remind readers and tourists that myths and storytelling are at the heart of narrating a Southern past as the region continues to reconcile its violent legacies with modern progress and activist reform. Miles, Hillyer, Rose, and Bush show that Southern voices provide the foundation for storytelling, and their recovery of lost Southern voices, particularly those of African Americans, raises more questions about the nature of tourism in the South. Is recovery of such voices enough to "carry on the integrity of our ancestors," as Miles asks (132), or will the ghosts of the past and the tourists of the present continue to wrestle with duality when touring the South?

Remembering and Honoring Marv Gettleman

Van Gosse

(given at a memorial in New York city on January 13, 2017)

I think of Marv as the exemplary radical historian. Long before anyone else, he understood what it meant to be "public, political, and popular," our motto at the *Radical History Review*, the goal towards which we strive. Over nearly fifty years, Marv hit that mark over and over, a remarkable achievement. He made the practice of doing history historically consequential.

I met Marv twenty-five years ago, when I interviewed him for my book in Cuba. He had led a group of skeptical students there in summer 1960, and afterwards became a leader of the Student Fair Play for Cuba committee at City College. As always, Marv got there early, and effectively. Back then, I knew him because, as a CISPES activist, his collection, *El Salvador: Central America in the New Cold War* was key to our work—it was what we gave people to read.

What I didn't know then was that the El Salvador (and Guatemala) collections of the 1980s were part of a longer trajectory of movement building. I was too young to remember his remarkably prescient volume from 1964, *Vietnam: History, Documents, and Opinions on a Major World Crisis*, which became the documentary bible for the antiwar movement of that time, with hundreds of thousands of copies in print.

And when it came time to rebuild the antiwar movement again, in 2003, Marv was there helping to found Historians Against the War, producing the first

Radical History Review
Issue 129 (October 2017)   DOI 10.1215/01636545-4187098
© 2017 by MARHO: The Radical Historians' Organization, Inc.

pamphlet with Stuart Schaar, an *Annotated Bibliography of English-Language Sources and Studies on The Middle East and Muslim South West Asia*, and playing a major role for six years on our Steering Committee. As the HAW statement says, "Marv brought to our collective work decades of experience in struggles for peace, human rights and social justice. His energy, optimistic spirit and wisdom enabled us to form a strong organization of historians, offering clear opposition to the Iraq War and other US military interventions in the aftermath of 9/11. Marv combined the militancy of an activist, tempered by a life of scholarship and reflection. In discouraging times, he was a fountain of good ideas. And when frustration nurtured excess, his was the voice of common sense. Though a profound critic of the social order, he did not give way to cynicism. And he was never too self-important to skip the necessary tasks."

Which brings me to the present. A few months ago I decided to teach a new "Vietnam and the Cold War" course aimed at first-years and sophomores. I started looking around for the newest and best historiography, and there is plenty. But at a certain point, I thought "I need to go back to the documents; after all, in my survey, I keep using the excerpt from General Vo Nguyen Giap's *People's War, People's Army* and Colonel Robert Heinl's 1971 article, 'The Collapse of the Armed Forces.'" So for my new course starting next week, I ordered the book from which those documents are drawn, Marv's 1995 *Vietnam and America* (on which he collaborated with Marilyn Young and Jane and Bruce Franklin). Marv is still there, with us, doing the long, patient work of radical history. *Presente, companero.*

Van Gosse teaches history at Franklin & Marshall College and is a longtime member of the *RHR* Editorial Collective.

Honoring Marilyn Young

Carolyn Rusti Eisenberg

Over decades Marilyn Young shared her wisdom about issues of "war and peace" with students, colleagues, friends, and the wider public. An extraordinary historian and a razor-sharp critic, she was able to convey the urgency of these matters to multiple generations and by so doing strengthened the impetus to activism.

Marilyn Young's 1991 book *The Vietnam Wars* remains a classic, still assigned in college courses. Written before the relevant archives were open, the historical judgments it contains are remarkably accurate. The book retains its vibrancy because of Marilyn's breath of vision and emotional engagement. More than others, she had an acute sense of how high policy, forged in claustrophobic Washington rooms, was translated into the lived experience of both Vietnamese and Americans.

Her effectiveness in linking the complexities of policy with the human consequences of official decisions underpinned her long career. While many left historians abandoned the study of "powerful white men" for the more appealing vistas of social history, Marilyn Young stayed with it. Recognizing the propensity for war and intervention, she was determined to track it—with her pen, computer, and distinctive voice.

Marilyn managed to be a careful scholar, a subtle analyst, and an eloquent dissenter. In every possible forum (her books, articles, anthologies, document collections, public lectures, and television appearances) she challenged her audience to think more deeply about the American role in the world. Until the end of her life, she was in great demand as a public speaker—always funny, smart, insightful, and passionate.

Radical History Review
Issue 129 (October 2017) DOI 10.1215/01636545-4187110
© 2017 by MARHO: The Radical Historians' Organization, Inc.

During these many appearances—in Dublin, Rome, Beijing, Montgomery, Santa Fe, and Austin (to name a few), she was struggling with illness, but was absolutely determined to do a fine job. When she belatedly realized that a conference at the LBJ Library in Austin included Henry Kissinger on the program, she hastily revised her remarks to fit the occasion. In the wee hours of the night, she went hunting for the figures on Cambodia, reminding her audience that the damage far exceeded the "five mile strip," he had blithely described.

Despite her maverick nature, in 2011 Marilyn Young was elected president of the Society of Historians of Foreign Relations. It was a richly deserved honor. More than practically everyone, Marilyn was an inspiring teacher and generous colleague. There are few major books on the Vietnam War, or post World War II US foreign policy, that she didn't somehow assist.

I was among these beneficiaries. For the past eighteen months, as I wrote my book on the "national security policy" of Nixon and Kissinger, Marilyn was both a friend and intellectual companion—constantly in touch with her questions, ideas, arguments, and quips. I could never convince her that the SALT talks were truly fascinating. And I cherished the illusion that if we could just keep discussing the nuclear balance that she would be fine.

That wasn't to be. But her voice lingers—asking questions, raising objections—forever outraged by the abuses of American power and relentlessly pursuing those hidden truths.

Carolyn Rusti Eisenberg is a professor of US foreign policy and history at Hofstra University. She is the author of the prize-winning *Drawing the Line: The American Decision to Divide Germany, 1944-49* and a forthcoming book on *Nixon, Kissinger and the Illusion of National Security.* She is a Steering Committee member of Historians Against the War and legislative coordinator for United for Peace and Justice.

After #Ferguson,
After #Baltimore:
The Challenge of Black
Death and Black Life for
Black Political Thought

An issue of
South Atlantic Quarterly (116:3)
Barnor Hesse and
Juliet Hooker, issue editors

Drawing primarily on the US #blacklivesmatter movement, contributors
to this issue come to terms with the crisis in the meaning of black
politics during the post–civil rights era as evidenced by the unknown
trajectories of black protests. The authors' timely essays frame black
protests and the implications of contemporary police killings of black
people as symptomatic of a crisis in black politics within the white limits
of liberal democracy.

Contributors: Barnor Hesse, Juliet Hooker, Minkah Makalani, John D. Márquez,
Junaid Rana, Debra Thompson, Shatema Threadcraft

Buy the issue at **dukeupress.edu/saq**.

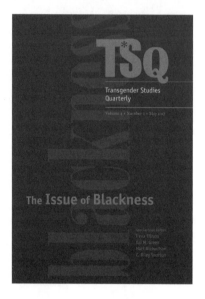